APOCALYPSE

THE COMING JUDGMENT *of the* NATIONS

GRANT R.
JEFFREY

BEST-SELLING AUTHOR OF *Creation*

WATERBROOK
PRESS

APOCALYPSE
PUBLISHED BY WATERBROOK PRESS
2375 Telstar Drive, Suite 160
Colorado Springs, Colorado 80920
A division of Random House, Inc.

Scripture taken from the *New King James Version.* Copyright © 1982 by Thomas
Nelson, Inc. Used by permission. All rights reserved. Scripture also taken from the
King James Version.

ISBN 0-921714-03-3

Apocalypse was originally published by Frontier Research Publications in 1992.

Library of Congress Cataloging-in-Publication Data
Jeffrey, Grant R.
Apocalypse

1. Apocalypse   2. Eschatology   3. Revelation
1. Title

Printed in the United States of America
2004

10 9 8 7 6 5

COMMENTS ON GRANT JEFFREY'S PREVIOUS BESTSELLERS:

ARMAGEDDON: APPOINTMENT WITH DESTINY
HEAVEN: THE LAST FRONTIER
and MESSIAH

"We need to have a biblically-based outlook on Bible prophecy. That's why we're featuring Grant Jeffrey in our magazine. His book "Armageddon: Appointment With Destiny" explores the amazingly accurate fulfilment of past prophecies, and examines the prophecies that relate to this time period leading to the Second Coming of Christ."

Jerry Rose: President,
National Religious Broadcasters

"**Armegeddon - Appointment With Destiny** has been our hottest single religious title." -- "We took it on with tremendous enthusiasm because there was something very exciting about the way Grant wrote, and it was something that we thought might go beyond the traditional religious audience.

Lou Arnonica, Vice President
Bantam Books - mass market division
New York Times - Oct. 22, 1990
Toronto Star Newspaper – August 1, 1992

Grant Jeffrey...is now a bestselling author throughout North America...His breakthrough book was his first, **Armageddon – Appointment With Destiny**...Bantam Books later picked it up, and it turned out to be their No. 1 religious bestseller in 1990."

Philip Marchand, Book Review Editor
Toronto Star Newspaper – August 1, 1992

"It is absolutely the most eye-opening book on end-time events I've come across in a long, long time. It's terrific!"

Dan Betzer: Host,
Revivaltime Media Ministries

"We are excited about Grant Jeffrey's new book. Back in the early seventies, the book that became a run-away best seller was "**Late Great Planet Earth**." Now the book with the latest information on prophetic fulfilment, the book for the nineties, is "**Armageddon: Appointment With Destiny**." It will show that God is in control and, most importantly, it will also prove to be a powerful witnessing tool to those who need Christ."

David Mainse: President,
100 Huntley Street

ACKNOWLEDGMENT

APOCALYPSE reflects a lifetime of research and Bible study on the visions of the book of Revelation. This thirty year study has convinced me that the coming Kingdom of God is the ultimate goal of human history. Over the last two thousand years, hundreds have written commentaries on John's visions which have guided my own explorations. Many of these books are listed in the select bibliography. However, the inspired Word of God has been my major source in these studies. I am thankful that the Lord has allowed me to see Him as the victorious Messiah, the Lord of hosts and King of kings.

I dedicate this book to my wife Kaye for her selfless work in the production of this book. Her loving concern is demonstrated in every aspect of our publications, television programs and teaching ministry. My parents, Lyle and Florence Jeffrey, inspired me with a great longing for our coming Messiah. Kaye's mother, Amelia Graham, who recently went home to be with the Lord, instilled in both of us a profound love for the coming reunion of the saints at the glorious Rapture of the Church.

I trust this book will encourage you to study the book of Revelation and discover the tremendous promises of Christ's triumphant victory.

TABLE OF CONTENTS

APOCALYPSE
The Coming Judgment of the Nations

The Apocalypse - the Unveiling of Jesus the Christ

The book of Revelation is the most fascinating and perplexing of all the books of the Bible. It contains awesome and terrifying visions of the final apocalyptic judgment at the end of time. These tremendous visions promise that man's last crisis will end in Jesus Christ's complete victory over the forces of evil. John's revelations unveil the wonderful prophecies of the millennial Kingdom when Christ will restore all things. Despite the difficulties in interpretation, this book has drawn the interest and curiosity of Christians for nearly two thousand years. The world is now rushing toward an abyss of civil war, totalitarian world government and the final devastation of nuclear, chemical and biological warfare. The book of Revelation is our key to understanding the cataclysmic events unfolding in the closing decade of this millennium.

Most writers describe the last book of the Bible as "The Revelation of St. John the Divine." However, God's title for the book is "The Revelation of Jesus Christ." The two words "Revelation" and "Apocalypse" are identical in meaning. They are both derived from the Greek word *apokalupsis* which suggests the unveiling of something that has previously been hidden, a revelation, an appearing, the manifestation of something. The Apocalypse is therefore the Revelation of Jesus Christ. In 1 Corinthians 1:7 the Apostle Paul used the same word *apokalupsis* to describe the Second Coming of Christ, encouraging Christians to "eagerly wait for the 'apocalypse' of our Lord Jesus Christ." The focus of

Revelation is the personal appearing or coming of our Lord and Savior Jesus Christ. It isn't the revelation of John or, even, of John's visions. It is the revelation of the nature, the triumph, the office and the final victory of Jesus the Messiah. Christ is both the subject and the object of this series of prophetic visions describing the final victory of God's anointed Messiah over the forces of evil. The theme of the book is the *Parousia*, the "coming of Christ in Glory." The purpose of the Apocalypse is to reveal God's plan to redeem the earth from the curse of sin through the triumphant victory of Christ over Satan and his Antichrist.

Many people approach this book with an apprehension that they will be unable to understand its visions. The great Reformer, John Calvin, wrote a complete commentary of every book of the Bible, except for the book of Revelation which he did not understand. However, a correct application of the principles of Bible interpretation will enable us to understand and benefit from the marvelous visions of the Prophet John. Revelation occupies a unique position in the Scriptures in the richness of its imagery. While its mysterious symbols have caused some to avoid the study of this book, it has fascinated many Christians over the centuries, including Martin Luther, the great Reformer. "We can profit by this book and make good use of it... We can rest assured that neither force nor lies, neither wisdom nor holiness, neither tribulation nor suffering shall suppress Christendom, but it will gain the victory and conquer at last" *(Luther's Works 35.409)*.

The Challenge of the Book of Revelation

Revelation is certainly the most difficult of all the books of the Bible to interpret properly. These difficulties in interpretation have caused many Christians to ignore the Apocalypse completely. Yet this is not an acceptable position for one who believes God's declaration that "all Scripture is given by inspiration of God, and is profitable for doctrine, for reproof, for correction, for instruction in righteousness" (2 Timothy 3:16). The Apocalypse is the only book that contains a promise of blessing for those who study it.

We live in a time when opinions have taken the place of convictions for many people. In the absence of personal, dedicated Bible study, some believers are unable to develop convictions regarding many of the fundamental aspects of prophetic truth. If their faith is based solely upon opinions of men, then people will be tossed about on the winds of doctrine in these last days. While opinions come and go, biblical truth remains absolute. God's truth is worth living for and, if necessary, it is worth dying for. Our age is quite different from the early centuries of the Christian era. During the terrors of the pagan persecution and the medieval Inquisition, hundreds of thousands of Christian believers went to a martyr's death in absolute confidence in the Bible's truth and the hope of Christ's return. Today, many are confused. They are tossed to and fro with every new book that hits the market or every new fad doctrine introduced by some celebrity preacher. Many in our generation, who refuse to pay the price of daily Bible study and an intimate prayer life, wonder why they lack conviction and purpose in their spiritual life.

Consider the difference between the message of the Apostles and the prevailing spirit of our age. "But even if we, or an angel from heaven, preach any other gospel to you than what we have preached to you, let him be accursed" (Galatians 1:8). The confidence of the inspired Apostle rests upon his unshakable faith in Christ. He knows the truth; it has set him free. God did not give opinions to the biblical writers. He gave them inspired "revelations" concerning His truth. Christianity is not based on opinions or philosophy. Our faith and spiritual life are founded on the unshakable revelation of the Almighty God who cannot lie. Regarding the historical truth of the life, death and resurrection of Jesus Christ, our belief is founded on the inspired revelation of the Scriptures. Our faith is confirmed by incontrovertible historical evidence. In my book *Messiah* I examine the incredible historical evidence about the life of Jesus from Roman, Pagan and Jewish sources. The Apostle Peter declared: "For we did not follow cunningly devised fables when we made known to you the power and coming of our Lord Jesus Christ, but were eyewitnesses of His majesty" (2 Peter 1:16).

The Bible declares that prophecy is the absolute proof that God inspired the Word of God and distinguishes it from any other religious writing. God declared that fulfilled prophecy is His signature on the inspired Scriptures because no one, not even Satan, can prophecy the future. The Lord declares that He is the only one who can prophecy the future in detail and bring it to pass. "Remember the former things of old, for I am God, and there is no other; I am God, and there is none like Me, Declaring the end from the beginning, and from ancient times things that are not yet done, saying, 'My counsel shall stand, and I will do all My pleasure'" (Isaiah 46:9,10).

Methods of Prophetic Interpretation

How are we to correctly interpret the prophecies of the Bible? Since one-quarter of the Bible is prophetic, it is vital for us to come to a proper understanding of this important portion of God's revelation to His Church. There are two basic methods of interpretation which men use to understand the Bible's prophecies. The first method is the literal or common-sense method. This approach takes the verses in their normal, common-sense meaning and assumes that the writer wrote his prophecy to be understood as any other portion of writing. While the literal method acknowledges that prophecy contains figures of speech and symbols, these symbols will point to a literal reality. This method looks to the Bible to interpret its own symbols and avoids speculation. The New Testament interprets the Old Testament prophecies in the same normal, common-sense manner. Jesus Christ and the Apostles who wrote the New Testament interpret the Old Testament prophecies in a literal and common-sense manner.

Some believe that prophecy is confusing and contradictory. The confusion is produced when men refuse to interpret the Bible's passages in the same way they interpret normal writing. They believe that we should reject a literal method and interpret these prophecies in an allegorical or "spiritual" manner. This second method of allegorical interpretation rejects the clear meaning of the prophecies that point to the second coming of Christ in our generation. The allegorical approach is used by Kingdom Now and Dominion theologians because it frees them from the literal interpretation of the prophecies. For example, in Matthew 24, Jesus Christ describes a series of signs that will characterize the generation when He will return to establish His millennial Kingdom on earth. However, the allegorical method rejects this literal interpretation. It interprets Christ's words in an allegorical fashion that allows the interpreter to assign whatever meaning he likes to the specific prophecies. Kingdom Now teachers reject the premillennial return of Christ, the key role of Israel, the rebuilt Temple, the personal Antichrist and Battle of Armageddon. When they interpret Matthew 24 allegorically, they believe that all of these prophetic signs were fulfilled in A.D. 70 when the Roman armies destroyed Jerusalem. They believe that the awesome signs of worldwide earthquakes, famines, pestilence, the Abomination of Desolation and the Sign of the coming of the Son of Man were fulfilled in the burning of the Temple and Jerusalem two thousand years ago. Obviously, this interpretation rejects totally the normal, common sense and literal interpretation of Christ's prophetic words.

A Literal Interpretation

Every single prophecy that has seen its fulfillment was fulfilled in a normal and literal manner. In the life, death and resurrection of Jesus of Nazareth we witness the fulfillment of forty-eight distinct predictions from the Old Testament prophets. It is significant that not one of those predictions was fulfilled in an allegorical or "spiritual" manner. They were fulfilled with an amazing degree of precision, as detailed in my book *Armageddon - Appointment With Destiny*. I have spent tens of thousands of hours over the last thirty years in a detailed study of the prophecies of the Bible and their precise fulfillment as proved by ancient historical records and archeology. My conclusion, which is shared by thousands of respected Bible scholars over the centuries, is that the Bible's prophecies are to be interpreted in a literal sense. Later in this book I will share the overwhelming evidence that the early Church of the first two centuries understood the prophecies of the premillennial return of Christ in the same literal manner I share with you in this book.

Prophecy was not intended to be so difficult to interpret that only specialists could understand it. The prophecies authenticate the truthfulness and inspiration of the Word of God. They also allow us to look into the future to understand the events that are transpiring in our generation leading to the Second Coming of Jesus Christ. Two thousand years ago, Jesus Christ severely criticized the religious leaders of Israel for failing to interpret the "signs of the times" that indicated that the Messiah was at hand. As we approach the final crisis of this age, it is vital that we study this portion of God's "love letter" to His beloved Church to understand the times we live in and His instructions to us in light of His Second Coming.

The Purpose of Prophecy

In 2 Peter 1:19-21 the Apostle Peter declared: "We also have the prophetic word made more sure, which you do well to heed as a light that shines in a dark place, until the day dawns and the morning star rises in your hearts. Knowing this first, that no prophecy of Scripture is of any private interpretation, for prophecy never came by the will of man, but holy men of God spoke as they were moved by the Holy Spirit." In this significant passage, Peter explained that prophecy is intended to be a light to Christians to enable them to understand their dark times and to motivate them to appropriate action in light of His soon coming. In addition, Peter tells us that prophecy does not come "by the will of men" or "of any private interpretation." The significance of prophecy is an inspired message from the Holy Spirit to the Church to live expectantly in light of His imminent return. The expectancy of His coming should motivate believers to action in two specific areas. First, living in the expectation of His Second Coming should motivate us to walk in purity before a Holy God. John, the author of the Revelation, wrote that "everyone who has this hope in Him purifies himself, just as He is pure" (1 John 3:3). Second, if we truly believe that Christ is coming, we will be motivated to witness as never before, while there is still time.

The Language of the Apocalyptic

The book of Revelation is a portion of a distinct form of religious literature called *apocalyptic*. This literature is characterized by a recognition of a ongoing battle in this age between God and Satan that will conclude with God's cataclysmic victory over the forces of evil. This viewpoint takes a somewhat pessimistic view of current events but looks forward optimistically to the coming age when God's Messiah will triumph. While the Revelation contains hundreds of specific prophecies about the events leading to the Second Coming of Christ, it uses highly symbolic language and figures. Fortunately, the Bible always interprets its own symbols so we are not left to guess at their meaning. For example, in Revelation 12:7 we read John's vision that "Michael and his angels fought against the dragon." Instead of leaving us to wonder what the dragon symbol represents, Revelation 12:9 reveals the identity of the symbolic dragon. "And the great dragon was cast out, that serpent of old, called the Devil and Satan." It is important to keep in mind that these prophetic symbols point to a literal reality that will occur at the end of this age. If we carefully apply the principles of prophetic interpretation we will be able to understand Jesus Christ's last message to His Church.

The Theme of the Apocalypse

The purpose of the Revelation is summed up in the first verse of the book. John was told by God "to show His servants things which must shortly take place." This prophecy about "things which must shortly take place" was inspired by God who looks at time quite differently than we do. King David indicated the divine time sense in these words: "A thousand years in Your sight are like yesterday when it is past, and like a watch in the night" (Psalm 90:4). The Apostle Peter, specifically speaking about Christ's delay of His Second Coming, told us, "Beloved, do not forget this one thing, that with the Lord one day is as a thousand years, and a thousand years as one day" (2 Peter 3:8). When God promised to show us "things which must shortly take place" the emphasis is on the "showing" of a panoramic vista of apocalyptic events laid out before us. This phrase, "things which must shortly take place," may also refer to the seven letters to the churches which John received immediately after his initial vision. The messages to the seven churches recorded in the first three chapters of Revelation are concerned with events at the time of John's vision during the first century and in the decades that followed. However, the majority of Revelation's prophecies, from chapter 6 to the end, will not be fulfilled until the final generation of this era. The phrase "must shortly take place" may also indicate that the prophesied events "must take place shortly" (with speed) or quickly. Once they commence, the fulfillment of Revelation's prophecies will occur in relatively short order over a period of seven years.

The Keys of Heaven and Hell

"I have the keys of Hades and of Death" (Revelation 1:18).

Keys are a universal symbol of power and authority, possession, and government. Satan can create nothing because he himself is a created angel. Only God has the power to create "out of nothing." The Scriptures promise that "at the name of Jesus every knee should bow, of those in heaven, and of those on earth, and of those under the earth, and that every tongue should confess that Jesus Christ is Lord, to the glory of God the Father" (Philippians 2:10,11).

Jesus Christ is the Lord and Creator of the universe. Everything that exists in heaven, the earth and hell was created by Jesus. As Colossians 1:16 declares: "For by Him all things were created that are in heaven and that are on earth, visible and invisible, whether thrones or dominions or principalities or powers. All things were created through Him and for Him." In Revelation 1:18 we read Christ's declaration that "I have the keys of Hades and of Death." A paraphrase of this statement is that "I have the sole authority over Hades and the Grave." Hades is the repository of the souls of the wicked dead waiting for the final Great White Throne judgment. The Grave is the place of waiting for the bodies of those who have died. By this statement, Christ declares His Lordship over the destiny of all men and women. He is the King of kings, Lord of lords.

13

Chapter One

Interpreting Revelation

The Problem of Interpretation

There are four major interpretive approaches to the prophecies of Revelation that have developed over the last two thousand years. The first approach, the "futurist view," was held by the Christians during the first few centuries following the writing of the New Testament. This is also the view that will be followed throughout this study of the tremendous promises of Apocalypse.

The Futurist View

The "futurist view" is the view which most prophecy teachers follow today. Futurists interpret the visions of Revelation to refer primarily to the future prophetic events that will culminate in Christ's Second Coming at the end of this era. Jesus and the Apostles described the coming of Christ in the last days. This futurist view was also believed and taught by the early New Testament Church, as I will demonstrate in this book. Unfortunately, as the Church gradually departed from the evangelical faith in the fifth and sixth centuries, they also abandoned the teaching of prophecy. The literal and futurist view gave way to the allegorical method of interpretation introduced widely by Augustine of Hippo (A.D. 410). During the medieval age very little was written on prophecy. After the Reformation in A.D. 1520 and the re-discovery of the literal view of biblical interpretation, the futurist view increasingly came into favor. The Reformers progressively recovered many of the key doctrines of the faith that were lost during spiritual darkness of the medieval period when Bibles were forbidden to laymen. After the 1830s the literal and futurist method of interpretation became the dominant Protestant method of interpreting Bible prophecy. This method strongly re-adopted the premillennial view of the early Church. It looks for the Second Coming of Jesus to precede His establishment of a one-thousand-year kingdom on earth.

The Historical View

The historical method interprets Revelation's visions as referring primarily to events that have affected the Church over two thousand years from the first century until the end of this era. A fundamental aspect of this view is the Year = Day Principle which interprets the 1260 days of Daniel and Revelation as being 1260 years. As an example, this position interprets the 1260 days of Revelation, not as real future days in the three-and-a-half year rule of a personal Antichrist, but rather as a 1260 year period of Anti-Christian rule from the rise of Papal Rome until the defeat of Papal troops by Napoleon around A.D. 1800. This historical view, tentatively developed in the twelfth century, became extremely popular with the early Reformation writers and prevailed up until approximately 1820. Since many of these writers had lost family and friends to the Inquisition, they naturally saw their enemy in the prophecies of the book of Revelation. This view mistakenly interpreted the Papacy as both the Antichrist and Babylon. However, Revelation 17 clearly prophesies that the future Antichrist and the ten nations will destroy the false church of the Great Whore of Babylon. Obviously, the Antichrist will not destroy himself or his own creation. When all possible termination periods for the 1260 day-year period expired without fulfillment, most Christians abandoned this method of interpretation.

The Preterit or Kingdom Now View

The word "preterit" comes from the Latin word *praeter* which means "past." The preterit view interprets virtually all of the visions of Revelation as referring to the events that were fulfilled in the destruction of the Temple and city of Jerusalem in A.D. 70 by the Roman armies. However the historical evidence contradicts this theory. The internal evidence within the book of Revelation and the overwhelming testimony of the early Church confirms that John's prophecy was written in A.D. 96, some twenty-six years after the fall of Jerusalem. Since the Apocalypse contains detailed prophecies about future events, John's predictions cannot possibly refer to events that occurred decades earlier. The true reason Kingdom Now and Dominion theology vehemently rejects the A.D. 96 date for the writing of Revelation is that it contradicts their position. Their theory requires them to place the date of Revelation's writing in A.D. 68, before Jerusalem was destroyed. Otherwise, John's prophecies must refer to future events at the end of this age of grace. Later, we will examine the critical evidence that Revelation was written by John in A.D. 96. This evidence will prove that the preterit and Kingdom Now position is untenable.

This preterit view of the Kingdom Now and Dominion teachers holds that the prophecies of Revelation were fulfilled in the distant past and that they have no predictive value for the Church today. Those who hold this postmillennial or amillennial view believe that Christ will not return to earth for thousands of years until the Church converts the world to Christianity and creates the Kingdom of God on earth. However, the visions of Revelation, if taken literally, describe Christ violently conquering an evil, rebellious earth in the future and setting up His millennial Kingdom. Those who reject our premillennial view are forced to adopt another interpretation of the prophecies of Revelation to avoid this conclusion. This Kingdom Now view suggests that John's apocalyptic visions of world-wide war, famine, pestilence killing one-third of humanity, etc. were fulfilled by the burning of Jerusalem in A.D. 70. Since the literal method of interpretation totally contradicts their preterit view, Kingdom Now teachers are forced to adopt an allegorical and spiritualizing method of interpretation. Later in this book, we will deal with the inadequacies of this preterit view.

The Idealist or Allegorical View

Lastly, some writers treat the Apocalypse as a symbolic

description of the ultimate war between good and evil, promising that good will finally triumph. To hold this idealist position, they must interpret the visions and prophecies of Revelation as allegories and figures of speech. In other words, they do not expect any of Revelation's detailed prophecies of the Antichrist, False Prophet and the Battle of Armageddon to ever be fulfilled in the future. Many postmillennial and amillennial writers interpret Revelation's prophecies in this purely allegorical manner to avoid the clear predictions of Christ coming to defeat Satan's Antichrist before the Millennium to set up His rule from the Throne of David.

The Premillennial Hope of the Early Church

Without exception, for the first two and a half centuries the early Church universally held a belief in the premillennial coming of Christ to defeat Satan's Antichrist and establish His glorious millennial Kingdom. They expected an apostasy in the last days followed by a personal Antichrist and False Prophet, a Great Tribulation and the victorious Battle of Armageddon. In the Appendix I list more than eighty specific literal and futurist interpretations of biblical prophecy held in common by the early Christians and premillennial believers today.

Webster's dictionary defines premillennialism as a system of prophetic interpretation that the second coming of Christ will precede the millennial Kingdom. The first-century Christians interpreted the Bible literally, exactly as Christ and the Apostles interpreted the Old Testament prophecies in the New Testament. The literal method of interpretation is the foundation of the premillennial position. Some complain that a literal view kills spiritual understanding. However, this is false because the New Testament interprets Old Testament passages literally, revealing God's stamp of approval on this literal system. In fact, every single prophecy that has been fulfilled, has been fulfilled literally. There are no examples of an allegorical fulfillment of prophecy. The literal method is biblical, practical and valid as we seek to understand God's message to the Church.

The evidence is incontrovertible that the early Church believed universally for two hundred and fifty years in the doctrine of a literal one-thousand-year reign of Christ's saints on the earth. After the conversion of Emperor Constantine, his Edict of Toleration made the Christian Church the official state church of the Roman Empire in A.D. 325. From that point on, political considerations and power politics entered the councils of the Church. The premillennial view of Christ coming to defeat the evil governments of this world became unpopular with rulers once Roman emperors and their successor kings entered into a mutually profitable, but unholy alliance with church leaders. They did not want to hear that God would overthrow their kingdoms and replace them with His eternal Kingdom on earth.

Amillennialism and the Allegorical Method

The third-century theologian Origen adopted and popularized an allegorical method of teaching borrowed from the Greek pagan writers. He was brilliant but quite unbalanced. At one point he castrated himself to ensure he lived a pure life. He taught many false doctrines, including reincarnation of men into animals and a rejection of a literal interpretation of the Scriptures. Augustine of Hippo, a very important theologian from North Africa, was influenced by Origen. He wrote his pivotal book *The City of God* in the beginning of the fifth century which rejected the literal interpretation of Scripture and the premillennial return of Christ. He proposed an allegorical method of interpretation to escape the clear teaching of premillennialism. This allegorical method refuses to interpret the words of Scripture in the common-sense, literal manner we apply to normal language and writing. The allegorical method interprets the words of Scripture in any manner the interpreter desires. There are no rules. Everything is symbolic and can be interpreted according to the preconception of the interpreter without reference to the normal sense of the prophecies.

Augustine adopted an amillennial view which rejected any literal period of a thousand years before or after Christ's return. This amillennial position became the dominant view of the Roman Catholic Church for fifteen hundred years until today. The study of prophecy was virtually abandoned except for an occasional mention by writers that the Antichrist would come. Following the Reformation in A.D. 1520, the Protestant Reformers rejected the theological heresies that had developed during the medieval period. Unfortunately, most of them did not seriously study the area of prophetic truth, except to describe the Papacy and the Popes as both Antichrist and the Great Whore of Babylon. Most of the early reformers continued with an amillennial view inherited from the medieval Church.

Irenaeus, in his *Against Heresies*, wrote a rebuttal of the heretical teaching that was beginning to corrupt the Church's hope of the second coming of Christ. Just as we find today, the allegorical method of interpretation led teachers to abandon the literal promises and prophecies of the Scriptures. Irenaeus held to a literal, common-sense interpretation of the prophecies of both the Old and New Testament. "If, however, any shall endeavor to allegorize [prophecies] of this kind, they shall not be found consistent with themselves in all points, and shall be confuted by the teaching of the very expressions." Allegorical interpretation produces confusion because each teacher will supply his own interpretation according to his imagination, rather than the normal sense of language.

The Literal Method of Interpretation

As the Reformers recovered a literal interpretation of the Holy Scriptures, they developed a systematic theology of the Bible's great truths. Eventually, they began to focus on the area of eschatology, the study of last things. Bishop Hooker, a key Reformation writer, claimed that if given a choice between a literal and an allegorical interpretation, the literal was closest and the allegorical farthest from the biblical truth. The great scientist and writer Sir Isaac Newton was fascinated with prophecy. He wrote of his belief that in the last days God would raise up men who would devote their efforts to the study of the prophetic portions of Scripture and "insist upon their literal interpretation in the midst of much clamour and opposition." The early Church and the writers on prophecy during the last two centuries both believed firmly in the premillennial return of Christ because they interpreted the Bible literally.

The recovery of a literal hermeneutic and the truth of the premillennial return of Christ transformed the Church back to its early zeal for evangelism. The fruits of this earnest hope for the Lord's return resulted in an explosion of evangelism, enormous missionary efforts to reach the world with the gospel and a commitment to "occupy till He comes." Some have criticized premillennialism, claiming that those who expect Christ to come at any moment would ignore the ills of society and abandon evangelism. Experience shows that this fear is misplaced. The truth is apparent for all who will examine the historical record. For the last two centuries, denominations that held to the literal premillennial and pretribulation return of Christ have been at the forefront of the worldwide missionary efforts to reach the lost. Premillennial Church leaders led the tremendous social reforms that ended child labor and created a strong Christian educational system. Far from leading to escapism, the hope of the return of Christ at any moment motivates Christians to live in purity. This expectation will encourage believers to witness to their world while there is still time.

The Certainty of Prophetic Fulfillment

Hundreds of detailed prophecies were fulfilled precisely when Jesus Christ came two thousand years ago. As we examine the literal and normal method in which these prophecies came to pass, we gain confidence that the prophecies that remain to be fulfilled in the last days will occur in exactly the same fashion. In the early Church, Justin Martyr wrote about the certainty of prophetic fulfillment. "Since, then, we prove that all things which have already happened had been predicted by the prophets before they came to pass, as we must necessarily believe also that those things which are in like manner predicted, but are yet to come to pass, shall certainly happen. For as the things which have already taken place came to pass when foretold, and even though unknown, so shall the things that remain, even though they be unknown and disbelieved, yet come to pass. For the prophets have proclaimed two advents of His: the one which is already past, when He came as a dishonored and suffering Man; but the second, when according to prophecy, He shall come from heaven with glory" (*First Apology* 25).

How Are We to Understand John's Visions?

Revelation brings together many diverse prophetic strands and explains many of the prophecies that were veiled in the Old Testament. Each symbol in the book of Revelation is interpreted by other passages and verses. We find parallels to these visions and symbols in the other biblical prophets. Many of the earlier prophets admitted that they did not fully understand the visions God had given them. Daniel declared, "I was astonished by the vision, but no one understood it" (Daniel 8:27). An unusual aspect of prophetic revelations is that they may not be fully understood till a point in time far removed from the life of the prophet. Some prophecies will not be understood until they are completely fulfilled. In Deuteronomy 29:29 the Bible tells us: "The secret things belong to the Lord our God, but those things which are revealed belong to us and to our children forever, that we may do all the words of this law."

The first verse of Revelation declares: "The Revelation of Jesus Christ, which God gave Him to show His servants — things which must shortly take place. And He sent and signified it by His angel to His servant John." The message of the Apocalypse was transmitted as follows: from God to Christ to His angel to John to His servants. The words "signified it" are critical because they acknowledge the fact that the book of Revelation contains more symbols than any other book of the Bible. If we are to understand this important apocalyptic vision we must learn to interpret the prophetic symbolic language used by John. As we explore the visions of the Apocalypse we will systematically examine and explain each symbol.

One curious feature of biblical prophecy sometimes confuses Christians. When predicting some event far in the future, the prophet will often speak about the event in the past tense, as if it had already occurred. For example, in

Revelation 21:1 John writes about the transformation of the earth at the end of the Millennium, over a thousand years in the future. "And I saw a new heaven and a new earth, for the first heaven and the first earth had passed away." Several early Christian writers, including Justin Martyr (A.D. 150), spoke of this phenomenon, "The things which He [God] absolutely knows will take place, He predicts as if already they had taken place" (*First Apology*).

The Principle of Recapitulation

Another key to understanding Revelation is the principle of recapitulation. Although the details and stages of John's visions follow each other sequentially, frequently you will see a prophetic recapitulation of a previous vision, though seen from a different vantage point. For example, the seventh Seal Judgment introduces and contains the next series of seven Trumpet Judgments. Quite often, the prophet John will follow a particular line of God's judgment and then go back to the beginning to describe another view of the same judgment period. This principle was recognized by early Christian writers such as Lactantius in his *Commentary on the Apocalypse of the Blessed John* (chapter 7). He wrote as follows: "What, therefore, he said too little in the trumpets, is here found in the vials. We must not regard the order of what is said, because frequently the Holy Spirit, when He has traversed even to the end of the last times, returns again to the same times, and fills up what He had before failed to say." A similar method is used today in novels and movies where several subplots are woven together by an author. The book or film will follow one character's actions, then backtrack earlier in time and follow another character through the day's activities until they meet at a common crisis.

Angelic Messengers

The word "angel" appears many times in the Apocalypse but we must carefully examine the context to determine its meaning. Angel can refer to a spiritual heavenly being or it can indicate one who has the role of a divine messenger. A large part of the Revelation concerns conversations between "His angel" and John. Who is this angel? He cannot be an angel like the other heavenly angels described by John because, later in his vision, John revealed that this particular "angel" was human. When John tried to worship this "angel," he stopped him saying, "I am your fellow servant, and of your brethren who have the testimony of Jesus" (Revelation 19:10). This passage indicates that this particular "angel" was a man, John's "fellow servant." Possibly he was a Jewish Christian, because Revelation records that he was "of your brethren who have the testimony of Jesus." He could be one of the many Old Testament saints who were resurrected from Abraham's bosom by Christ at His resurrection (Matthew 27:52, 53). It's also possible that the messenger was Moses or Elijah who appeared on the Mount of Transfiguration to witness to the glory of Jesus Christ.

Daniel's Prophecy of the Seventy Weeks
An Outline of Prophecy

"Seventy weeks [490 years] are determined for your people and for your holy city, to finish the transgression, to make an end of sins, to make reconciliation for iniquity, to bring in everlasting righteousness, to seal up vision and prophecy, and to anoint the Most Holy. Know therefore and understand, that from the going forth of the command to restore and build Jerusalem until Messiah the Prince, there shall be seven weeks and sixty-two weeks; the street shall be built again, and the wall, even in troublesome times. And after the sixty-two weeks Messiah shall be cut off, but not for Himself; and the people of the prince who is to come shall destroy the city and the sanctuary. The end of it shall be with a flood, and till the end of the war desolations are determined. Then he shall confirm a covenant with many for one week; but in the middle of the week he shall bring an end to sacrifice and offering" (Daniel 9:24-27).

Throughout this book we will often refer to Daniel's vision of the seventy weeks. This key prophecy is fundamental to our understanding of the order of events that will unfold in the last days. Daniel is unique among the prophets of the Bible because he was given an unusually detailed view of time in his predictions. When Nebuchadnezzar, King of Babylon, conquered Jerusalem in 606 B.C. he returned to Babylon with the Jewish royal captives, including Daniel. The prophet was given a vision that outlined the entire history of God's dealing with Israel and the nations. Daniel's vision of the seventy weeks foretold to the day when Israel would reject and "cut off" their Messiah. He also predicted the second coming of Christ to "seal up the vision and prophecy" and establish His everlasting kingdom. The time element is quite specific and demonstrates the precision of fulfilled prophecy. The word "weeks" referred to a seven-year period. This method of counting time was as common with the Jews as decades are with us because God commanded Israel to keep the Sabbath of the land every seven years.

The 360-Day Biblical and Prophetic Year

The true length of the prophetic year is vital in determining the chronology of prophecy. The Jews in biblical times used a lunar-solar year with only 360 days. The solar calendar year, of course, has 365.25 days. However, this solar year was not used by the ancient nations in the Middle East. The *Encyclopedia Britannica*'s article on Chronology confirms that Abraham used a 360-day year in Chaldea and the Promised Land. The Genesis history of Noah's flood reveals a thirty-day month and a 360-day year were in use at that time. The flood waters were at the full for "150 days," the five-month interval (of thirty days each) between the seventeenth day of the second month to the seventeenth day of the seventh month. We still need to calculate using the same biblical lunar-solar year of 360 days if we wish to understand the detailed time prophecies of Daniel. Similarly, in the book of Revelation, John refers to the last three-and-one-half years of the Great Tribulation as precisely 1260 days (Revelation 12:6). He writes about the three and a half year Great Tribulation period as "a time, times and half a time" where a "time" stands for a year of 360 days, "times" represents two years and "half a time" means six months. This period is also described as "forty-two months" of thirty days each (13:5). These references confirm that the 360-day biblical year, is the one by which we must calculate biblical prophecy.

The Precision of Prophecy

There are four important parts in Daniel's vision. The first part commences with "the commandment to rebuild the walls of Jerusalem" (Daniel 9:25). This decree of the Persian King Artaxerxes Longimanus was given to Nehemiah "in the month of Nisan, in the twentieth year" of his reign (Nehemiah 2:1). According to the *Talmud,* "The first day of the month Nisan is the New Year for the computation of the reign of kings and for festivals." In other words, if no day is given, the assumption is that the first day of the month applies. The first day of Nisan in King Artaxerxes' twentieth year was calculated by the Royal Observatory, Greenwich, United Kingdom, to be March 14, 445 B. C.

The second part of the vision extends "from the going forth of the commandment to restore and to rebuild Jerusalem" (March 14, 445 B.C.) and includes an initial period of seven "weeks" of years (7x7=49 years) in which Jerusalem was rebuilt "even in troublous times." A second period of sixty-two "weeks" (62 x 7= 434 years) immediately followed the first seven "weeks" bringing us to a combined total of sixty-nine weeks of years (69 x 7 years = 483 Biblical years). This sixty-nine week period of 483 biblical years is equal to 173,880 days (483 x 360 days = 173,880 days). The third part of the vision concludes with the Messiah being "cut off" at the end of the sixty-nine "weeks" (483 years). Exactly 483 biblical years later, precisely 173,880 days from the command on March 14, 445 B.C., brings us to the tenth day of Nisan, April 6, A.D. 32. On that day, Palm Sunday, Jesus Christ fulfilled this prophecy as He entered Jerusalem presenting Himself to Israel as their Messiah. The precision of prophecy is illustrated by the fact that Jesus was rejected by Israel on the precise day that ended the sixty-ninth week of Daniel 9:24-27.

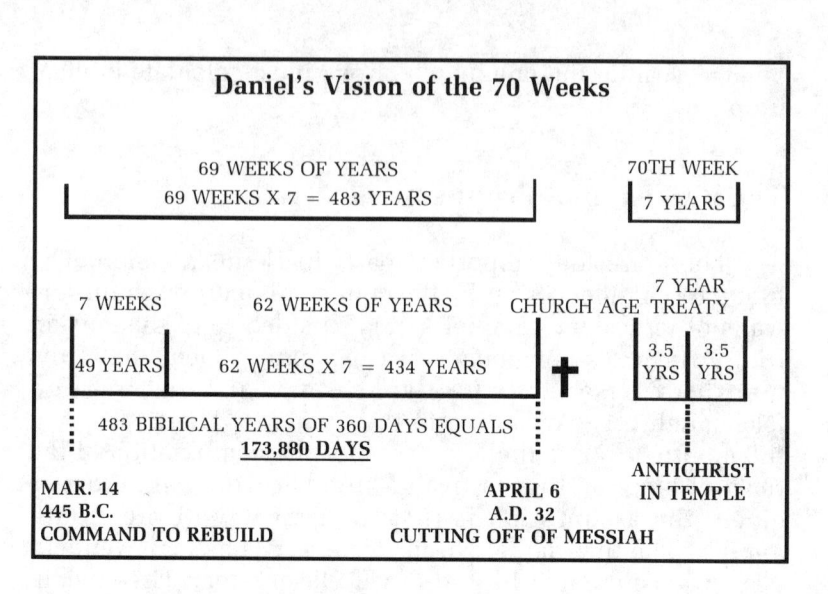

Daniel's Vision of the 70 Weeks

| 69 WEEKS OF YEARS | 70TH WEEK |
| 69 WEEKS X 7 = 483 YEARS | 7 YEARS |

| 7 WEEKS | 62 WEEKS OF YEARS | CHURCH AGE | 7 YEAR TREATY |
| 49 YEARS | 62 WEEKS X 7 = 434 YEARS | ✝ | 3.5 YRS | 3.5 YRS |

483 BIBLICAL YEARS OF 360 DAYS EQUALS
173,880 DAYS

MAR. 14
445 B.C.
COMMAND TO REBUILD

APRIL 6
A.D. 32
CUTTING OFF OF MESSIAH

**ANTICHRIST
IN TEMPLE**

Israel's Time of Visitation

The Messiah rode into Jerusalem on the back of a foal on the precise day Daniel's sixty-nine "weeks" of years ended. Christ's disciples acknowledged Him as their Messiah, proclaiming, "Blessed is the King who comes in the name of the Lord! Peace in heaven and glory in the highest!" (Luke 19:38). However, the majority of Israel and the Gentiles tragically rejected Him as their Messiah. When Jesus approached Jerusalem "He saw the city and wept over it, saying, 'If you had known, even you, especially in this your day, the things that make for your peace! But now they are hidden from your eyes. For the days will come upon you when your enemies will build an embankment around you, surround you and close you in on every side, and level you, and your children within you, to the ground; and they will not leave in you one stone upon another, because you did not know the time of your visitation" (Luke 19:41-44). Almost forty years later, the Roman legions burned Jerusalem and ripped up every stone of the Temple.

In this passage, Jesus told Israel that this day, Palm Sunday, the tenth day of Nisan, April 6, A.D. 32, was the "time of your visitation." This was their day of decision to choose to accept or reject Jesus as their Messiah-King. Despite the acclaim by Jesus' disciples and some citizens, the majority of the religious and political leaders rejected Him. Five days later this rejection culminated in the crucifixion of Jesus. Their promised kingdom was postponed for almost two thousand years.

To sum up, Daniel's vision spoke of a total of seventy "sevens" or seventy "weeks" of years, equalling 490 biblical years. This first period of sixty-nine weeks of years was fulfilled to the exact day. For those who want to confirm these calculations, I cover this topic in great detail in my book *Armageddon - Appointment With Destiny*. The last seventieth "week" of seven critical years remains to be fulfilled in our generation. Can anyone seriously doubt that the remaining "week" of seven years, Daniel's seventieth "week" of years, will be fulfilled just as precisely?

Daniel's Seventieth Week
The Seven Years of Tribulation

"Then he shall confirm a covenant with many for one week; but in the middle of the week he shall bring an end to sacrifice and offering" (Daniel 9:27).

Daniel's seventieth week will be fulfilled in the final seven years of this era. Jewish and Gentile history is moving inexorably toward a countdown to Armageddon. When Israel and the Gentiles rejected their promised Messiah on Palm Sunday, April 6, A.D. 32, "the time of your visitation" (Luke 20:44) on the last day of Daniel's sixty-ninth week of prophecy, God's prophetic clock stopped ticking. The Lord postponed their prophesied kingdom for almost two thousand years. During this interval between Daniel's sixty-ninth week and the final seventieth week, God created His Church composed of Jews and Gentiles from every nation to be a witness to all the world. During this interval, "Hardening in part has happened to Israel until the fullness of the Gentiles has come in" (Romans 11:25-26). However, while the kingdom was postponed, God's covenant with Israel remains unbroken. Their Messiah will return and usher in the Kingdom of God on earth. Israel will finally see her Messiah when Christ returns at Armageddon to conclude the seventieth week of years.

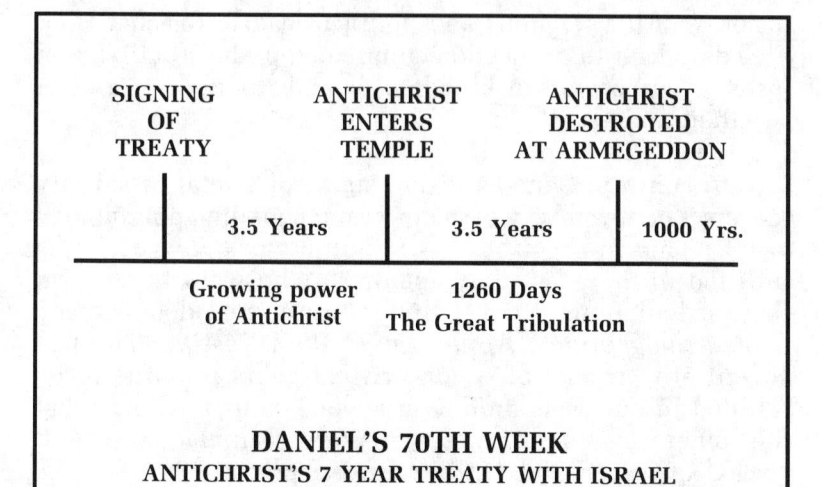

SIGNING OF TREATY	ANTICHRIST ENTERS TEMPLE	ANTICHRIST DESTROYED AT ARMEGEDDON	
	3.5 Years	3.5 Years	1000 Yrs.
	Growing power of Antichrist	1260 Days The Great Tribulation	

DANIEL'S 70TH WEEK
ANTICHRIST'S 7 YEAR TREATY WITH ISRAEL

The Prophetic Gap in Daniel 9:24-27

A number of modern critics of prophecy have complained about our belief that Daniel's seventieth week will involve seven years occurring in our future. They declare that the last three and a half years of Daniel's final seventieth week of years was fulfilled between A.D. 33 and A.D. 37. Their suggestion is that Christ's disciples somehow fulfilled the last three and one-half years by witnessing to the Jews until A.D. 37. This forced and awkward interpretation is an attempt to avoid the clear prediction of a future Antichrist and a seven-year tribulation period occurring just prior to Christ establishing His kingdom. They suggest that Christ made a seven-year "covenant" with the Jews despite the total lack of biblical evidence for such a conclusion. The New Testament knows nothing of a seven-year covenant with Israel. Furthermore, they declare that Jesus fulfilled Daniel 9:27 when He brought "an end to sacrifice and offering" by His death on the Cross. However, this interpretation is contradicted by the historical evidence that the daily sacrifice continued without interruption for 38 years until the Romans burnt the Temple in A.D. 70.

These critics totally reject our belief in a "gap" of almost two thousand years between the end of the sixty-ninth week with Christ's rejection and the signing of a seven-year treaty between the Antichrist and Israel. Several writers have ridiculed the "gap" theory claiming that it was invented by modern futurist prophecy teachers since A.D. 1820. However, the *Epistle of Barnabas* and many other early Christian writings prove that they are completely mistaken in their assumption. The concept of a future seven-year treaty between the Antichrist and the Jews (Daniel's seventieth week) and a "gap" between the sixty-ninth and seventieth week was widely accepted by the early Church.

Kingdom Now teachers criticize our interpretation that there is a "gap" of time in Daniel 9:24-27 allowing the Church Age to exist between the sixty-ninth week and the seventieth week. They claim that this "gap" in Daniel 9:24-27 is artificial, unnatural and without foundation in Scripture or the historic biblical interpretation of these prophecies. Some who oppose the pretribulation Rapture suggest that the "gap" between Daniel's sixty-ninth week and the beginning of the seventieth week has no foundation in the biblical text itself. However, an unprejudiced reader of Daniel's seventieth week prophecy will notice that there is a clear division between the two periods. Obviously, the Messiah being "cut off" is the critical event between these two periods.

Daniel's prophecy reads: "And after threescore and two weeks shall Messiah be cut off, but not for himself" (Daniel 9:26). A close examination will reveal that the Messiah is "cut off" at a point "after" the sixty-nine weeks are completed. However the cutting off of the Messiah does not take place within the duration of the seventieth week either. This indicates that it would occur during some "interval" or "gap" between both periods. A careful reading of the prophecy indicates that there is a break after the sixty-ninth week, rather than a continuous running of the sixty-ninth week right into the seventieth week of years.

Early Church Writers on Daniel's Seventieth Week

Several of the Ante-Nicene Fathers clearly taught that there was a "gap" between the two periods. They taught that the seventieth week of seven years under the rule of the Antichrist would follow many centuries later. Their writings

29

prove that this interpretation is not some recent innovation by either Jesuits, the Plymouth Brethren or others. An example can be found in the *Epistle of Barnabas* which was written about A.D. 100. The widespread acceptance of this writing indicates that this book accurately reflected the thinking of the ancient apostolic Church regarding prophecy. It was clearly written after the destruction of Jerusalem by the Roman army in A.D. 70 because the writer of the epistle refers to the burning of the Temple. "Moreover, He [Jesus] again says, 'Behold, they who have cast down this temple, even they shall build it up again.' It has so happened. For through their going to war, it was destroyed by their enemies; and now they, [the Jews] as the servants of their enemies, shall rebuild it" (16). He also describes the future Temple that will be built, "For it is written, 'And it shall come to pass, *when the week is completed, the Temple of God shall be built in glory* in the name of the Lord" (16, italics added).

Note that this *Epistle of Barnabas* refers to Daniel's "week" of years, seven years leading to Armageddon, in the last days. He also indicates that the future Temple described by Ezekiel 40 to 48 will be built by God "when the week [seven years] is completed." Early Christian writers spoke of Daniel's vision of the seventy weeks having their initial fulfillment in Christ's passion with His cutting off at the end of the first sixty-nine weeks. This prophecy of Daniel 9:24-27 described a final seventieth "week" of seven years to be completed just before the return of Christ in glory. This *Epistle of Barnabas*, written long after Christ's resurrection and the destruction of Jerusalem in A.D. 70, refers to the prophesied "week" as still future. Many other first century writers also wrote of Daniel's seventieth "week" being fulfilled in the last days.

Hippolytus, a disciple of Irenaeus, was one of the authoritative Christian writers in the second century. In his *Commentaries* he wrote about the coming Antichrist and the seventieth week of Daniel 9:27. "For when the threescore and two weeks are fulfilled, and Christ is come, and the gospel is preached in every place, the times being then accomplished, *there will remain only one week, the last, in which Elias [Elijah] will appear, and Enoch, and in the midst of it the abomination of desolation will be manifested, viz. Antichrist,* announcing desolation to the world" [italics added] (*Ante Nicene Fathers*, Vol. v, p.182). This manuscript clearly proves that the Church during the first centuries understood that there would be a "gap." In addition to these writers, Irenaeus in his book *Against Heresies* and Justin Martyr in his *Dialogue With Trypho* also taught that there would be an interlude before the future seventieth week of Daniel 9:27.

Other "Gaps" in the Fulfillment of Prophecy

A close examination of other prophecies reveals a number of "gaps" in the durations of prophetic times or historical enumerations found in the Scriptures. Throughout the Bible's prophecies we find several predictions that contain a dual nature regarding the time factor. In other words, within a single passage, a prophet will speak of two future events that will be separated by thousands of years. As an example, Isaiah 9:6-7 declares: "For unto us a child is born, unto us a son is given: and the government will be upon His shoulder: and His Name will be called Wonderful, Counselor, Mighty God, Everlasting Father, Prince of Peace. Of the increase of His government and peace there will be no end, upon the throne of David, and upon His kingdom, to order it, and establish it with judgment and justice from that time forward even forever."

Note that the statement, "For unto us a Child is born, unto us a Son is given" was fulfilled at the birth of Jesus of Nazareth. However, the second portion of his prophecy, beginning with "and the government will be upon His shoulder" and "Of the increase of His government and peace there will be no end, upon the throne of David" was not fulfilled in Christ's first advent. Those future events, separated by a "gap" of almost two thousand years, will find their fulfillment at the return of the Messiah at the end of this age.

The prophecy of Daniel 12:2 also manifests the phenomenon of a single prophetic passage containing predictions covering events more than a thousand years apart. "And many of those who sleep in the dust of the earth shall awake, some to everlasting life, some to shame and

31

everlasting contempt." As Revelation 20:4-6 reveals, the first resurrection of life will be followed a thousand years later by the resurrection unto spiritual death at the White Throne Judgment. Another example of a gap is found in Zechariah 9:9-10: "Rejoice greatly, O daughter of Zion! Shout, O daughter of Jerusalem! Behold, your King is coming to you; He is just and having salvation, lowly and riding on a donkey, a colt, the foal of a donkey. I will cut off the chariot from Ephraim and the horse from Jerusalem; the battle bow shall be cut off. He shall speak peace to the nations; His dominion shall be 'from sea to sea, and from the River to the ends of the earth.'" The first part of Zechariah's prophecy "your King is coming to you; He is just and having salvation, lowly and riding on a donkey, a colt, the foal of a donkey" — was fulfilled precisely in Christ's Palm Sunday entry to Jerusalem. However, the second portion of the prediction included "I will cut off the chariot from Ephraim and the horse from Jerusalem; the battle bow shall be cut off," and the statement that "His dominion shall be 'from sea to sea.'" This second portion is separated by a "gap" of some two thousand years and will be fulfilled at the triumphant return of Christ.

Other prophetic gap passages include: Isaiah 11:1-6; Isaiah 40:3-5 and Isaiah 52:13-15. However, of all the "gap" prophecies, the one prediction that clearly reveals this phenomenon is found in Isaiah 61:1-2: "The Spirit of the Lord God is upon Me, because the Lord has anointed Me to preach good tidings to the poor; He has sent Me to heal the brokenhearted, to proclaim liberty to the captives, and the opening of the prison to those who are bound; to proclaim the acceptable year of the Lord, and the day of vengeance of our God."

Our authority for interpreting this prophecy as containing a gap of thousands of years is found in the actual words of Jesus Christ. It is noteworthy that Jesus began His public ministry in the synagogue in Nazareth by reading this great Jubilee prophecy from Isaiah 61. After reading the first part of the prophecy ending with "the acceptable year of the Lord" Jesus "closed the book, and gave it back to the attendent, and sat down. And the eyes of all who were in the synagogue were fixed on Him. And He began to say to them,

'Today this scripture is fulfilled in your hearing" (Luke 4:18-21). Note that Jesus did not read Isaiah's concluding prophetic phrase — "and the day of vengeance of our God." This remarkable passage in Luke reveals that Jesus knew that the last part of Isaiah's prophecy "the day of vengeance of our God" would not be fulfilled in His first advent. It would be delayed almost two thousand years until His second coming in glory to establish His kingdom. Thus, the New Testament records that Jesus Christ acknowledged through His interpretation that there was a prophetic "gap" of thousands of years between His first coming and His second coming.

Reasons for the Prophetic Gap in Daniel 9:24-27

Over the last thirty years of studying Bible prophecy I have often pondered the mystery of this "gap" between the First and Second Advents of Christ. Surely God knew from the beginning of time how events would work out. Why do we find this strange parenthesis of an undefined duration? I believe the reason for this gap in Bible prophecy is due to the problem of predestination and free will. God is sovereign and all-knowing. He knows the ultimate outcome of every course of action man could take. However, for reasons known only to Him, God created mankind with the freedom to choose to obey or rebel against Him. The Lord knew that our freedom would result in sin, the loss of Paradise, the Cross and finally redemption. This freedom is of such value to God that He risked everything to allow us to freely obey Him.

When Jesus Christ came to earth two thousand years ago He presented to both the Jews and Gentiles a genuine, bona fide offer of the Kingdom of heaven on earth if they would accept Him as their Messiah-King. If they had chosen to accept Jesus and crown Him as their Messiah on Palm Sunday, A.D. 32, He would have entered the Eastern Gate and announce the restitution of all things, the cancellation of all debts and the proclamation of liberty to the captives. It was a genuine possibility that Israel could have accepted Him as Messiah and He would have ushered in the millennial Kingdom. Somehow, Jesus would have been crucified at some later point to fulfill the prophecy and provide salvation of all those who repent of their sins.

The tragedy is that both the Jews and Gentiles rejected God's offer of the Kingdom of heaven and murdered His Son, the Messiah. The result was two thousand years of exile for Israel and centuries of war and ruin under a series of evil Gentile empires. God turned to the Church, composed of both Gentiles and Jews, to fulfill His Great Commission to reach all mankind with the saving gospel of Christ's salvation. When the Church completes its mission God will rapture the Christians home to heaven. Then, the Lord will motivate Israel to be "a light to the nations" during the last seven years of this age. Since man was free to choose, the Bible's prophecies in Daniel 9:24-27, Isaiah 9:6-8, and Matthew 24, etcetera were constructed with a "gap" of undetermined length that could have lasted one hour or two thousand years. If mankind had accepted Christ at His first coming, Daniel's seventieth week would have immediately followed the close of the sixty-ninth week without a break. However, when they rejected their Messiah, God postponed the Kingdom. This created a gap that lasted almost two thousands years until the final seventieth week will run its course. Possibly, if the Church had faithfully fulfilled Christ's Great Commission in an earlier generation, God would have raptured the saints to heaven prior to our generation.

Israel Is the Focus of the Seventy Weeks

"For so the Lord has commanded us: 'I have set you to be a light to the Gentiles, that you should be for salvation to the ends of the earth'" (Acts 13:47).

The Lord will use Israel as "a light to the Gentiles" to reach the world during the tribulation period. God told Daniel that the "seventy weeks" are determined upon "your people," the Jews, and "your holy city," Jerusalem (Daniel 9:24). The first sixty-nine weeks of years focused upon God's dealing with the Jewish people and His witnessing to the world through His "chosen people." In a similar manner, the major focus of this final seventieth "week" of seven years will return to God's dealing with Israel. During the first sixty-nine weeks of years the Church was a "mystery" hid from the Old Testament prophets. Equally, the Church has no role on earth during the seventieth week of the seven-year tribulation period.

As detailed later in this book, Daniel revealed that the Antichrist, the "prince who is to come," will make a seven-year treaty with Israel, the "many," guaranteeing her security. However, at the mid-point of the seventieth week, after three and a half years, the Antichrist will break his covenant and defile the holy Temple in Jerusalem (Daniel 9:26,27). This event will trigger the beginning of the worst period of persecution in history. While the first three-and-a-half years will be a terrible time of persecution and judgment, the last three-and-a-half years leading to Armageddon will be unbearable. When Israel rejects the Antichrist's claim to be "god," He will persecute the Jews wherever he can find them. After the horrors of the persecution and the wrath of God during the Great Tribulation, Daniel's seventieth week will end with Christ's triumphant return to establish His eternal kingdom. As indicated in another chapter, the rapture of the Church will occur before Daniel's seventieth week. After the Marriage Supper of the Lamb Jesus will return from heaven with His army of saints to sit on the throne of David.

CHAPTER TWO

The Visions of Revelation

The Seven Titles of Jesus Christ in Revelation

The Apocalypse proclaims that Christ will defeat Satan's Antichrist and establish His glorious Kingdom on the earth forever. Seven distinct titles in the introductory chapter of the Apocalypse progressively reveal the nature of Jesus Christ. These seven titles confirm that the judgments of the Great Tribulation will be focused on the rebellious sinners in all the nations, not the Church. Each of the seven titles appears within the first chapter. A close examination of these names will enable us to more fully understand the prophetic role of the coming Messiah.

The Son of Man

"I saw...in the midst of the seven lampstands One like the Son of Man" (Revelation 1:13).

Of all the titles of Jesus Christ in the Apocalypse, probably the most important is "the Son of Man." It usually occurs in connection with His position in relation to the Kingdom of God on earth. Significantly, the designation "the Son of Man" appears eighty times in the four Gospels and the book of Acts in reference to Christ as King of the coming millennial Kingdom. However, in Paul's Epistles to the churches, he never used this title "Son of Man." His focus in the Epistles was on Christ's role as the Head of His Church during the Age of Grace. Interestingly, in Revelation 14:14, we see this title used again because the focus returns to Jesus Christ coming as a triumphant monarch to claim His Kingdom: "And I looked, and behold, a white cloud, and on the cloud sat One like the Son of Man, having on His head a

36

golden crown, and in His hand a sharp sickle." This Kingdom title, "the Son of Man" also appears in Matthew 24:30 and 25:31, in prophetic passages focused on the Great Tribulation. This title confirms that the focus of these prophecies is Christ's coming Kingdom, not the role of the Church.

The Almighty

"I am the Alpha and the Omega, the Beginning and the End," says the Lord, "who is and who was and who is to come, the Almighty" (Revelation 1:8).

This title, "the Almighty," expresses the tremendous power of God, that He "has dominion over all." It parallels the Old Testament expression, "the Lord of hosts," that presents Christ as the Captain of the mighty angelic legions of heaven coming to rule the earth. This designation, the "Almighty," appears nine times in Revelation emphasizing the enormous military power that will be exercised by Christ at the Second Coming. This stands in sharp contrast to Christ's role at His First Coming as the "suffering servant." Paintings and statues of the suffering Savior on the Cross have caused millions of Christians and non-believers to think of Jesus Christ solely as a weak, suffering victim on the Cross. Many Christians have forgotten that Christ is no longer on the Cross or in the Tomb. Jesus Christ sits at the right hand of the Father in heaven awaiting the moment when He will reclaim the kingdoms of this world forever. "Jesus said to him...'hereafter you will see the Son of Man sitting at the right hand of the Power, and coming on the clouds of heaven'" (Matthew 26:64).

The Lord God

"Then he said to me, 'These words are faithful and true.' And the Lord God of the holy prophets sent His angel to show His servants the things which must shortly take place" (Revelation 22:6).

This expression, "the Lord God" appears in Genesis in

the passages describing the original Kingdom of God on earth, the Garden of Eden. It appears again in the New Testament for the first time in the Apocalypse, as the prophet describes the approaching redemption of the earth introducing the true Kingdom of God. This recurring title, "the Lord God," connects Genesis and Revelation, the "Alpha and Omega," the "beginning and the end." In Genesis 3:15 God prophesied the ultimate defeat of Satan's "seed," the Antichrist. This title confirms that Christ will finally redeem His promise. The message of Revelation is that Satan's rule of sin, evil, suffering and death is about to end. The final victory of Christ is assured. The "Lord God" will keep His promise to create a Kingdom of righteousness and justice forever.

Alpha and Omega

"I am the Alpha and the Omega, the First and the Last" (Revelation 1:11).

The unusual title, "the Alpha and the Omega, the First and the Last," is used in the Scriptures to describe the Messiah in His connection with Israel. John used this title four times in Revelation to emphasize Christ's ultimate authority over the earth and His coming Kingdom. From the "Alpha" of the Garden of Eden to the "Omega" of the Apocalypse, the Bible's progressive revelation tells us of God's plan to redeem His suffering creation from the curse of sin. This title, "Alpha and Omega," is uniquely related to Christ's role as the coming Messiah of Israel. Consider the words of Isaiah 44:6: "Thus says the Lord, the King of Israel, and his Redeemer, the Lord of hosts: 'I am the First and I am the Last; besides Me there is no God.'" This phrase, "Alpha and Omega," indicates that the focus of John's prophecies is the final redemption of Israel and the Gentile nations, not the Church.

King of Kings and Lord of Lords

"He has on His robe and on His thigh a name written: King of kings and Lord of lords" (Revelation 19:16).

Of all the titles given to Christ, this is the greatest. For thousands of years Israel and the nations rejected the claim of Jesus as their promised Messiah. The Day of the Lord will reveal Christ's glory and victory over every other power in the universe. Although the world will still contain nations and kings in the millennial Kingdom, Christ alone will bear the supreme title "King of kings and Lord of lords." All power will belong to Christ forever. The kings and the saints will rule the nations under His delegated authority. Although many in the world today delight in blaspheming His name, someday soon the heavens will open and reveal Jesus Christ coming with all His royal splendor. On that day of victory the universe will witness the fulfillment of Christ's great prophecy: "For it is written: 'As I live, says the Lord, every knee shall bow to Me, and every tongue shall confess to God'" (Romans 14:11).

The Coming One

"Holy, holy, holy, Lord God Almighty, Who was and is and is to come!" (Revelation 4:8).

The prophetic title, "the Coming One," appears in many different forms throughout the Scriptures and in the Jewish writings about the coming Messiah. In Matthew 3:11 we read John's prediction about the coming Messiah in these words: "But He who is coming after me is mightier than I, whose sandals I am not worthy to carry." In John's Gospel account (4:25) the woman of Samaria told Jesus about her messianic expectation of "the Coming One" in these words: "I know that Messiah is coming (who is called Christ). When He comes, He will tell us all things" (John 4:25). Variations of the title "the Coming One" appear throughout the Old Testament in connection with Jewish messianic expectations. In the New Testament it is used sixteen times in the Gospels, the book of Acts and the Revelation. However, in keeping with its connection with Israel, it is never used by the Apostle Paul in any of his letters to the Christian Church.

The One Who Lives Forever

"The living creatures give glory and honor and thanks to Him who sits on the throne, who lives forever and ever" (Revelation 4:9).

We find variations of this title "the one who lives forever" six times in the book of Revelation. From the moment of man's creation, God intended that man should be immortal and live forever in obedience to Him. However, the rebellion of Adam and Eve introduced universal sin and death for mankind. The prophecies of Revelation declare that Christ will defeat the rule of sin and death. He will win immortality for all who trust in His salvation. Paul declared Christ's victory over death: "For since by man came death, by Man also came the resurrection of the dead. For as in Adam all die, even so in Christ all shall be made alive" (1 Corinthians 15:21,22).

The Bible's identification of Jesus Christ as "the one who lives forever" signifies His complete victory over Satan, sin and death. Christ defeated the curse of sin and death, not only for Himself, but for all those who will trust in His salvation and accept Him as their Lord and Savior. In total opposition to Satan, whose career ends with death, Jesus Christ is "the one who lives forever." He is the One who won eternal life for all those who trust in Him. Christ's victory over death through His resurrection is the central fact of Christianity. As Paul acknowledged: "If in this life only we have hope in Christ, we are of all men the most pitiable" (1 Corinthians 15:19). The Apostle Paul affirmed the truth of the resurrection of Christ with evidence of eyewitnesses who presented "infallible proofs" that Christ rose from the dead. His triumphant conclusion is this: "But now Christ is risen from the dead, and has become the firstfruits of those who have fallen asleep" (15:20). Jesus rose from the dead and lives forever. All who trust in Him will also be "ones who live forever" in Christ's eternal kingdom.

The Lord's Day

John introduced his book with his vision of Christ: "I was in the Spirit on the Lord's Day and I heard behind me a loud voice as a trumpet saying 'I am Alpha and the Omega, the First and the Last'" (Revelation 1:10). What does John mean by this phrase "the Lord's Day?" The answer to this question will go a long way toward illuminating the meaning of the visions of Revelation. His expression "the Lord's Day" may be a simple rearrangement of the common expression "the Day of the Lord." He may have used this expression to remind us that the Apocalypse will involve the awesome events of the great Day of the Lord during the Great Tribulation.

Another possibility is that John's expression, the "Lord's Day," referred to the fact that he received his incredible vision on "the Lord's Day," Sunday, the first day of the week. The arguments in favor of this view stem from several facts. The early Church began to use this expression, the "Lord's Day," during the first century to refer to Sunday as our common day of worship. This reference in Revelation 1:10 is the only place in Scripture that we find the expression "the Lord's Day." Other biblical references to Sunday used the common expression, "the first day of the week." Some suggest that John's use of the phrase "the Lord's Day," as Christ begins His message to the seven churches, indicates that the focus of these introductory chapters is the present Church age and that Sunday is the natural meaning rather than the future day of judgment.

In the centuries following Christ, the expression "the Lord's Day" became a synonym for Sunday. Ignatius lived from A.D. 30 to A.D. 107 as a fellow disciple with Polycarp under the leadership of the Apostle John. In his non-canonical book, *The Epistle of Ignatius to the Magnesians* (approx. A.D. 101) Ignatius twice called Sunday "the Lord's Day." He wrote: "After the observance of the Sabbath, let every friend of Christ keep the Lord's Day as a festival, the resurrection-day, the queen and chief of all the days (of the week). Looking forward to this, the prophet declared, 'To the end, for the eighth day,' on which our life both sprang up again, and the victory over death was obtained in Christ...'"

However, there is no evidence that the Church customarily called Sunday "the Lord's Day" until the second century, at some point after the book of Revelation was written (A.D. 96). Sunday was invariably called "the first day of the week' throughout the New Testament (Matthew 28:1; Luke 24:1; 1 Corinthians 16:2; for example). Most significantly, John, the author of Revelation, twice used the expression "the first day of the week" in his Gospel of John to designate Sunday, rather than use the second-century-Church expression "the Lord's Day" (John 20:1, 19).

The Day of the Lord - The Focus of the Apocalypse

Therefore, the burden of evidence suggests that John's use of the expression "the Lord's Day" refers to the coming great "Day of the Lord" which is referred to by all the prophets. In the same manner that John was lifted up in vision to heaven "in the Spirit" in chapter 4:1, we read in the introductory chapter that he was "in the Spirit on the Lord's Day." He recorded the great voice saying, "Come up here and I will show you things which must take place after this." John's reference to being "in the Spirit on the Lord's Day" probably suggests that he was taken in vision to the future Day of the Lord where he witnessed the climactic events that will end with Christ's triumph over evil.

The incredible events of the Day of the Lord are the focus of the majority of the Bible's prophecies about the "last days." There is no essential difference between John's expressions "the Lord's Day" and "the Day of the Lord." As an example of a New Testament writer reversing an expression, consider Peter's words about "Christ's suffering" in 1 Peter 4:13 and his description eight verses later in 1 Peter 5:1 about "the sufferings of Christ." Obviously, the meaning is the same although he reversed the order of the words. In the Hebrew language of the Old Testament, the expression always appears as "the Day of the Lord" rather than "the Lord's Day" because the adjective "Lord's" does not exist in Hebrew. The only way to express the concept "the Lord's Day" in Hebrew is to use both nouns, "the Day of the Lord." However, in the Greek language used in Revelation, John could express the concept using the Greek adjective as "the Lord's Day." The book of Revelation reveals more about the details of this future day of judgment than all of the other prophets. This subject of the Day of the Lord is extensively discussed by all the Old and New Testament prophets, Jesus Christ, and the early Church fathers. In fact the book of Revelation could be subtitled "The Great Day of the Lord." Whether or not John received his tremendous vision on Sunday, the focus of the book of Revelation is a series of fascinating prophetic visions manifesting the glory of Jesus Christ during the approaching great Day of the Lord.

Saturday Sabbath or Sunday Worship

John's use of the phrase "the Lord's Day" reminds us of the continuing dispute about whether the Church is correct to worship on Sunday rather than the Saturday Sabbath. Over the years, various groups — including the Seventh Day Adventists, the Seventh Day Baptists and others — have claimed that Christians have sinfully abandoned the true Saturday worship of God's Sabbath and adopted Sunday worship, "changing the times and laws" of God. They claim that God commanded us to worship on Saturday and that the early Church worshipped on Saturday for many decades until it arbitrarily changed the day of worship to Sunday without any command from God. Some suggest that the Church worshipped on Saturday for two centuries and suddenly changed to Sunday when a decree was issued by a Church Council. This is false. The argument over Saturday or Sunday worship has often confused Christians who do not have access to the history of the early Church. The truth is that the Church never "changed" the day of worship. From the beginning the Christians celebrated communion on Sunday.

Why Did the Early Church Worship on Sunday?

Following Christ's Resurrection, the early Church began to worship on Sunday, the first day of the week, because this was the day that Jesus rose from the grave. "On the first day of the week Mary Magdalene came to the tomb" (John 20:1). The Church was also empowered by the Holy Spirit on

Pentecost Sunday, the fiftieth day counting from the Feast of Firstfruits (Leviticus 23:16 and Acts 2:1). Pentecost always fell on Sunday because it occurs fifty days after the beginning Sabbath day. Beginning with the initial Sabbath of the Feast of Firstfruits, they counted fifty days (seven weeks of seven days plus one day) which ended on the first day of the week, Sunday. Thus, the two most important days initiating the birth of our Christian faith, the Resurrection and the coming of the Holy Spirit at Pentecost, both occurred by God's providence on Sunday, rather than on the Saturday Sabbath. The early Christian writer Chrysostom wrote a commentary on Psalm 119 declaring that Sunday "was called the Lord's Day because the Lord rose from the dead on that day."

Additional evidence is provided by an early commentary on the works of Irenaeus (A.D. 120 - 202) about the Church worshipping on Sunday from the beginning. "This custom of not bending the knee upon Sunday, is a symbol of the resurrection, through which we have been set free, by the grace of Christ, from sins, and from death, which has been put to death under Him. Now this custom took its rise from apostolic times, as the blessed Irenaeus, the martyr and bishop of Lyons, declares in his treatise *On Easter*, in which he makes mention of Pentecost also; upon which feast we do not bend the knee, because it is of equal significance with the Lord's day, for the reason already alleged concerning it" (*Fragments From Lost Writings of Irenaeus - Ante-Nicene Fathers*).

Why Did Jewish Christians Worship on Saturday and Sunday?

In the first century Jewish Christians continued to observe the Saturday Sabbath because Christ and His disciples never instructed them to stop this practice. From the beginning the Jewish believers also joined with their Gentile Christian brothers in worshipping at the Lord's Supper on Sunday. In other words, Jewish Christians worshipped on both Saturday and Sunday. Many Church writers differentiated between the Jewish Sabbath and the Christian's Lord's Day of Sunday. Theodoret wrote about the Jewish Christian Ebonite groups (*Fab. Haeret.* 2:1). He claimed, "They keep the Sabbath according to the Jewish law and sanctify the Lord's Day in like manner as we do." In other words, these Jewish Christians continued to worship on the Sabbath as their Jewish fathers, but also joined the Jewish and Gentile Christians in their customary worship on Sunday, the "Lord's Day." They worshipped on both Saturday and Sunday.

Gentiles, when they became Christians, never worshipped on the Saturday Sabbath of the Jews. They simply began to worship on Sunday, the day of His Resurrection and the Day of Pentecost. However, they realized that their Sunday worship was not a matter of law, but an act of loving observance of His resurrection. As an example, if a Christian's military service makes it impossible to worship on Sunday, he might choose to have a quiet time with the Lord on Wednesday. The key point to remember is that we are no longer under Law; we have been saved by God's Grace.

Although many Jewish Christians continued to observe the Saturday Sabbath as well as Sunday worship, some ceased Saturday worship. No one ever commanded Gentile Christians to worship on the Saturday Sabbath. When the issue arose about the demands that should be placed upon Gentile followers of Jesus, the book of Acts records the inspired decision of the council of the Jerusalem Church. "For it seemed good to the Holy Spirit, and to us, to lay upon you no greater burden than these necessary things: that you abstain from things offered to idols, from blood, from things strangled, and from sexual immorality. If you keep yourselves from these, you will do well. Farewell" (Acts 15:28-29). In these instructions to the Gentile converts, there was no requirement to follow the Old Testament Law regarding Saturday Sabbath worship. In fact, the early Church, inspired by the Holy Spirit and led by Jewish disciples of Christ, declared that "it seemed good to the Holy Spirit, and to us, to lay upon you no greater burden than these necessary things" only.

There are no commands or suggestions in the New Testament that Gentile Christians must observe the Jewish Sabbath. Where does this desire to observe the Saturday

Sabbath come from? The Seventh Day Adventists and several other groups suggest that the abandonment of the Saturday Sabbath worship was a great sin of the Antichrist system, "the changing of times and laws." This is a blatant appeal to the spiritual pride of mankind to return to the system of law that proved a total failure for Israel. The commandment for the observance of a Saturday Sabbath was given to Israel. It was never given as a direct commandment to the Gentiles. Paul addressed the Galatian church on this very same issue of whether Christians should try to follow the old Mosaic Law or place our entire hope in faith in Christ. "Are you so foolish? Having begun in the Spirit, are you now being made perfect by the flesh? (Galatians 3:3). We can never succeed in obeying the law 100 percent and, therefore, we can never please God by obedience to the dead Law. The purpose of the Old Testament Law was to prove to us, as a "schoolmaster," that we could never meet the mark of perfect obedience. The word "sin" is derived from the concept "to miss the mark." Our only hope of salvation lies in the completed redemption of Christ on the Cross to all who believe in Him. The attempt to observe Saturday Sabbath worship, rather than the two-thousand-year-old custom of Sunday worship, is an attempt to return to the failed Mosaic Law, rather than rely on Christ's Grace.

As the Church increasingly became dominated by Gentile converts the number of Jewish Christians who observed both Saturday and Sunday became fewer and fewer. Finally, after the A.D. 135 Bar Kochba Rebellion, the Jewish Christians were no longer accepted in the synagogues as legitimate Jews by the non-Christian Jews. Fewer and fewer Jews converted to Christianity until the Church became 99 percent Gentile after the first two centuries. Since God never placed the Gentile Christians under the obligation of the Mosaic law, they continued to worship Christ only on Sunday as they had from the first. The changing demographic balance between Jewish believers and Gentile believers in the Church eventually resulted in a primarily Gentile Christian Church worshipping solely on Sunday. The idea of some writers that the early Church worshipped on Saturday for the first century or so and later switched their worship to Sunday is an invention. There is no evidence that the Church ever made a massive switch from Saturday to

Sunday worship. The Church councils simply confirmed the historic practice of worshipping the Lord on Sunday.

The Author of the Apocalypse

The author of the Apocalypse was John, the son of Zebedee (Matthew 10:2), the beloved disciple of Jesus. John declares four times in the text that he is the author. He used the word "I" over seventy times throughout the twenty-two chapters. "The Revelation of Jesus Christ, which God gave Him to show His servants -- things which must shortly take place. And He sent and signified it by His angel to His servant John" (Revelation 1:1). The book of Revelation is the best attested book in the New Testament according to ancient Church authorities. In Justin Martyr's *Dialogue With Trypho* (A.D. 146) about his debate in Ephesus, he clearly identified the Apocalypse as John's. "There was a certain man with us, whose name was John, one of the apostles of Christ, who prophesied by a revelation that was made to him, that those who believed in our Christ would dwell a thousand years in Jerusalem." Irenaeus, who lived shortly after John, referred to the Revelation over thirty times in his extensive writings, indicating that these visions of John were well known to the early Church.

Although some speculate that another John may be the author, there is no historical evidence that anyone else wrote this prophecy. Papias, a disciple of John (A.D. 135) wrote that the author of the Apocalypse was "the elder John," indicating that he was speaking about the "elder" or aged, beloved disciple. John was the only Apostle to live into old age and died in his nineties. However, the early Church historian Eusebius (A.D. 325), misunderstood this quotation and concluded that the author was someone named John the Elder. However, if Papias was referring to another man, the form of the name in Greek would have been "John the Elder," not "the elder John." This usual form is also indicated by the name "John the Baptist."

The Apocalypse was addressed by John to the seven churches of Asia that were under his direction as bishop. These early Christians would have instantly detected a fraud if the book was not written by their bishop, the Apostle John. The universal testimony of the early Church was that the Apocalypse was written by "the disciple that Jesus loved" (John 21:20). Virtually every major Christian writer in the first two and a half centuries accepted Revelation as the inspired work of the disciple John. Tertullian, Papias, Clemens Alexandrinus, Origen, Jerome and Augustine together with the vast majority of orthodox believers accepted John as the inspired author of these unique visions. In Wordsworth's commentary on Revelation (*Wordsworth on Apocalypse*) he states: "There is scarcely a book in the whole Bible whose genuineness and inspiration were more strongly attested on its first appearance than the Apocalypse. No doubts whatever seem to have been entertained on these points. Suffice it now to say, that Papias, Justin Martyr, Irenaeus, Melito, that is, eminent teachers in the Church, in the next age to that in which it was written, proclaim that its writer was St. John, the beloved disciple of Christ. Such was then the voice of the Church."

In his manuscript, Andreas Caesariensis writes: "With regard to the inspiration of the book of Revelation, we deem it superfluous to add another word; for the blessed Gregory Theologus and Cyril, and even men of still older date, Papias, Irenaeus, Methodius, and Hippolytus, bore entirely satisfactory testimony to it" (Lardner, 5. 77).

Opposition to the Book of Revelation

While Satan hates the whole Bible he especially despises Genesis and Revelation, the beginning and the end of the Word of God. He hates Genesis because it reveals God's glorious creation and Christ's ultimate defeat of Satan in the last days. The book of Genesis has suffered one hundred and fifty years of continuous attacks by those who hate the Bible. Satan hates the book of Revelation more than any other in the Bible because it reveals his true character, his deceptions, his devices and his ultimate overthrow. The Apocalypse details Satan's defeat at the Battle of Armageddon, his imprisonment for a thousand years and his final destruction in the lake of fire. Satan's attack on the Revelation has focused on getting the Church to ignore the book as something too mystical and mysterious to be practical. Genesis and Revelation are "the Alpha and the Omega," the beginning and ending of God's message to the Church. The message of these two books contains our key to understanding God's plan of redemption for the earth from the curse of sin. Although the canonical authority of Revelation as an inspired book is the best attested of all New Testament books, those who hated its message then and now are prejudiced against it. If we as Christians wish to understand our role in history and prophecy we must understand the truths of Genesis and Revelation.

The Date of the Revelation

The consistent opinion of the early Christian writers closest to John's lifetime was that he wrote the Revelation in A.D. 96 while imprisoned on the isle of Patmos in the Mediterranean off the coast of Asia (modern Turkey). The evidence for the A.D. 96 date is overwhelming. *The Fragment of Muratori*,written by Caius (A.D. 200) a presbyter of Rome, is one of the earliest direct sources of evidence about the Apocalypse (*Antiquities Italicae*, 3.854). It proves the Revelation was received in the church at Rome in the middle of the second century during the times of Pius (A.D. 160). Caius refers to John's Revelation as follows: "And John too, indeed, in the Apocalypse, although he writes only to seven churches, yet addresses all." The author of the *Fragment of Muratori* says, "We receive also the Apocalypse." Irenaeus, an early (A.D.120 to 202) Christian writer of great authority, stated that John wrote the Revelation under imprisonment from the Emperor Domitian. He described John as, "him that beheld the apocalyptic vision. For that was seen no very long time since, but almost in our day, towards the end of the Domitian's reign" (*Against Heresies*, 30.3). This evil emperor was the second son of Emperor Vespasian, who conquered Jerusalem with his son Titus. After the death of Emperor Titus, his brother Domitian became the sole ruler of the Empire. Emperor Domitian ended his tyranny at his death in September A.D. 96. During his reign the Church experienced the first organized empire-wide persecution authorized by government decree from Rome. Many Christian leaders such as the Apostle John were exiled to places like the isle of

Patmos to work under brutal conditions in the mines on the island. History records that those exiled and banished were released from imprisonment following Emperor Domitian's death in fall of A.D. 96. Christian tradition states that John returned from Patmos to his church in Ephesus and finally died peacefully in his nineties. John was the only one of the original disciples who did not end his life as a martyr for the faith.

Some writers suggest that John was exiled to the isle of Patmos during the reign of Emperor Nero, before the destruction of Jerusalem. However, the persecution under Emperor Nero in A.D. 68 was fairly limited. It was fueled by Nero's personal hatred and madness, not by official Roman governmental decree. After Nero burned Rome, he blamed the Christians in an attempt to deflect blame from himself. Although he killed many Christian martyrs, the persecution was quite limited in duration and extent. There is no historical record of banishment of exiles under Nero. He killed his enemies, rather than banish them. However, the banishment of John to Patmos is consistent with the widespread exiling of opponents by Emperor Domitian which occurred almost thirty years later.

During the fifteen year tyrannical reign of Emperor Domitian (A.D. 81 to 96), the persecution existed throughout the Roman Empire as large numbers of Christians were banished to the mines by government decree. In his evil madness, Domitian called himself "god" and demanded that statues be erected everywhere in all the temples of the Empire. Naturally the Christians refused to worship him as god and were persecuted and banished for their faith. After Jerusalem was burnt to the ground in A.D. 70 the majority of the active churches that survived were in Asia (Turkey). The persecution was greatest there. The early Christian writers record that John, as bishop of these churches, was banished to Patmos from A.D. 95 to 96 during the final years of Domitian's rule. Jerome in his book *Lives of Illustrious Men* (chapter 9) wrote about John's banishment. "In the fourteenth year then after Nero, Domitian having raised a second persecution, he [John] was banished to the island of Patmos, and wrote the Apocalypse, on which Justin Martyr and Irenaeus afterwards wrote commentaries. But Domitian having been put to death and his acts, on account of his excessive cruelty, having been annulled by the senate, he [John] returned to Ephesus under Pertinax and continuing there until the time of the emperor Trajan, founded and built churches throughout all Asia, and, worn out by old age, died in the sixty-eighth year after our Lord's passion and was buried near the same city." Another Christian writer, Victorinus, Bishop of Petau (A.D. 240-304) wrote an extensive *Commentary on the Apocalypse*. In this book he revealed the date that John wrote his prophecy in his comment on the seven kings of Revelation 17. "The time must be understood in which the written Apocalypse was published, since then reigned Caesar Domitian..."

The greatest historian of the Christian Church, Eusebius (A.D. 265-339) had access to all of the existing records of the Church. While he questioned John's authorship at one point, later he concluded that the Apostle John was the author of the Apocalypse. He wrote about John's book of Revelation as follows. "After Domitian had reigned fifteen years, Nerva succeeded. The sentences of Domitian were annulled, and the Roman Senate decreed the return of those who had been unjustly banished and the restoration of their property. Those who committed the story of those times to writing relate it. At that time, too, the story of the ancient Christians relates that the Apostle John, after his banishment to the island, took up his abode in Ephesus. After Nerva reigned a little more than a year he was succeeded by Trajan...At this time that very disciple whom Jesus loved, John, at once Apostle and Evangelist, still remained alive in Asia and administered the churches there, for after the death of Domitian, he had returned from his banishment on the island. And that he remained alive until this time may fully be confirmed by two witnesses, and these ought to be trustworthy for they represent the orthodoxy of the church, no less persons than Irenaeus and Clement of Alexandria." The Christian writer Irenaeus, in his book *Against Heresies* wrote about John's prophecies in the book of Revelation about the name and number of the Antichrist. After warning against trying to name the Antichrist he wrote, "We will not, however, incur the risk of pronouncing positively as to the name of Antichrist; for if it were necessary that his name should be distinctly revealed in this present time, it would have been announced by him who beheld the apocalyptic vision. For that was seen no very long time since, but almost in our day, towards the end of Domitian's reign" (30.3).

Kingdom Now and Dominion Theology Opposition

Kingdom Now postmillennialists and amillennialists reject the clear historical evidence for dating Revelation in A.D. 96. They insist that Revelation must have been written in A.D. 68 before the destruction of the city of Jerusalem. They believe the prophetic visions of Revelation were fulfilled during the events of the burning of the city of Jerusalem by the Roman armies in A.D. 70. Kingdom Now teachers reject the A.D. 96 date and cling to A.D. 68, despite the lack of historical evidence supporting their position. The reason they desperately need the earlier date of A.D. 68 is to avoid the conclusion that John's Apocalypse prophesies of a future destruction in the Day of the Lord in the last days. Kingdom Now postmillennial writers admit that their whole system will fail if it can be proved that the book of Revelation was written after the A.D. 70 burning of Jerusalem. They admit that its prophecies would then have to point to the future coming of Christ to set up His millennial Kingdom. Kenneth L. Gentry, in his enthusiastic review of David Chilton's Dominion Theology book, *Days of Vengeance* wrote: "If it could be demonstrated that Revelation was written twenty-five years after the fall of Jerusalem, Chilton's entire labor would go up in smoke" (*The Council Chalcedon*, 11.4.11).

If the prophecies of Revelation were written after the fall of Jerusalem in A.D. 70, then it clearly predicts a future Great Tribulation and Armageddon at the end of this era. Kingdom Now proponents will be forced to come to terms with the Bible's clear premillennial teaching that Christ will come in the future to defeat Satan's Antichrist and establish His millennial Kingdom on earth. Those who are committed to a postmillennial or amillennial position reject the teaching of the future Second Coming of Christ to defeat the Antichrist and set up a kingdom. Teachers of the Kingdom Now and Dominion Theology position reject the biblical hope of an imminent Second Coming of Christ. In David Chilton's book

Paradise Restored, where he espoused his Dominion Theology, he rejected this historic hope of the Church. Speaking about God's promise of the coming Messiah he wrote, "The God of the covenant told His people that He would bless them to the thousandth generation of their descendants (Deuteronomy 7:9). That promise [the Second Coming] was made (in round figures) about 3,400 years ago. If we figure the biblical generation at about 40 years, a thousand generations is forty thousand years. We've got 36,600 years to go before this promise is fulfilled." This position directly contradicts the prophecies of Jesus Christ and the New Testament writers.

The Kingdom Now position declares that the predictions of Revelation and the parallel prophecies in Matthew 24 were totally fulfilled in the burning of Jerusalem and the Temple in A.D. 70. The only way that could be true is to hold to the position that Revelation was written by the Apostle John in A.D. 68 before Jerusalem was burned by the Roman soldiers. Their problem is that not one historical witness bears evidence for this A.D. 68 dating of Revelation. While they quote men who conjecture this early dating, there are no hard witnesses to prove it. There is a huge problem in their theory of such an early date for the Apocalypse. The problem lies in the spiritual state of the seven churches in Asia that John writes to in the first three chapters of Revelation. In A.D. 68 the Apostle Paul was writing his second letter to Timothy at a time prior to John's involvement with these churches. Consider John's first letter to the church at Ephesus (Revelation 2:1-7). He told them that "you have left your first love," that they had "fallen," they must return to "the first works" and "repent." This depressed spiritual condition could only occur after the passage of a number of years since the church's establishment during Paul's missionary trips. John's description is consistent with a church that has existed for decades. When Paul wrote to the Ephesians in the late sixties the spiritual life of this church bore no resemblance to the spiritual backsliding described by John in Revelation. For example, in John's Apocalypse he warns of the Nicolaitans while Paul makes no mention of them. The obvious conclusion is that John wrote his Revelation in A.D. 96 as an encouragement to the Church to stand against the terrible persecution of Domitian and the trials that would follow.

Another objection raised by Dominion teachers against the A.D. 96 date is that John records very accurate details about the Temple worship in Jerusalem. They suggest that John, who was a priest, could not have written such an accurate account of Temple worship more than twenty-five years after the Holy Sanctuary was destroyed in A.D. 70. In David Chilton's *Days of Vengeance*, he makes the astonishing suggestion that John's intimate knowledge of the details of the Temple worship indicates that the Apocalypse must have been written before the Temple services ceased. He suggests that John could not possibly remember these details decades after the Temple's destruction. This is a ridiculous argument on several accounts. First, as a righteous Jew, let alone a priest, John would have attended Temple services at least three times every year at the major feasts where all Israelite males must attend. Over the course of sixty years he would have visited the Holy Sanctuary at least one hundred and eighty times as a layman; as a priest he would have attended thousands of times. Why would he not retain an accurate memory of the details? Furthermore, John was inspired by the Holy Spirit and would thereby write only the perfect truth.

The awesome prophecies of Revelation reveal the great wrath of God poured out on the earth, the destruction of two-thirds of humanity, the devastation of two-thirds of the planet, and the battle of Armageddon. None of these prophecies or John's predictions of Israel fleeing into the wilderness for 1260 days or the descent of Christ with His heavenly army were fulfilled when Jerusalem fell to the Roman armies. It is hard for anyone who interprets the Scriptures seriously to agree that these tremendous prophecies could be fulfilled by the burning of Jerusalem and the Temple in A.D. 70. Such an interpretation must assume that the inspired Scriptures contain vast exaggeration and massive overstatement. This conception violates every principle of biblical interpretation and is contradicted by the hundreds of precisely fulfilled prophecies found throughout the Scriptures. The prophecies of the Bible that have already been fulfilled have been fulfilled with an amazing degree of precision. None of the biblical prophecies that have been fulfilled bear these characteristics of exaggeration or overstatement that these men believe exist in Revelation's predictions.

The evidence is overwhelming that the book of Revelation was written by John around A.D. 96. Therefore these prophecies promise that Christ will return in the future to defeat Satan's Antichrist and establish the Kingdom of God on earth forever.

The Mystery of the Numbers of Revelation

A detailed examination of the Bible reveals a profound and complicated structure of mathematical features throughout the Scriptures from Genesis to Revelation. In another book I will examine this mathematical phenomenon in detail. It is obvious that a precise pattern of sevens underlies the book of Revelation and the rest of the Bible. The number seven suggests completion and divine perfection. The ancient Jewish sages thought of seven as a divine number symbolizing God's creation and power. Throughout His creation we discover a series of sevens within the seven basic musical notes and the mathematical structure of orbits. From the moment of creation God stamped His seven-fold design upon all things and sealed it with His command for a Sabbath rest every seven days.

The Apocalypse completed God's written revelation to man. It is fitting that the number seven occurs so frequently within the structure of this prophecy. John's vision began with seven letters to the seven churches represented by seven lampstands. The seven stars stand for the seven angels of the seven churches. The judgments in the Apocalypse were revealed in a seven-sealed scroll containing seven series of sevens: seven seals, seven trumpets, seven bowls, seven personages, seven dooms, seven thunders and seven new things. The Beast from the sea possesses seven heads representing seven nations while the Great Whore of Babylon sits on seven mountains. The Dragon, representing Satan, has seven heads and seven crowns on his heads. John declared that the mystery of God will be completed in the seventh bowl of the seventh trumpet of the seventh seal. Fittingly, the prophecy ends with seven new things in the New Heaven and New Earth. In John's prophecy, the seven years of Daniel's seventieth week is divided into a three-and-a-half-year period of 1260 days. This is described as the duration of the testimony of the Two Witnesses as well as the period when the Woman, Israel, flees to escape Satan. The Antichrist will receive power to persecute the Tribulation saints during this same period of forty-two months, seven times six months. The whole of the seven-year Tribulation period contains 2520 days which is equal to seven times 360 days. Obviously God has stamped this divine seven-fold pattern on His revelation to confirm that it is His message to the believers of all generations.

The Apocalypse Illustrated

When Martin Luther printed his first German Bible in A.D. 1534, it was accompanied by a series of fascinating woodcut illustrations. We do not know the identity of this particular artist but he created twenty-six pictures illustrating the Book of Revelation. Many subsequent Bibles included similar pictures. Several of these are included throughout this book to indicate how Christian artists visualized John's incredible visions. These curious woodcuts acted as filmstrips to enhance the readers understanding of the biblical text.

"in the midst of the seven lampstands One like the Son of Man..." (Revelation 1:13).

CHAPTER THREE

CHRIST'S MESSAGE TO THE SEVEN CHURCHES

"John to the seven churches which are in Asia" (Revelation 1:4).

The letters to the seven churches in Revelation contain the last written message directly from Jesus Christ to His Church. These seven short epistles are similar to the parables and His prophecy on the Mount of Olives in that they are composed of Christ's own words. Christ's message is confirmed by His seven-fold command to "hear what the Spirit says to the churches." Despite the clear command of Christ to pay close attention to these messages, it would be difficult to find any other area of Scripture that has been so universally ignored by the Church over the centuries. As an example, in the Church of England the structure of required Sunday Bible readings covers the whole of the New Testament during the course of a year. Strangely, the only part of the Bible that will not be read in the course of the liturgical year are chapters two and three in Revelation, which contain Christ's last specific commands to His Church. According to Archbishop Trench in the book *Epistles to the Seven Churches*, "Under no circumstances whatever can the second and third chapters ever be heard in the congregation." Commentaries and teachers on the book of Revelation often silently pass over these seven letters to the churches. They sometimes act as though the book begins in chapter 4 with the vision of the Four Horseman of the Apocalypse. However, these words of Christ should speak to us because they address the spiritual challenges and problems faced by every church and Christian in every age.

Significantly, the Apocalypse begins with Christ's last epistles to the seven churches in Asia. These seven churches flourished during the first century in the geographic region of modern-day Turkey. Why did Christ send messages to these particular churches? There were many other churches in Asia at this time under the care of the Apostle John, who was bishop of the area. As an example, John records a letter to the church of Laodicea in his book but doesn't mention the church at Hierapolis which was on the other side of a river from Laodicea (Colossians 4:13). The church at Colosse is also not mentioned. Obviously, the book of Revelation is addressed to these seven particular churches for a specific reason. These first century churches were undergoing a series of spiritual problems and challenges that motivated the Lord to address them with chastening, warnings and promises. These seven individual churches were chosen because their specific problems and conditions were characteristic of the spiritual situation of the Church at various times throughout the last two millennia.

The seven stars represent seven angelic messengers while the seven stars point to the seven spirits (or aspects) of God. There is an obvious connection with the vision of Zechariah 4:10 concerning the seven eyes and seven lampstands. His vision described the seven eyes: "They are the eyes of the Lord, which scan to and fro throughout the whole earth." This expression, the "seven eyes" refers to seven distinct characteristics of the one triune God. The words of the prophet Isaiah 11:2 describe the coming Messiah, the Son of God, and reveal the meaning of these seven spirits. "The Spirit of the Lord shall rest upon Him, the Spirit of wisdom and understanding, the Spirit of counsel and might, the Spirit of knowledge and of the fear of the Lord." Each of these seven "spirits" described a Divine characteristic of the coming Son of God.

The Lord commanded John to write about "the mystery of the seven stars which you saw in My right hand." Although we often ignore the spiritual realm in which we live, Christ emphasized His control over the spiritual and angelic realm by holding the seven stars — the seven angels — in His hand. Before introducing the message to the seven churches, John revealed the meaning of the stars. "The mystery of the seven stars which you saw in My right hand, and the seven golden lampstands: The seven stars are the angels of the seven churches, and the seven lampstands which you saw are the seven churches" (Revelation 1:20). The stars are the angels and the lampstands represent the seven churches. These lampstands are not candlesticks as we know them, but are oil lamps like the ancient candelabra.

The number seven stands in Scripture for divine completion and perfection. It is the "signature of God" declaring that everything in Revelation is proceeding toward the fulfillment and completion of the Lord's perfect plan. In accord with this divine mathematical plan, John recorded seven messages from Jesus to seven churches representing the complete Bride of Christ throughout the centuries.

A Three - Fold Application of the Letters

There is a threefold application to these seven letters. The first and most obvious application is to the specific local churches under John's care. We know that these seven churches existed when John wrote the Apocalypse in A.D. 96. As bishop or overseer of the churches in the Roman province of Asia, John was in charge of the spiritual health of these churches that were founded three decades earlier through the missionary labors of the Apostle Paul. These churches struggled against outside attacks from paganism, idolatry and Roman persecution while contending for the true faith against internal corruption and heresy. It is fascinating to observe that human nature remains unchanged after two thousand years. The same struggle for obedience and spiritual faithfulness continues in the Church today. The problems that afflicted the seven churches in Asia are still found in our local congregations in this decade. Therefore, these messages from the past are as applicable to us as they were two thousand years ago.

The second application involves Christ's prophetic message to the universal Church existing from its creation on the Day of Pentecost until the Rapture. In Revelation 1:19-20 the Lord tells John, "Write the things which you have seen...the mystery of the seven stars..." If this was simply a message to the local churches in A.D. 96 with no prophetic message to the universal Church, it would not be a "mystery." The prophecies throughout the rest of Revelation are addressed to the seven churches because they represent the greater Church. The conclusion of the message to the first of the seven churches contains these words addressed to the universal Church: "He who has an ear, let him hear what the Spirit says to the churches. To him who overcomes I will give to eat of the tree of life, which is in the midst of the Paradise of God" (Revelation 2:7).

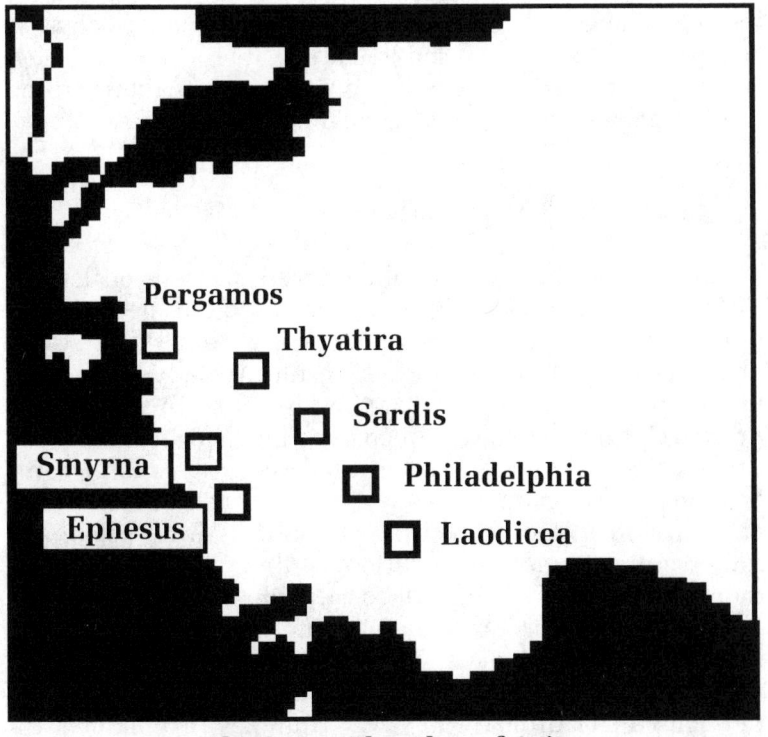

The Seven Churches of Asia

Some writers conclude that the seven churches prophetically represented seven distinct future ages or epochs of the Church. There is an interesting parallel between the state of the Church at different historical periods and the spiritual state of these seven churches. However, there have always been churches in every city and in every age that manifest the characteristics of each of the seven churches of that first century. These spiritual commendations and warnings apply to all Christians in every century, including ours.

The third application of the message to these churches is to each believer as an individual. The spiritual problems and challenges faced by these seven churches confronting the trials of the first century speak to Christians in every age. The message of Christ is a call to awaken spiritually, to commit ourselves to a life of witness and obedience. Just as the Church must examine its heart regarding its faithfulness to the Lord, we as individual Christians must ask ourselves if we "have left our first love." Christ's warnings and promises are also addressed directly to each believer.

The Structure of the Letters

There is a similar structure to each of the seven letters. They begin with the identification of the Church and the speaker, Jesus Christ. Commencing with praise for whatever is praiseworthy in their situation, the Lord then reproves them for their errors. This is followed by a promise of the Second Coming of Christ and its effect on that Church. The letters conclude with a command to "hear what the Spirit is saying to the churches" and a promise to those who overcome these spiritual challenges. The seven letters are addressed to "the angel" of that particular church. The name "angel" can refer to a spiritual creature of heaven or it can refer to one who fulfills the office of a messenger. It is possible that the word angel refers to the pastor or messenger of the individual church. In support of this position, we find John addressing a man as an "angel" in Revelation 19:10. This "angel" is a man because he tells John, "I am your fellowservant and of your brethren who have the testimony of Jesus."

The other possibility is that the messenger of each church is actually a heavenly angel assigned to that Church. There is no conclusive reason to assume that the word angel refers to a man when holy spiritual beings are called angels throughout the balance of the book. The prevalence of angels is indicated in the words of Christ in Matthew 18:10. Even little children have their assigned angels, as Christ promised that, "their angels always see the face of My Father who is in heaven." The great nations have angels assigned to them, according to Daniel 10:13, 20,21. The disciples thought that their friend had seen Peter's angel (Acts 12:15). The servant of Elisha had his spiritual eyes opened and he was enabled to see a vast legion of angels greater than the army of the Syrians (2 Kings 6:16, 17). There is nothing strange about God assigning an angel to oversee His churches. Angels are much more involved with our life on earth than most of us realize. Many of the details of John's vision were revealed by angels. Although the message is directed to the congregation and pastors, it is quite possible that Christ would address these churches in the form of letters to the angels charged with the spiritual oversight of each church. Each of the letters concludes in the same manner. Seven times we are admonished "Hear what the Spirit says to the churches."

The Church at Ephesus

"To the angel of the church of Ephesus write, 'These things says He who holds the seven stars in His right hand, who walks in the midst of the seven golden lampstands'" (Revelation 2:1).

Outside the Promised Land itself, the city of Ephesus was the most important city in the life of the early Church. The Apostle Paul and John both labored for the Lord in this city, the capital of the Roman province of Asia. As bishop or overseer of the churches of Asia, Ephesus was John's home church, so it was natural that he would begin his first letter to this church. The name *Ephesus* means "desirable" but also suggests the meaning "to let go" or "relax." It was an incredibly wealthy city with its famous Temple of Diana, one of the seven wonders of the ancient world. For centuries pagan worshippers brought their gifts of gold, statues and art treasures to dedicate to their Greek gods. Over the centuries Ephesus became an important commercial and political center until it was destroyed by the Goth invasion in A.D. 252. The church was founded by the missionary labors of Paul as recorded in Acts 19 and 20. Paul wrote his Epistle to the Ephesians during his first imprisonment in Rome.

Timothy was the first pastor of this early church.

The church of Ephesus is the "church of the first love." It represents the church as a bride, the object of the love of the bridegroom. It is separate from the world yet has become careless. The Lord commends it for its genuine good works, its toil and patient enduring, not simply lipservice to God. Jesus praises the Ephesians for their fidelity that refused to tolerate evil men. They continually tested and rejected the false claims of "so-called" apostles. This commendation reminds us of Paul's warning to this church (Acts 20:29,30) about "savage wolves," men "speaking perverse things, to draw away the disciples after themselves." Revelation records their faithful bearing of Christ's name without growing weary in the struggle.

The Doctrine of the Nicolaitans

Jesus also mentions that "you hate the deeds of the Nicolaitans, which I also hate." The other side of love is hatred for that which will destroy the object of our love. A mother hates the danger to her child. How can we not hate an evil heresy that seeks to separate us from our spiritual destiny? There is a lot of disagreement about who these Nicolaitans were. Some believe that they were identical with those who follow the doctrine of Balaam. However, this is impossible because the Nicolaitans are mentioned separately from followers of Balaam in Revelation 2:14 and 15. Christ created a universal "holy priesthood" (1 Peter 2:5) where every believer is a priest. The Nicolaitans attempted to recreate the hierarchy of the Old Testament priesthood. They sought to establish a priestly authority over laymen. The Greek word is derived from *Nike* meaning "victory" and *laos* meaning "people." It suggests a group of people who seek to elevate themselves into a special class of priesthood over other Christians. Jesus told us in 1 Timothy 2:5: "For there is one God and one Mediator between God and men, the Man Christ Jesus." Such men sought the sole right to interpret the Scriptures for other Christians. Centuries later, after Emperor Constantine's conversion, this Nicolaitan heresy produced the Babylonian hierarchy of priests, leading to the spiritual "Dark Ages" of the medieval period.

Christ criticized the church at Ephesus for abandoning their "first love." Their doctrine was uncorrupted but their passion for the Lord who saved them was growing dim. Paul had taught them that "Christ is all in all" and that our focus should be "not I, but Christ who dwells within me." When our heart departs from Christ, it begins a slow step-by-step rejection of His Lordship of our lives. This withdrawal begins when we put something other than Christ in the place of preeminence in our heart.

The church at Ephesus is commanded to "remember therefore from where you have fallen, repent and do the first works." When we have lost a love, the best way to find it is to return to where we last experienced it. Christ commands them to "remember" how they felt when Christ first saved them from the despair of paganism and to "do the first works." When we have lost our passion, the best way to recover it is to obey His command and begin to witness, to worship and to serve our Lord. If we will obey His command, we will recover our spiritual passion for our Savior. Christ promised "to him who overcomes I will grant to eat from the tree of life." Revelation 22:1,2 tells us that the tree of life is now in Paradise, the New Jerusalem in heaven. Jesus, the second Adam, promises spiritual overcomers the possession of the tree of life that the first Adam lost by his sinful rebellion against God.

Christ's warning is that if they do not repent and return to their first love, He "will remove your lampstand from its place." Note that the threat is not to extinguish its light but to "remove" the light of God's truth to another place. This threat was fulfilled when the spiritual light of the lampstand of Ephesus was withdrawn and transferred westward to the growing churches of the western Roman Empire. In A.D. 431 a chaotic Third General Council at Ephesus condemned various false doctrines. A second council in A.D. 449 was disastrous and violent. The church at Ephesus faded away. Their lampstand was removed as the prophecy warned.

The Church of Smyrna

"And to the angel of the church in Smyrna write, 'These

things says the First and the Last, who was dead, and came to life'" (Revelation 2:8).

According to the early Christian writer Polycarp, the Apostle Paul founded the church at Smyrna on his missionary journey to Ephesus. Acts 19:10 tells us that "all who dwelt in Asia heard the word of the Lord Jesus, both Jews and Greeks." The only mention we have of this church comes in the book of Revelation. Of the seven churches, only two escaped condemnation by Christ, Philadelphia and the church of Smyrna. The message to both is one of praise and commendation. Surely it is no accident of history that Smyrna and Philadelphia are the only two cities of the seven that have survived despite tribulations as important, populous trading centers over the centuries. Smyrna was an extremely wealthy and beautiful port city known for its devotion both to Rome and its pagan gods. It is presently a city of over three hundred thousand souls of whom some two-thirds belong to various Christian denominations.

The church in Smyrna represents the "persecuted church." The name *Smyrna* comes from "myrrh," a fragrant aromatic sap that comes from a thorny tree in the Middle East. It was very valuable and was used as one of the ingredients for holy ointment. Myrrh was used in the embalming of the dead in ancient times. It was one of the gifts brought to the Christ Child by the wise men from the East. In honoring Him with the precious gift, the Magi also foreshadowed Christ's ultimate gift to us in His death on the Cross. Myrrh was widely used as a sacrificial gift in religious ceremonies because of its connection with death and resurrection. The church in Smyrna was persecuted almost to the point of death by the Roman pagans. Although the church was poor in worldly goods, it was rich in spiritual gifts as measured by Christ. "I know your works, tribulation and poverty, but you are rich." We need to view our situation spiritually as our Lord evaluates it. Though they lacked worldly goods, the Christians in this church were rich in the esteem of Christ. He told us to "lay up for yourselves treasures in heaven...For where your treasure is there your heart will be also (Matthew 6:20,21).

As a church suffering persecution and tribulations,

Smyrna was surviving through its steadfast faith in its Savior. While the Lord does not criticize this stalwart congregation, neither does He commend it for any special victories. The church maintained its love and faithfulness to true doctrine against the continuous assault of pagan persecution. In addition, some of the Jews joined in persecuting the newly formed church. Instead of worshipping the true God, some, according to Revelation 2:9, were part of "a synagogue of Satan." Though outwardly professing faith in Jehovah, these particular people were blaspheming God by their actions. However, many Jews listened to the message of the gospel and accepted Christ as their Messiah. Notice that Christ warned that "the devil is about to throw some of you in prison that you may be tested." Although Satan used human instruments to oppress the Church, their real enemy was the Devil.

Shortly after the death of John, a series of great waves of persecution fell on this church. The aged pastor of Smyrna, Polycarp, a convert and pupil of John, was burned at the stake in A.D. 168 in that city because he would not renounce his faith in Christ. The Roman proconsul promised him, "Swear by Caesar and I will release thee. Revile Christ." The serene Polycarp replied as he was led to the stake to be burned, "Eighty and six years have I served him and He never did me wrong: how can I revile my King and my Savior?" As the flames rose around him they offered him freedom if he would reject Christ. He died victoriously with these words on his lips, "I am a Christian." While we rejoice in the religious liberty that exists in North America we should remember that over the last two thousand years some fifty million believers have paid the supreme price of martyrdom for their faith in the Lord. Even in this century, some three hundred thousand Christians have died as martyrs to Christ every year until today. If the Lord delays His return for His Church, we may see persecution in America such as our brothers experience daily in Syria, Lebanon, Peru and Africa.

Jesus encouraged the Christians of Smyrna not to fear what man can do to their bodies in the coming tribulations. He promised those of Smyrna that "you will have persecution ten days." This probably referred to a future specific attack on that church. It might also hint at the fact that Smyrna and the rest of the churches in Asia would have to endure ten great waves of persecution until the Edict of Toleration of Emperor Constantine in A.D. 324. Jesus commanded the overcomers: "Be faithful until death, and I will give you the crown of life." Christ promised the faithful a crown of life that will never tarnish or lose its glory throughout eternity. While physical pain and death are terrible, they finally must end. Jesus gave this promise to the Christians facing persecution, "He who overcomes shall not be hurt by the second death." The second death is the spiritual death of the soul who rejects the life and salvation of Jesus Christ. The Bible reminds us that we should not fear those who can only destroy our physical bodies, but rather the one who controls the eternal destiny of our soul. "Do not fear those who kill the body but cannot kill the soul. But rather fear Him who is able to destroy both the soul and body in hell (Matthew 10:28). The reference to an eternal "crown of life" contrasted vividly with the perishable wreath or crown given to the winning athlete in the Smyrnean Olympic games which took place every five years.

For many Christians today, their entire focus is on their present life and problems. They look to God to solve every problem in their daily life. Many modern converts accepted Christ because Christianity seemed to offer a better alternative lifestyle than their earlier sinful, problem-filled life. As carnal, earthly-minded Christians they have never considered the fact that they may someday have to face terrible persecution for their faith. If we live only in the consciousness of this earthly life we will never learn to serve Christ as He demands. In Hebrews 11:13 to 17, we read that God praised the Old and New Testament saints because they believed His heavenly promises: "These all died in faith, not having received the promises, but having seen them afar off were assured of them, embraced them, and confessed that they were strangers and pilgrims on the earth...But now they desire a better, that is, a heavenly country. Therefore God is not ashamed to be called their God, for He has prepared a city for them."

The Church of Pergamos

"And to the angel of the church in Pergamos write, 'These things says He who has the sharp two-edged sword'" (Revelation 2:12).

Pergamos, presently called Bergama, was a three day journey north of Smyrna in the province of Mysia (Turkey). Pergamos was noted for its tremendous temples and statues of pagan gods. After two thousand years an incredible number of white marble columns and blocks remain as silent evidence to its wealth. Even its coins declared its idol worship and that it was a "temple-keeper" for licentious worship of pagan deities. The special god whom Pergamos worshipped was called *Aesculapius*, the god of healing, or "savior." His chief symbol was a serpent. This debased worship included a huge serpent in the temple and a serpent image on many of the coins of the city. In a pagan city like Pergamos the problem of eating meat offered to idols was very real. Most food entering the city would be ritually offered in front of the pagan gods before being sold in the open market or restaurants. If you refused to partake of this "idol-blessed" food, you would have to refrain from any of the public festivals and ceremonies in the pagan city. Together with idols, these festivals centered around licentious parties and temple prostitution.

Satan's Throne

"I know your works, and where you dwell, where Satan's throne is" (Revelation 2:13). Christ refers to "Satan's throne" because Pergamos had become a center of the Babylonian mystery religion after the fall of the city of Babylon. Satan attempted to destroy the young Christian Church with a huge pagan revival led by the idolatrous temples of Pergamos. Some scholars suggest that one of the temples actually contained a throne dedicated to Satan in one of his many pagan guises. Pergamos contained one of the ancient wonders of the world, a massive and famous altar to Zeus, the greatest of the Greek gods. It was over ninety feet by forty feet in size. Additionally, Pergamos devoted three huge temples to pagan emperor-worship. This worship of the emperor will be revived in the last days as the whole world worships the Antichrist.

The Doctrine of Balaam

Jesus commends the church at Pergamos for faithfulness to His Name and their good works in the midst of the continuing spiritual assault from Satan. It represents "the confessing church." He warns them against tolerating in their midst those who hold the "doctrine of Balaam" that encouraged them to "eat things sacrificed to idols and to commit sexual immorality." During the Exodus the pagan prophet Balaam, who failed to curse Israel directly, tried to destroy the Chosen People through his diabolical advice to Balak, the Moabite leader. His plan was to entice Israel to defile their separateness by seducing them with pagan women and causing them to abandon their call to God's service.

In a similar manner, the Christians of Pergamos were enticed by Satan's servants to join the world and its "pleasures of sin for a season." Christ warned the church about tolerating in their midst those who held to Balaam's doctrine. The church of Pergamos was in danger of losing its sanctified and holy walk with God by allowing these people to continue as part of the congregation while tempting others. Today, we are surrounded by a world that continually offers sensuality and sexual temptation. Like the church at Pergamos, many Christians are succumbing today to these sinful temptations leading them to spiritual disaster. While God will forgive our sins, the consequences of sin will continue to destroy families and peace of mind, leading to disease and death. God will pardon a sinner who repents, but He will not change the consequences of sin. The Christians of Pergamos were compromised when they partook of the food that was first sacrificed in part to the pagan gods. In a similar manner Satan continually attacks the separate, sanctified walk of the Christian believer today, suggesting that it is unrealistic to attempt to live a pure, undefiled life. The devil suggests that you can have Christ and the world also. God demands that we must make a choice between following Him or following the world. The Lord offered Israel the same choice He offers each of us. "See, I have set before you today life and good, death and evil, in that I command you today to love the Lord your God, to walk in His ways, and to keep His commandments, His statutes, and His judgments, that you may live and multiply; and the Lord your God will bless you in the land which you go to possess" (Deuteronomy 30:15,16).

Christ cautioned this church about the growing doctrine of the Nicolaitans, as He did the church at Ephesus. Despite the church's love of Christ, its works and faithfulness, Christ warned that it was tolerating His enemies in its bosom. The Lord commanded them to "repent, or else I will come to you quickly and will fight against them with the sword of My mouth." The letter ends with a promise to those who overcome that He will give them "hidden manna," the bread of life, the spiritual food from heaven, if they turn from food offered to idols. In Pergamos, the people used special crystals or stones with pagan symbols marked on them for healing and protection just as the New Agers do today. In contrast, Christ promised the faithful overcomers, "I will give him a white stone, and on the stone a new name written which no one knows except him who receives it." Throughout the Bible we see the incredible importance that God places on the names of people and things. God's love for us, though universal, is so personal that He has chosen a special spiritual name for every single Christian that remains faithful to Him.

The Church of Thyatira

"And to the angel of the church in Thyatira write, 'These things says the Son of God, who has eyes like a flame of fire, and His feet like fine brass...'" (Revelation 2:18).

The city of Thyatira is called *Ak-hissar* in modern Turkey. It was founded as a Greek colony by Seleucus Nicator, the founder of the Greek-Syrian monarchy that followed the death of Alexander the Great. He named it Thyatira in commemoration of his daughter's birth. The only other time Thyatira is mentioned in the New Testament is in Acts 16:14 speaking of the conversion of "Lydia, a seller of purple, of the city of Thyatira." This city was known for its purple dye factories and its great wealth.

Christ began by commending the church for its "works, love service, faith and your patience; and as for your works, the last are more than the first." This church, in contrast to the church at Ephesus, grew stronger in its works, while the Ephesians "left their first love." The church of Thyatira proved its love in practical service to the Lord and others. However, this church tolerated sin within its community without resisting it to the full. It lacked a zeal for the true doctrine of Christ and church discipline. A wicked woman, named Jezebel, was allowed by the leadership to act as a self-appointed "prophetess, to teach and seduce My servants to commit sexual immorality and eat things sacrificed to idols." Just as Jezebel led Israel astray from God in the Old Testament, this woman Jezebel tried to lead the church at Thyatira into gross immorality.

Perhaps because the church was founded by the woman Lydia, they were more open in later years to the feminine leadership of this reprobate woman, Jezebel. In their love and charity, the leadership of the church failed to quickly expel the woman who was leading Christians to spiritual ruin. After telling us that He had given her "time to repent," but she refused, Christ declared her punishment. He will "cast her into a sickbed and those who commit adultery with her into great tribulation...and kill her children." Men often think that they have gotten away with sin because God mercifully delays His punishment for a time. However, after giving him "time to repent," God's judgment will always catch up with him. Jezebel crossed that final line of rejection of God's mercy. For every man or woman, there is a line, a "time to repent." If you reject God's mercy that last time, His grace will never draw you back to Him. The Lord declares that we should "know that I am He who searches the minds and hearts. And I will give to each one of you according to your works." There is nothing that can be kept in secret from Christ. He knows every action, every thought, every motive.

To those who have rejected Jezebel's sinfulness and the "depths of Satan," Christ promised a reward. The "depths of Satan" referred to the antinomian heresy that suggested that

Christians could indulge in all manner of immorality to the depths of sin with safety because their sins were forgiven. They forgot that "without holiness, no man shall see the Lord." Christ tells His faithful followers to "hold fast what you have till I come. And he who overcomes and keeps My works until the end, to him I will give power over the nations." The Lord promises that Christians who remain faithful will rule and reign over the nations forever in His eternal Kingdom. Christ's final promise to the overcomer is that "I will give him the morning star." Just as the morning star refers to Christ Himself, it also describes a star that appears just before dawn, while night still lingers. Like the morning star, Jesus will come for His Bride, the Church, without warning before commencing the great and terrible Day of the Lord.

The Church of Sardis

"And to the angel of the church in Sardis write, 'These things says He who has the seven Spirits of God and the seven stars: "I know your works, that you have a name that you are alive, but you are dead" (Revelation 3:1).

The city of Sardis was the capital of King Croesus, the extremely wealthy ancient monarch. The city may have received its name from the sardis stones found in this area that were commonly used as pagan amulets to drive away evil spirits. Some scholars believe that the name may relate to "the remnant." Certainly, only a remnant of this church truly followed their Lord. Although we do not find open sexual immorality or paganism within the church, it has lost it spiritual vitality and life. Tragically, this church became caught up in materialism and carnal concerns. Christ's only words of commendation were to the remnant "a few names who have not defiled their garments." Though they boast in their outward accomplishments, God's verdict is that their spiritual life was almost extinguished. "You have a name that you are alive, but you are dead." God examines the heart of His church and its members. While we tend to look at outward things like buildings, finances and numbers of worshippers, Christ evaluates the true spiritual health of His Church. Unlike the earlier commendations to the churches, this church of Sardis is told that "I have not found your works perfect before God."

The Lord commands, "Be watchful and strengthen the things which remain, that are ready to die." Unless we are watchful for our Lord's return, our eyes will begin to turn solely to this world and its cares. The church in Sardis is the "church of uncompleted works." In a practical way, Christ encouraged them to "strengthen the things that remain." If there is to be a revival in a spiritually dying church, we must start with the small remnant and build upon their faithful prayers and devotion to Jesus Christ. Just as in Gideon's army, God delights to accomplish His great victories with a small remnant. Then, it will be obvious to all that it is God who has won the victory, not man. The message to the church at Sardis reminds us that no matter how dead a church or denomination may be, God still has "a few names...who have not defiled their garments; and they shall walk with Me in white, for they are worthy." The prayer of every believer should be that we shall join that faithful remnant and walk with Him.

The Church at Philadelphia

"And to the angel of the church in Philadelphia write, 'These things says He who is holy, He who is true, "He who has the key of David, He who opens and no one shuts, and shuts and no one opens" (Revelation 3:7).

Thirty miles inland from Sardis, King Attalus II - Philadelphus founded the city of Philadelphia in 140 B.C. The name means "brotherly love" suggesting that the church partakes of the love that flows from the Father to motivate the "household of faith." It lies on the river Cogamus in a valley surrounded by mountains, an area subject to earthquakes for millennia. This was a small flock of Christians, poor in wealth but rich in the eyes of God. It represents the missionary and evangelical church. Of the seven churches, this church and Smyrna are the only ones that escaped criticism. Christ commends the Philadelphian church because they "have a little strength, have kept My word, and have not denied My name" (Revelation 3:8). Jesus says to them as He says to all Christians: "I know your works." Someday every Christian will stand before the Judgment Seat of Christ to receive rewards for our faithful service. Some believers will receive no rewards at all because they lived carnal lives of service to self rather than service to the Lord. God has given his Church a Great Commission to "go into all the world and preach the gospel to every creature."

The church at Philadelphia is the "faithful church." To the Philadelphians Christ said, "See, I have set before you an open door, and no one can shut it." Where Jesus opens a door the powers of Satan cannot shut it. If we will walk in the power of the risen Savior and "put on the whole armor of God" we will be empowered to go through the "open doors" that Christ sets before us. In the beginning of the second century, Ignatius, an early Christian writer commended the victorious conversion of Gentiles and Jews by the church of Philadelphia in his *Epistle to the Philadelphians*. This church was commended by Christ for believing in the promise of His Second Coming and practicing patient watching until the day of His appearance.

An incredible promise was offered by Christ to the Philadelphian Christians who had given everything in faithful missionary service to Him: "Because you have kept My command to persevere, I also will keep you from the hour of trial which shall come upon the whole world, to test those who dwell on the earth" (Revelation 3:10). In its primary application, this promise offered escape from persecution to these Christians in Philadelphia in the first century. However, the unusual phrase "the hour of trial which shall come upon the whole world" obviously extends the promise to encompass the whole Church of Jesus Christ. Many scholars believe this passage confirms the other promises that show that Christ will rapture His Church home to heaven before the Great Tribulation "which shall come upon the whole world, to test those who dwell on the earth."

Christ promises: "Behold, I come quickly!" He then admonishes the believers to "hold fast what you have, that no one may take your crown" (Revelation 3:11). The saints at Smyrna, as well as Philadelphia, were promised the Crown of Life for their faithfulness. As indicated in the chapter on Rewards and Judgments, Christians are promised a number of golden crowns for faithful service to the Lord. Jesus warned that we are to "hold fast" lest we lose our crowns. This indicates that it is possible to lose the eternal rewards and blessings that God prepared for those who love him. While our salvation is assured today by our accepting Christ as our Savior and Lord, our future reward will be determined at the Judgment Seat of Christ after the Rapture. We are encouraged to hold on to these rewards through continued faithful service. The Lord promises the overcomer that he will be made a pillar in the Temple of God in heaven. This promise has a special meaning for this church because of their curious method of honoring illustrious leaders. Any citizen that accomplished something noteworthy as a magistrate or benefactor was honored by having his name inscribed on a pillar that was placed in one of the great temples of the city of Philadelphia.

The book of Revelation warns the tribulation believers to refuse the Mark of the Beast, a seal upon the forehead or right hand. In fact, the Bible warns that any that receive Satan's mark will be damned forever to the lake of fire. The forehead of every believer in Christ is reserved for the "name of My God." The promise of Christ is, "I will write on him the name of My God and the name of the city of My God, the New Jerusalem...And I will write on him My new name" (Revelation 3:12). The Greek word *grapho* means to engrave or write with a visible mark. It is used 186 times in the New Testament and always means a visible mark, not a spiritual engraving. Those who accept the Mark of the Beast, will lose the hope of heaven forever. Those who choose to follow Jesus Christ will proudly wear His Name on their foreheads forever.

The Church at Laodicea

"And to the angel of the church of the Laodiceans write, 'These things says the Amen, the Faithful and True Witness, the Beginning of the creation of God'" (Revelation 3:14).

Christ declared that there were serious spiritual faults in

five of the seven churches. Yet He also has a word of commendation for every church except the church in Laodicea. Only two churches, Smyrna and Philadelphia, were praised without any criticism. When we come to the church of Laodicea, we find a church that has nothing to commend it whatsoever, save for the remnant of a few souls who remain within it that still love Christ. The chastening of these souls is a mark that Christ still loves them. "As many as I love, I rebuke and chasten. Therefore be zealous and repent" (Revelation 3:19). When believers are chastened for their sins, it is a sign that our heavenly Father still loves us enough to try and bring us back to a place of obedience and fellowship.

The city of Laodicea was formed by King Antiochus II who named it for his wife, Laodicea. Its position on the Meander River controlling the Lycus Valley gave it a profitable trade in various commercial items, including a special medicinal product, an eye ointment used widely throughout the Roman Empire. It also produced a unique rich, black wool that was an important part of a large flourishing garment industry. The city of Laodicea was so wealthy that, when it suffered massive damage in an earthquake in A.D. 60, the Roman historian Tacitus says that it proudly refused the financial assistance of the emperor and chose to rebuild with its own huge resources.

The church of Laodicea represents the "lukewarm church." The majority of the church of Laodicea were caught up in a "prosperity gospel" that developed out of a combination of worldly wealth and spiritual pride. The name *Laodicea* means "judgment of the people" or "mob rule." Instead of following its head, Jesus Christ and His pastors, the Laodicean church followed the popular will of the laity. It represents the self-sufficient and self-satisfied church that is heading for spiritual disaster. The wealth and health of its outward condition and circumstances had produced an inward spiritual cancer that eats away at the vitality of the Body of Christ. Our inward faith will always manifest itself in our "works." Unlike the church of Philadelphia that was concerned with the need to evangelize a lost world, the Laodicean church was focused inward on its own needs and desires. As a result, the Laodiceans mistakenly believed they were almost perf'ct as a church. This picture mirrors the "prosperity gospel" of today with its "name it and claim it" mentality. It is utterly blinded to its true spiritual condition.

Christ declares: "I know your works, that you are neither cold nor hot. I could wish you were cold or hot. So then, because you are lukewarm, and neither cold nor hot, I will spew you out of My mouth" (Revelation 3:15). They had lost their passion for Christ in a general lukewarm "goodness" that tolerated a compromised worship of materialism and Christ. God hates "lukewarm" people who are spiritual wimps. Study the Bible from Genesis to Revelation. It is difficult to find any "wimps" who became great men of God. God would rather take dynamic men and women of passion like David or Saul, even if they are headed in a wrong, sinful direction and turn them around 180 degrees to accomplish His will in their lives. Satan was very clever in his attack on ancient Israel and on the Church. He did not tell Israel to reject God and worship Baal instead. That was too dangerous an approach because many would awaken to the eternal consequences of such a betrayal of God. Rather, Satan deceitfully suggested that "you can have God and Baal too." The devil tells Christians today that they can have Christ and the New Age with its astrology, its spiritualism and "little gods" theology. Christ's answer is, "Absolutely Not!" God declared that He is a jealous God. His word has never changed from the commandment uttered from Mount Sinai: "You shall have no other gods before Me" (Exodus 20:3). The Lord's judgment fell on Israel because they tried to follow Jehovah and Baal. God's judgment will always fall on a church that compromises with evil.

Spiritual blindness caused the Laodiceans to focus on their worldly wealth and to believe that their success was evidence that they were pleasing God. However, Jesus Christ looks on the inward heart of men. He declared: "You say, 'I am rich, have become wealthy, and have need of nothing' — and do not know that you are wretched, miserable, poor, blind, and naked — I counsel you to buy from Me gold refined in the fire, that you may be rich; and white garments, that you may be clothed, that the shame of your nakedness may not be revealed; and anoint your eyes with eye salve, that you may see" (Revelation 3:17,18). Jesus spoke to this church in terms they understood perfectly. After declaring their spiritual poverty and nakedness He counsels them to buy the true "gold refined in the fire" referring to true righteousness. To a city dependent on a garment industry and medicinal eye salve, the Lord advised that they put on "white garments" of righteousness and "anoint your eyes with eye salve" to heal their spiritual vision.

In summary, of the seven churches, only the church at Philadelphia received complete approval from Christ for their faithfulness, love and works. God promised that they would escape the fierce trial coming on the whole earth. Christ declared, "I will make him a pillar in the temple of My God, and he shall go out no more" (Revelation 3:12). An extraordinary statement is found in the writings of the great historian Edward Gibbon. "The captivity or ruin of the seven churches of Asia was consummated, and the barbarous lords of Ionia and Lydia still trample on the monuments of classic and Christian antiquity. In the loss of Ephesus, the Christians deplored the fall of the first angel and the extinction of the first candlestick of the Revelation. The desolation is complete and the temple of Diana, or the church of Mary, will equally elude the search of the curious traveller. The circus and the three stately theatres of Laodicea are now peopled by wolves and foxes. Sardis is reduced to a miserable village. The god of Mohammed without a rival or a son, is invoked in the mosques of Thyatira and Pergamos. The populousness of Smyrna is supported by the foreign trade of the Franks and Armenians. Philadelphia alone has been saved by prophecy or courage...Among the Greek colonies and churches of Asia, Philadelphia is still erect — a column in the scene of ruins" (Gibbon's *Decline and Fall of the Roman Empire* 64). Two thousand years later, Smyrna and Philadelphia, the only churches that received Christ's unqualified praise, are still thriving cities with Christian churches.

Christ concludes His letters to the seven churches with an invitation to the Marriage Supper of the Lamb. Jesus asks us to respond to His call to repentance and salvation: "Behold, I stand at the door and knock. If anyone hears My voice and opens the door, I will come in to him and dine with him, and he with Me" (Revelation 3:20). Although the letter to the Laodiceans is filled with warnings, Jesus concludes His last letter to the churches with a promise of eternal salvation and glory for any that will turn from their spiritual pride and give themselves totally to Christ as their Lord and Savior. "To him who overcomes I will grant to sit with Me on My throne, as I also overcame and sat down with My Father on His throne" (Revelation 3:21).

CHAPTER FOUR

The Imminent Rapture of the Saints

The Purpose of the Translation of the Saints

The Rapture is one of the most important doctrines in the Bible. However, many have avoided studying this subject because it is the most supernatural event in the Scriptures. Unfortunately, most discussions about the translation of the saints have focused exclusively on the question of the timing of the Rapture relative to the Tribulation. While the timing is very important, many Christians have lost sight of the true purpose of the Rapture. Although this event will remove the living saints to heaven to escape the Antichrist, its primary purpose is to provide all believers, living and departed, with their eternal resurrection bodies.

The "translation of the saints" will transform our mortal and corruptible body into a new resurrection body that will be immortal and incorruptible. Our present body is subject to disease, accident and death. The Scripture assures us that our present mortal and corruptible body is not suitable for heaven, nor is it suitable for us to reign and rule with Christ on the earth forever. In order that we may partake of all that Christ has promised His Bride, the Church, we must receive a new resurrection body. "Now this I say, brethren, that flesh and blood cannot inherit the kingdom of God; nor does corruption inherit incorruption. Behold, I tell you a mystery: We shall not all sleep, but we shall all be changed -- in a moment, in the twinkling of an eye, at the last trumpet. For the trumpet will sound, and the dead will be raised incorruptible, and we shall be changed" (1 Corinthians 15:50-52).

In Philippians 3:20,21 the Apostle Paul informs us that our eternal resurrection body will be similar to the glorious body that Jesus possessed when He rose from the grave. "For our citizenship is in heaven, from which we also eagerly wait for the Savior, the Lord Jesus Christ, who will transform our lowly body that it may be conformed to His glorious body, according to the working by which He is able even to subdue all things to Himself." In Romans 8:29 Paul again tells us that our body will be "conformed" to the resurrection body of our Lord. "For whom He foreknew, He also predestined to be conformed to the image of His Son, that He might be the firstborn among many brethren." The Old Testament did not reveal many details about the future life and bodies of the saints in heaven. However, the Apostle John received a vision about the nature of our resurrection body. "Beloved, now we are children of God; and it has not yet been revealed what we shall be, but we know that when He is revealed, we shall be like Him, for we shall see Him as He is. And everyone who has this hope in Him purifies himself, just as He is pure" (1 John 3:2,3).

The Promise of the Rapture

"For the Lord Himself will descend from heaven with a shout, with the voice of an archangel, and with the trumpet of God. And the dead in Christ will rise first. Then we who are alive and remain shall be caught up together with them in the clouds to meet the Lord in the air. And thus we shall always be with the Lord" (1 Thessalonians 4:16-17).

Some who oppose the teaching of the Rapture declare that the word "Rapture" does not appear in the Bible. The original Latin translation of the Bible by Jerome, an early Christian scholar, used the Latin word *rapere* to correctly translate "shall be caught up." This word *rapere* was used later as the derivation for our English word "Rapture." Since the phrase "to be caught up" is clearly in the New Testament and was quoted extensively by the early Church, we can safely use the word "Rapture" to describe the translation of the saints as outlined in 1 Thessalonians 4:16, 17.

Christ's Resurrection Body

If we wish to understand what our body will be like in heaven we need to examine the Scriptures that record the appearance of the body of Christ after His resurrection. In the last chapter of the gospel of Luke we read of Christ's supernatural visitation to His disciples in the Upper Room. When they saw Him standing miraculously in the center of the locked room, they were astonished and thought they had seen a ghost. Jesus replied as follows: "And He said to them, 'Why are you troubled? And why do doubts arise in your hearts? 'Behold My hands and My feet, that it is I Myself. Handle Me and see, for a spirit does not have flesh and bones as you see I have.' When He had said this, He showed them His hands and His feet" (Luke 24:38-40). Jesus explained that He wasn't a ghost or spirit but that His resurrection body was as real as His body before His death. To prove this, Christ challenged them to examine his hands and feet. He declared He had flesh and bones. Christ's resurrection body was similar in appearance to His body before His crucifixion. However, now His body was immortal, not subject to death, and incorruptible, not subject to pain, disease or injury. He showed His followers that His new body could travel at the speed of thought and appear at will in the middle of a room. Later, He appeared suddenly in Galilee.

Yet, despite these supernatural qualities, Christ requested food from His disciples to demonstrate His reality and to give them a foretaste of the reality of their future life in heaven. Though Christ did not need food biologically, He could enjoy the taste of food and joyfully partake of food in a social setting with His friends. "But while they still did not believe for joy, and marveled, He said to them, 'Have you any food here?' So they gave Him a piece of a broiled fish and some honeycomb" (Luke 24:41,42). The Revelation promised that believers will participate in the Marriage Supper of the Lamb. Jesus, when He celebrated the Last Supper with His followers, told them, "For I say to you, I will not drink of the fruit of the vine until the kingdom of God comes" (Luke 22:18). This statement of Christ tells us that He will partake of real food with us in that great marriage banquet in heaven. We will enjoy a twelve-fold variety of fruit from the Tree of Life in the New Jerusalem. "In the middle of its street, and on either side of the river, was the tree of life, which bore twelve fruits, each tree yielding its fruit every month" (Revelation 22:2). Christ's reference to "supping with Abraham, Isaac, and Jacob in the Kingdom of heaven," gives us a foretaste of the incredible reality of our new resurrection body. We will possess a body without pain, without suffering and having the miraculous qualities Christ demonstrated in His post-resurrection appearances.

The Early Church and the Time of the Rapture

The *Parousia*, the coming of Christ, is a message of tremendous hope, joy and comfort. The early Christians were commanded to be watchful and to live in purity in light of His coming "at any moment." If the apostles believed that Christians would be forced to endure the Mark of the Beast and the beheading of the saints in the Great Tribulation, why would their expressions concerning the coming of Christ be couched in terms of hope, comfort and joy? However, if the early Church taught that Christ would translate His Church to heaven to escape the horrible persecution, it is consistent that they would discuss the *Parousia* in terms of hope and joy.

In 2 Timothy 2:18 we read the words of Paul to the Church correcting doctrinal error about the Rapture. Certain heretics had misled believers, teaching that the Rapture had already occurred and that they had missed it. Speaking about these heretics Paul wrote, "Hymenaeus and Philetus are of this sort, who have strayed concerning the truth, saying that the resurrection is already past, and they overthrow the faith of some." The only "resurrection" that would concern the Christians would be the Rapture of the living and dead saints to meet Christ in the air. In analyzing Paul's teaching about the timing of the Rapture, as indicated in this passage, the best method is to consider his statements in terms of two different possibilities. (1) Imagine that Paul had taught the Christians the posttribulation Rapture position: that the Rapture would not occur until the completion of the Great Tribulation, the seven year treaty, the Antichrist and the wrath of God leading to Armageddon. How could Hymenaeus and Philetus possibly "overthrow the faith of some" by "saying that the resurrection is already past" if the Church "knew" that many detailed prophecies of worldwide catastrophes must occur before the Rapture? Their teaching that "the resurrection is already past" would fall on deaf ears to the Church if Paul had taught a posttribulation Rapture.

However, consider the second possibility. (2) Imagine that Paul taught about an imminent, pretribulation Rapture that could occur at any time from Pentecost until the revealing of the Antichrist. It is easy to understand how Hymenaeus and Philetus could "overthrow the faith of some" by "saying that the resurrection is already past" if the Christians understood Paul to have taught that there will be no warning prophetic signs before the Rapture. Since such an imminent pretribulation "resurrection" could occur at any time, this would allow these false teachers to confuse the Christians by telling them that believers in other communities had been raptured, leaving them behind. These heretics would "overthrow the faith of some" by making them believe that they had "missed" the Rapture (perhaps because of sin) and must now endure the Great Tribulation and the coming Antichrist. Paul corrects this false view of the "missed Rapture" and also rejects the view that only some of the "elite" Christians will be translated. In 2 Timothy 2:19 Paul declares "Nevertheless the solid foundation of God stands, having this seal: The Lord knows those who are His."

In another passage, Paul talks about the coming Rapture of the Church as a translation and resurrection of all Christians simultaneously. In 1 Corinthians 15:22,23, "For as in Adam all die, even so in Christ all shall be made alive. But each one in his own order: Christ the firstfruits, afterwards those who are Christ's at His coming." When Christ returns in the air for His Bride, the Church, He will translate "those who are Christ's at His coming." Only Jesus Christ and you know if you have committed your life and soul to Him, but if you have, you are Christ's, regardless of how righteous your works. If you belong to Christ, you will be raptured on that glorious day. The Bible does not teach a partial Rapture, nor does it describe a partial Bride at the Marriage Supper of the Lamb. The Rapture is not a prize for good works of Christians, it is the moment and the method by which Christ translates our mortal and corruptible bodies into a glorious resurrection body fit for an eternity in the Kingdom of heaven. All Christians, those who died in the faith in the last two thousand years, and those who are alive when He comes in the air, will be supernaturally "translated" without warning. The Scriptures declare that Christ will bring all the departed saints with Him "in the air."

In the first three hundred years of the early Church the major theological battles concerned the gnostic heresies about the nature of Jesus Christ. The great theological contest established the biblical doctrine that Jesus Christ was "perfect man and perfect God." Very little time was spent in developing a detailed and systematic eschatology, the study of prophecy, such as we have today. The early Christians taught a literal interpretation of the Bible's prophecies about the Second Coming and His "catching away" of the saints to meet Him in the air. However, they did not try to lay out a detailed time line regarding these particular prophetic events. As we will discover in another chapter the early Church universally believed in the premillennial return of Christ to establish His Kingdom after defeating Satan's Antichrist.

The Hope of the Imminent Rapture

The clear teaching of the apostles as found in the New Testament is that Christ could come at any moment, without warning, to translate His Church to heaven. Many such verses can be cited. I will provide several such passages to illustrate the concept of the imminent return of Christ as taught by the New Testament writers. The word "imminent" simply means that Christ could translate His Church to heaven without the necessity of the fulfillment of any intervening prophetic events. In other words, imminency meant that His coming for the Church was an impending event that could happen without warning at any time following the birth of the Church on the day of Pentecost. The Apostle Paul continually talked about the Rapture expressing the hope that he himself would participate in the glorious event. As an example, he wrote, "In a moment, in the twinkling of an eye, at the last trumpet. For the trumpet will sound, and the dead will be raised incorruptible, and we shall be changed" (1 Corinthians 15:52). Paul is the most precise of writers in his use of accurate language to convey the smallest shade and nuance of meaning. When Paul said "we shall be changed," he clearly hoped that the promised translation of the Christians would occur during his lifetime.

Since Paul was inspired by the Holy Spirit in his New Testament Epistles, his writing conveyed the truth of God. Therefore I conclude that it was possible that the Rapture could occur during Paul's lifetime or any other point during the last two thousand years. To illustrate that this is not an isolated instance, Paul again refers to his personal hope of participation in the Rapture in 1 Thessalonians 4:15: "For this we say to you by the word of the Lord, that we who are alive and remain until the coming of the Lord will by no means precede those who are asleep." Again, he shared his fervent hope that he will still be alive to see the coming of the Lord through the use of the words, "we who are alive and remain until the coming." While Paul knew Christ could delay His coming for a very long time, he hoped the Rapture would occur quickly. Some have objected that the Lord could not rapture the Church at that time because the Great Commission had not yet been completed, nor had the predicted apostasy occurred. However, the gospel was transmitted to many lands within and outside the Roman Empire during the first century. A glance at the writings of Paul to the church at Corinth and the messages to the seven churches in the book of Revelation reveals that a "falling away" from the true gospel message began to occur within the generation of the Apostles.

The Early Church's Belief in an Imminent Rapture

Some of the early Church writers wrote about the persecution of the Tribulation as if the saints will be present. However, a number of early Christian commentaries suggested that the Church will be delivered supernaturally before the Great Tribulation. Some posttribulation writers declare that the hope of a pretribulation Rapture and deliverance from the Great Tribulation was never taught until the Plymouth Brethren began to emphasize this around 1820. As this chapter will show, there is a great deal of evidence to illustrate that some writers in the first few centuries of the Church believed in Christ rapturing the saints to deliver them from this coming Tribulation. The doctrine of the imminent Rapture was clearly taught in the New Testament and by some writers in the first centuries of the early Church. There was a difference of opinion within the early Church about the timing of the Rapture just as we find today. However, the hope of the imminent Rapture clearly existed in the writings of the early Church.

The Didache

A Church manual from approximately A.D. 110, called the *Didache,* confirms the belief of these Christians in the imminent return of Christ for believers. This was written less than fifteen years after John wrote the Revelation.

In the *Didache* 16, we find the following instructions. "1. Be ye watchful for your life! Let not your lamps be extinguished nor your loins ungirded, but be ye ready! For ye know not the hour in which your Lord cometh. 2. Assemble yourselves frequently, seeking what is fitting for your souls. For the whole time of your faith will not be profitable to you, if you are not made perfect in the last time...then the world-deceiver shall appear as a son of god and shall work signs and wonders...6. And then shall the signs of the truth appear, first the sign of a rift in heaven, then the sign of the sound of a trumpet, and thirdly, a resurrection of the dead. 7. but not of all, but as it was said, 'The Lord will come and all His saints with Him.' 8. Then shall the world see the Lord coming on the clouds of heaven." In this short passage we see a strong belief in the imminent return of Christ: "Be ye ready! For ye know not the hour in which your Lord cometh." There is also a suggestion that the writer of the Didache was familiar with the teaching of Revelation 20 that the First Resurrection of the believers will be separated from the Second Resurrection of the wicked dead by the millennial period when he talks about "the resurrection of the dead, but not of all."

After warning Christians to prepare for "the hour in which your Lord cometh," the *Didache* said, "*Then,* the world-deceiver shall appear." This order of events suggests the Rapture will precede the appearance of the world-deceiver, the Antichrist.

Hippolytus' Treatise on the Christ and Antichrist

Hippolytus, who lived from A.D. 170 to 236, was the most brilliant of the early Christian writers. Writing in his *Treatise on the Christ and Antichrist* (section 66) about the Rapture he quoted extensively and approvingly from Paul's writing in 1 Thessalonians 4:12: "Then we which are alive and remain shall be caught up together with them in the clouds to meet the Lord in the air; and so shall we ever be with the Lord." He reminds his readers of the hope of Christ's imminent return. He wrote that we should be "'looking for that blessed hope and appearing of our God and Savior' when having raised the saints among us, He will rejoice with them glorifying the Father."

The Epistles of Cyprian

Cyprian lived from A.D. 200 to 258, and wrote extensively on Christian doctrine. In his Epistle 55, chapter 7, he wrote about his belief in Christ's ability to deliver the Church from the Antichrist's tribulation. "Nor let any one of you, beloved brethren, be so terrified by the fear of future persecutions, or the coming of the threatening Antichrist, as not to be found armed for all things by the evangelical exhortations and precepts, and by the heavenly warnings. Antichrist is coming, but above him comes Christ also. The enemy goeth about and rageth, but immediately the Lord follows to avenge our suffering and our wounds. The adversary is enraged and threatens, but there is One who can deliver us from his hands." Cyprian's declaration that Christ "is One who can deliver us from his [Antichrist's] hands" suggests the possibility of the Church being raptured before the Tribulation period. It is significant that he did not write about enduring the persecution of the Antichrist. Rather, Cyprian promised that Christ "is One who can deliver us from his hands."

Cyprian quoted Paul's prophecy about the translation of the saints, "For if we believe that Jesus died and rose again, even so them which are asleep in Jesus will God bring with Him" (1 Thessalonians 4:13). Speaking of the imminency of the Rapture, he wrote, "Who would not crave to be changed and transformed into the likeness of Christ and to arrive more quickly to the dignity of heavenly glory." After telling his readers that the coming resurrection was the hope of the Christian, he points out that the Rapture should motivate us as we see the last days approaching. Cyprian says that "we who see that terrible things have begun, and know that still more terrible things are imminent, may regard it as the greatest advantage to depart from it as quickly as possible." Referring to his hope of the approaching Rapture, he encouraged his readers as follows: "Do you not give God thanks, do you not congratulate yourself, that by an early departure you are taken away, and delivered from the shipwrecks and disasters that are imminent?" Cyprian concludes his comments on the translation of the saints with these words: "Let us greet the day which assigns each of us to his own home, which snatches us hence, and sets us free from the snares of the world, and restores us to paradise and the kingdom" (*Treatises of Cyprian* - 21 to 26).

Victorinus - Commentary of the Apocalypse

Victorinus, bishop of Petau, lived from A.D. 240 till his martyrdom during the last great persecution in A.D. 304. In his *Commentary on the Apocalypse* he interpreted chapter 6 of the Revelation to promise the deliverance of the Church from the tribulation period. "'And the heaven withdrew as a scroll that is rolled up.' For the heaven to be rolled away, that is, that the Church shall be taken away. 'And the mountain and the islands were moved from their places.' Mountains and islands removed from their places intimate that in the last persecution all men departed from their places; that is, that the good will be removed, seeking to avoid the persecution." In his comments on chapter 15, Victorinus wrote, "'And I saw another great and wonderful sign, seven angels having the seven last plagues; for in them is completed the indignation of God.' For the wrath of God always strikes the obstinate people with seven plagues, that is, perfectly, as it is said in Leviticus; and these shall be in the last time, when the Church shall have gone out of the midst." These comments reveal that this second century pastor also understood that the saints would be "removed" to escape the wrath of God "when the Church shall have gone out of the midst" of the coming tribulation.

The Shepherd of Hermes

Another example from the early decades of the second century is the writing known as *The Shepherd of Hermes* (A.D. 130). This book, as all writings outside the Bible, has no authority in terms of teaching doctrine. However, as an example of writing widely read by Christians in the period shortly after the death of the Apostles, it provides evidence of how some early Christians viewed the return of Christ. Part of this apocalyptic vision focused on the church's deliverance from the tribulation. The writer, after escaping a huge terrifying beast with four colors on its head (white, red, black and gold), met a virgin in his vision, "like a bride going forth from a bride-chamber, all in white...I recognized from the former visions that it was the church." The virgin explained that he escaped destruction from the beast (the Great Tribulation) because of God's special deliverance. "Thou hast escaped a great tribulation because thou hast believed and at the sight of such a huge beast hast not doubted. Go therefore and declare to the Elect of the Lord His mighty deeds and say to them that this beast is a type of the great tribulation which is to come. If ye therefore prepare yourselves and with your whole heart turn to the Lord in repentance, then shall ye be able to escape it, if your heart is pure and blameless." After explaining to him that "the golden colour stands for you who have escaped from this world," the virgin concluded her messages with, "Now ye know the symbol of the great tribulation to come. But if ye are willing, it shall be nothing." Despite the unusual details of this so-called vision, it clearly conveys the understanding of this early Christian writer that the faithful Church is promised a supernatural escape from the great tribulation. When posttribulationists make the claim that no one ever presented a pretribulation Rapture before 1830, they display their ignorance of a great deal of the history of prophetic interpretation. The French writer Joubert wrote: "Nothing makes men so imprudent and conceited as ignorance of the past and a scorn for old books."

Lactantius' Commentary on the Apocalypse

In Lactantius' *Commentary on the Apocalypse* (second century A.D.), he wrote about Revelation 6:14: "'And the heaven withdrew to be rolled away', that is, that the Church shall be taken away. 'And every mountain and the islands were moved from their places.' Mountains and islands removed from their places intimate that in the last persecution all men departed from their places; that is, that the good will be removed, seeking to avoid the persecution." While this passage is not definitive, it suggests through the words, "the Church shall be taken away" an anticipation of a supernatural Rapture of the Church from apocalyptic persecutions (probably the Tribulation period). Note that none of these writers quoted here suggests that the Church will experience the Great Tribulation and the Mark of the Beast system of the Antichrist.

The Teaching of the Twelve Apostles

Most scholars accept that this writing was composed before A.D. 120 and therefore indicates early Church attitudes. While this writing was never accepted as part of the canon of the New Testament its widespread popularity suggests that its ideas were held by many. Regarding the anticipation of the imminent return of Christ, consider this passage from chapter 16. "Watch for your life's sake. Let not your lamps be quenched, nor your loins unloosed; but be ye ready, for ye know not the hour in which our Lord cometh."

The Epistle of Barnabas

An epistle to the church at Corinth was written around A.D. 100 by someone named Barnabas. Although modern scholars reject the position that this Barnabas was the companion of Paul, the early Church believed that Paul's fellow worker wrote this book. Regardless of who wrote this letter, it represents one of the earliest writings of the Christians outside the New Testament. The writer certainly expected the Lord to come shortly as he indicated in these passages (chapter 4). "The final stumbling block approaches, concerning which it is written, as Enoch says, 'For this end the Lord has cut short the times and the days that His Beloved may hasten; and He will come to the inheritance...We take earnest heed in these last days; for the whole time of your faith will profit you nothing, unless now in this wicked time we also withstand coming sources of danger, as becometh the sons of God." Barnabas concluded his chapter 20 with these words: "On this account there will be a resurrection...For the day is at hand on which all things shall perish with the evil (one). The Lord is near, and His reward." This epistle clearly conveys the writer's hope of the imminent return of Christ to take the saints to heaven.

The First Epistle of Clement

Clement, a Gentile who became bishop of Rome, was a fellow laborer with the Apostle Paul at Philippi in A.D. 57. He lived from A.D. 30 to 100 and witnessed the explosive growth of the New Testament Church. In his first *Epistle to the Corinthians* he criticized the doubters who were expressing their disbelief in Christ's return because of the long delay since Christ's resurrection. In chapter 23 he wrote: "Far from us be that which is written, 'Wretched are they who are of a double mind, and of a doubting heart; who say, These things we have heard even in the times of our fathers; but, behold, we have grown old and none of them has happened unto us. Ye foolish ones.'" Comparing God's time to the time it takes a tree to mature, Clement then concludes with a clear expression of his belief in the imminency of the return of Christ that he had learned from the Apostle Paul. "Of a truth, soon and suddenly shall His will be accomplished, as the Scripture also bears witness, saying, 'Speedily will He come, and will not tarry;' and, 'The Lord shall suddenly come to His temple, even the Holy One, for whom ye look.'"

The Pretribulation Rapture Was Taught Three Hundred Years Ago

Many writers ignorantly assert that the pretribulation Rapture theory was invented in 1820. While the clearest statement of the pretribulation position was articulated by N. Darby at that time, they ignore these writings of the early Christians that anticipate Christ's coming to deliver His saints before the Tribulation period. Furthermore, many of these writers are ignorant of the other men who developed a clearer understanding of the Rapture in the centuries before 1820. Very few ideas appear out of nowhere. These concepts are usually "in the air" and are discussed for decades before someone publishes a manuscript.

Peter Jurieu

Peter Jurieu was a French Calvinist preacher and was considered "the Goliath of the French Protestants." He wrote in A.D. 1687 about the Rapture and the premillennial return of Christ. Jurieu discussed the coming of Jesus to translate the saints prior to the time He returns in judgment. He preached in Rotterdam as one of the greatest of the Reformers in his day. I found his rare and fascinating book, *Approaching Deliverance of the Church,* in a small bookstore in Wales. In his book, Jurieu refuted the amillennial teaching of his day and clearly argued for the premillennial position regarding Christ's return. He also believed that Christ would come in the air to rapture the saints and return to heaven before the Battle of Armageddon. While his teaching in this area was tentative, his book disproves the theory of the posttribulation teachers that assert that the pretribulation Rapture was first invented by Darby and the Plymouth Brethren. As my research indicates, the pretribulation Rapture was articulated in both the New Testament, the writings of some of the Ante-Nicene Fathers and Peter Jurieu, long before 1820.

Over one hundred and thirty years before Darby, Jurieu spoke of a secret Rapture, "a kind of a clandestine coming of Christ" prior to His coming in glory and judgment at Armageddon. In chapter 24:8:1 he wrote of John's prophecy about the Millennium, "The saints shall reign with Christ a thousand years." He commented, "But to me it seems very evident that this reign shall begin with some miraculous appearance of our Lord in His glory. After which He shall go back to Heaven." Expanding on his interpretation, he wrote, "There is a first coming of Christ, and it may be a first Resurrection. Lastly, who can be certain, that this coming of Christ, to establish His Kingdom upon Earth, shall not be in that manner, with the voice of an Arch-angel, and in great magnificence and Glory? Who can prove, that at that first coming of Christ He shall not raise some of the dead, as St. John seems expressly to have fore-told?"

Writing directly about the coming Rapture he compared it to the resurrection of the Old Testament saints when Christ rose from the grave. He asked, "Why may not Christ raise some of the New Testament Saints, at the coming of His Kingdom, as well as raise some of the ancient patriarchs, when He arose from the grave?" Jurieu rejected the view that Christ will stay in heaven until the final judgment of the world. He suggested that Christ will first "come down from heaven" in the air in "a glorious apparition, returning to heaven." While these comments are not conclusive, they do suggest that the idea of Christ coming in the air for His saints prior to Armageddon was under discussion over three hundred years ago. As the Reformers adopted a literal approach to interpreting the Bible's prophecies, they began to notice that the Rapture was a separate and earlier event from Christ's coming to defeat the forces of Antichrist at Armageddon.

The Three-Fold Division of the Book of Revelation

"Write the things which you have seen, and the things which are, and the things which will take place after this" (Revelation 1:19).

It is impossible to understand the meaning of the visions of Revelation unless we pay attention to this critical verse 19. Jesus Christ revealed to John that the book of Revelation was divided into three parts representing three periods of time.

1. The "things which you have seen"
    -- the introductory vision on Patmos - Chapter 1.

2. The "things which are"
    -- Christ's letters in chapters 2 and 3 to the seven
    churches.

3. The "things which will take place after this"
    -- the vision John received, when he was lifted up to
    heaven, of the terrible last-day judgments of God
    following the Church Age - Chapter 4 to the end of the
    book.

The word "church" appears seventy-four times in the
New Testament. In the first division of Revelation (chapters 1
to 3) dealing with the seven churches there is not one
mention of Israel while the word "church" appears seven
times. However, in the balance of the Revelation, the word
"church" does not appear and the focus returns to Israel and
the nations on earth. It is clear from this dramatic change that
the Church will not be on earth during the Tribulation period
described in Revelation 4 through 19. It is also significant
that the first three chapters dealing with the Church
constantly reveal the mercy of God. However, from chapter 4
through chapter 19, dealing with the Tribulation period, the
entire focus is on the wrath of God and His unreserved
judgment on unrepentant sinners.

John Lifted up to Heaven

"After these things I looked, and behold, a door standing
open in heaven. And the first voice which I heard was like a
trumpet speaking with me, saying, 'Come up here, and I will
show you things which must take place after this'"
(Revelation 4:1).

It is significant that, after completing the seven letters to
the churches, the next section of the visions of Revelation
begins with this phrase, "After these things..." Then the voice
from heaven calls John up to heaven and declares, "I will
show you things which must take place after this."
Obviously, the Scriptures are introducing a whole new

revelation. There is a complete shift of focus from the "things which are" - the seven churches of the first century, to "the things which must take place after this."

The first three chapters of the book of Revelation include seven letters addressed to the Church, the Bride of Christ. After the completion of the letters to the churches on earth, John was lifted up to heaven in his vision. This "lifting up" reminds us of the coming Rapture of the saints. He was given an amazing vision of the Throne of God and the Twenty-Four Elders. This commences a series of revelations focused on heaven and the coming Great Tribulation on earth. Chapters 4 through 19 of Revelation deal with the Tribulation period and the end-time events involving the Gentile nations and Israel on earth. It is significant that from the end of chapter three with the last message to the church of Laodicea until the vision of Armageddon in chapter 19, there is not one mention of the Church on earth. Then, in chapter 19, the Church is seen descending from heaven with Christ as part of a heavenly army to defeat the forces of Satan at Armageddon. These returning saints are clothed with "white linen" representing "the righteousness of Christ." This suggests strongly that the Church must have been translated to heaven at some earlier point in time to allow these saints to receive their resurrection bodies and white garments.

The Throne of God

"Immediately I was in the Spirit; and behold, a throne set in heaven, and One sat on the throne. And He who sat there was like a jasper and a sardius stone in appearance; and there was a rainbow around the throne, in appearance like an emerald" (Revelation 4:2,3).

The first thing John witnessed after being lifted up to heaven was God seated on His throne. The glorious vision described the literal reality witnessed by John in the best language available to the prophet. The word "throne" is found thirty-two times in Revelation and it always refers to a real throne. John described a "jasper and a sardine stone" as the colors in his heavenly vision. The stone called jasper by

96

the ancients is almost transparent, like crystal, while sardine possesses a beautiful red color. John saw a "rainbow around the throne" representing God's eternal covenant with mankind to refrain from ever again destroying the earth with a flood. The throne of God is the center of the authority of heaven and the focus of the coming judgments. "And from the throne proceeded lightnings, thunderings, and voices. And there were seven lamps of fire burning before the throne, which are the seven Spirits of God" (Revelation 4:5). The "seven Spirits of God" relate to the spiritual perfections and divine completeness of Jesus Christ. In Revelation 5:6 John describes Christ as follows: "A Lamb...having seven horns and seven eyes, which are the seven Spirits of God sent out into all the earth." In the Old Testament also, the prophet Zechariah described this seven-fold aspect of the Triune God: "Behold, I am bringing forth My Servant the Branch. For behold, the stone that I have laid before Joshua: upon the stone are seven eyes (Zechariah 3:8,9)" Throughout the Bible, God is clearly described as a Trinity, one God with three aspects or personalities.

What did John mean by "the seven Spirits of God"? While God is presented as triune, yet one, three Persons in One, the Father, Son and Holy Spirit, the prophet Isaiah was given an extraordinary vision of Jesus the Messiah revealing a multitude of unique qualities or "spirits." "There shall come forth a Rod from the stem of Jesse, and a Branch shall grow out of his roots. The Spirit of the Lord shall rest upon Him, the Spirit of wisdom and understanding, the Spirit of counsel and might, the Spirit of knowledge and of the fear of the Lord" (Isaiah 11:2). In this inspired vision we see seven different Spirits or qualities revealed in Jesus, the righteous "Branch." (1) The Spirit of the Lord; (2) The Spirit of wisdom; (3) The Spirit of understanding; (4) The Spirit of counsel; (5) The Spirit of might; (6) The Spirit of knowledge; and finally (7) The Spirit of the fear of the Lord. Each of these spirits or qualities, found in perfection in Christ, should be emulated by every follower of the Messiah.

The Twenty Four Elders

The Greek word *presbuteros,* translated "elder," appears

sixty-six times in the Bible. It almost always refers to the leading representative of a family, city, tribe or nation. This word is never applied to angels since they cannot grow old or mature in wisdom as human "elders." Jesus Christ, the twenty-four elders, and the saints are the only ones seen in heaven with crowns. Angels never receive crowns. Therefore, these elders must be men redeemed from the earth. The twenty-four elders represent the New Testament Church and the Old Testament saints who rose with Christ at His resurrection (Matthew 27:52,53). Victorinus, an early Church writer wrote in his *Commentary on the Apocalypse*: "They are the twenty-four fathers - twelve apostles and twelve patriarchs." Later, in John's vision of the New Jerusalem, we see the Old Testament saints and the Church of the New Testament united in the Holy City of God. "Also she [the New Jerusalem] had a great and high wall with twelve gates, and twelve angels at the gates, and names written on them, which are the names of the twelve tribes of the children of Israel"(Revelation 21:12). In addition, John sees the representatives of the Church in the heavenly city: "Now the wall of the city had twelve foundations, and on them were the names of the twelve apostles of the Lamb" (Revelation 21:14). In Revelation 5:8 John describes the twenty-four elders worshipping Jesus with harps and a new song. "The twenty-four elders fell down before the Lamb, each having a harp and golden bowls full of incense which are the prayers of the saints."

The Apocalypse mentions harps in numerous places in John's visions of heaven. The prayer of hundreds of millions of Christians — "Thy kingdom come" — has ascended to heaven over the centuries. The incense represents the faithful prayers of believers in the ultimate victory of the coming Messiah and reminds us of incense brought into the Holy Place of the Temple. When the twenty-four elders prophesy with their harps, they sing their new song declaring that God will "make us kings and priests to our God; and we shall reign on the earth" (Revelation 5:10). John's vision reminds us of the twenty-four courses of priests established by King David to serve in rotation in the Temple. Since the number twelve relates to human government, the number twenty-four, (twelve times two) suggests the perfection of the divine government of God's universe.

The Four Living Creatures

"And in the midst of the throne, and around the throne, were four living creatures full of eyes in front and in back. The first living creature was like a lion, the second living creature like a calf, the third living creature had a face like a man, and the fourth living creature was like a flying eagle. And the four living creatures, each having six wings, were full of eyes around and within. And they do not rest day or night, saying: 'Holy, holy, holy, Lord God Almighty, Who was and is and is to come!'" (Revelation 4:6-8).

In the King James Version the Greek word *Zoa* was translated "beasts" but a better translation is reflected in the New King James Version, quoted extensively in this book. In later chapters we find the Greek word *therion* correctly translated as "beasts" reflecting the symbolic visions of the Antichrist and his kingdom. These *Zoa*, or Living Creatures, are probably the same angelic beings described as seraphim (Isaiah 6:1-8) and cherubim (Ezekiel 1:4-28) in other related passages. Since these living creatures are described separately from the other classes of angels, they have a different and exalted role surrounding the throne of God. John describes these supreme angelic beings worshipping God, singing and praising the Lamb with harps. Later they call forth the Four Horsemen of the Apocalypse and provide the seven bowl judgments to the angels. All the heavenly creatures surrounding the throne worship God and give Him glory. The twenty-four elders will cast their crowns at the feet of Christ to give Him the glory. They announce the purpose of all of His creation: "You are worthy, O Lord, to receive glory and honor and power; for You created all things, and by Your will they exist and were created" (Revelation 4:11). Christ created man with a "God-shaped void" within each of our hearts, that nothing else will satisfy. As the old catechism declared: "What is the chief end of man. To glorify God and enjoy Him forever."

Differences Between the Rapture and Revelation

The Rapture and the Revelation are not the same event. Not one verse in the Bible refers to the translation of the saints and the Revelation as if they were a single event. Some suggest that the Bible's references to the Second Coming of Christ demand that everything happen simultaneously. They feel that His "coming" cannot logically include two events, the Rapture and, seven years later, the Revelation at Armageddon. However, the Scriptures clearly describe these two different events in a manner that makes it impossible that they occur simultaneously. We should remember that the First Coming of Christ involved a diverse set of events beginning with the birth of Jesus and ending with His Crucifixion, Resurrection and Ascension thirty-three and a half years later. Therefore, there is no contradiction in describing the Rapture and the Revelation as two events connected with the Second Coming of Christ. Additionally, we should remember that Christ comes in the air to rapture His Church back to heaven while He only comes once to the earth to establish His eternal Kingdom.

The Rapture and the Revelation are two distinct events with different purposes, locations, classes of participants and timing. The purpose of the Rapture is to transform the mortal, corruptible bodies of the saints of the Church into their new immortal, incorruptible bodies allowing them to reign with Christ forever. While the Rapture will remove the living Christians from the earth before the Tribulation period, its primary purpose is to bring about "the glorious liberty of the children of God" and "the adoption, the redemption of the body" (Romans 8:21,23). The location of the Rapture is "in the air." It will involve all living and dead Christian believers, "those who are Christ's at His coming" (1 Corinthians 15:23). The Scriptures reveal the Rapture will occur before the seven-year Tribulation period. It will produce a joyful reunion" in the air" as the living saints join together with the "dead in Christ." The Rapture of Enoch, Elijah, the Old Testament saints and Christ's ascension were private events. The Rapture of the saints will not be a public event. It is for the Church, not the world.

In contrast, the Revelation, the coming of Christ in glory, will produce a totally different reaction. "Then all the tribes of the earth will mourn, and they will see the Son of Man coming on the clouds of heaven with power and great glory" (Matthew 24:30). The different reaction will occur because, at the Revelation, Christ is coming with His heavenly army to destroy His enemies. The purpose of the Revelation is to defeat the forces of Antichrist, imprison Satan and establish the millennial Kingdom. The location of Christ's Revelation is on the earth, especially at Armageddon and Jerusalem. The people involved will include all the nations on earth together with His Chosen People Israel. Christ's Revelation will occur at the end of Daniel's seventieth week of years, the seven-year countdown to Armageddon. In every single item, the Rapture and the Revelation differ. In contrast to the private Rapture, the Revelation will be witnessed by the whole world.

The Blessed Hope of the Church

Throughout the New Testament and the writings of the Apostolic Church we find expressions of positive expectation and hope applied to Christ's coming at the Rapture. The word *Parousia* means "the personal appearance or coming" and is used to describe both His coming for the Church at the Rapture and His coming to the earth at His Revelation. We must examine the context and details of each passage to determine its meaning. The other word *Phaneros* means "to become manifest, to appear, to be seen or to shine forth." It is usually translated "to appear" and often refers to Christ appearing in the air with the souls of departed saints to meet the Christian saints rising in the air in their new resurrection bodies.

The promise of Christ's coming at the Rapture is the great hope of the Church. The Apostle Paul says: "For what is our hope, or joy, or crown of rejoicing? Is it not even you in the presence of our Lord Jesus Christ at His coming?" (1 Thessalonians 2:19). Paul describes the coming Rapture: "Then we who are alive and remain shall be caught up together with them in the clouds to meet the Lord in the air. And thus we shall always be with the Lord. Therefore comfort one another with these words" (1 Thessalonians 4:17,18). The Apostle certainly knew when the Rapture would occur relative to the Tribulation period. Why would he continually tell the Church that the coming of Christ was their "hope, joy, crown of rejoicing" and their "comfort" if he knew that the vast majority of the Church would be killed by the persecution of the Tribulation period? His words of comfort, hope and joy are consistent with his understanding that Christ will rapture His Church before the Tribulation.

As an example of the continuing hope of the Rapture in the early Church we find Polycrates, Bishop of Ephesus who wrote an epistle to the Church at Rome around A.D. 190. "For in Asia great luminaries have gone to their rest, who shall rise again in the day of the coming of the Lord, when He cometh with glory from heaven and shall raise again all the saints." Speaking of those departed saints at Sardis, he wrote that they are "awaiting the visitation from heaven, when he shall rise again from the dead" (*Remains of Second Century - Ante-Nicene Fathers*).

A fascinating homily written by Clement was found by Bryennios, Metropolitan bishop of Nicomedia over a century ago. Bishop Lightfoot concluded that it was written from Corinth about A.D. 130. The homily encourages believers to look for the imminent resurrection and Second Coming. "Let us expect therefore, hour by hour, the kingdom of God in love and righteousness, since we know not the day of the appearing of God."

The Qualifications for the Rapture

Some writers believe that the Rapture is a reward for good behavior by Christians. They observe the carnality of many Christians and believe that perhaps God will deliver justice by only rapturing the righteous believers and leaving the rest to be "purified" by enduring the Tribulation. While their attitude does them credit, the Bible reveals that we are purified by the completed work of Christ on the Cross, not by tribulation. God's justice will be displayed when every Christian will appear before the Judgment Seat of Christ to give an account of every action of our life. There the final rewards and crowns of the saints will be given or withheld on the basis of our works.

What is the qualification for the Rapture if our personal righteous deeds do not count? The only hope for salvation lies in our acceptance of Jesus Christ as our Lord and Savior. Christ told His disciples "the way" to heaven was through faith in Him. Jesus said:, "I am the way, the truth, and the life. No one comes to the Father except through Me" (John 14:6). When Christ returns in the air to rapture His Church, He will bring the souls of all departed Christians with Him to receive their resurrected bodies. All departed saints, from Paul to the last believer who dies before the Rapture, will be returning with Christ, regardless of the quality of their righteous deeds. Obviously, since all the departed saints, representing all levels of righteous works, will be present at the Rapture, then all living believers, regardless of their works, will also be raptured at the same time. The qualification for the Rapture is the same as for salvation itself. It is based solely on our faith and trust in Jesus Christ.

Can We Know the Time of the End?

As indicated in the earlier part of this chapter, the time of the Rapture is imminent and, hence, unknowable. Can we know the time of the Rapture? The answer is clearly no. If the translation of the saints can happen at any moment, then it has not been set in time or revealed in prophecy. It may be that God will delay His return for the Church until the last soul accepts Him as their Savior. Then Christ will say to His Church, "Come Home!" Where God has drawn a veil, we should not attempt to lift the veil and declare dogmatically what God has not revealed. If the Lord had wanted the Church to know the exact time of the Rapture, He would have told us. Since He did not choose to tell us, it must be that He believed it was best that the Church live in constant expectation of the speedy return of Christ to translate His saints. As Deuteronomy 29:29 tells us, "The secret things belong to the Lord our God, but those things which are revealed belong to us." The greatest secret is the timing of the Rapture. The absence of any detailed indication of the time of the Rapture, together with Christ's continual command to "Be watchful! You don't know the hour of My return!" tell us that it is useless to speculate on the day or hour of His return for His Church. If anyone claims they have discovered the date of the Rapture, they are wrong.

However, if the question is: Can we know the general time of Christ's coming to establish His millennial Kingdom? The answer is: Possibly. As indicated in my earlier book *Armageddon - Appointment With Destiny*, the early Christians and Jewish writers believed that the Bible taught that Christ would return to set up His kingdom at the end of six thousand years from the creation of Adam. During the first three hundred years of the Christian Era it was virtually the universal opinion of the early Christian writers that the Apostles and the Bible taught that the six days of creation were a microcosm of the Great Week of six thousand years of man's history. These writers taught that, just as God rested on the Sabbath, the seventh day of the week of creation, the Great Sabbath of man's history would enable mankind to enter into God's Sabbath rest of His one-thousand-year reign. In the book of Hebrews we are told that mankind has not yet entered into God's Sabbath rest. "There remains therefore a rest for the people of God" (Hebrews 4:9). However, when God's time comes, we will enter into His perfect Sabbath rest of the Millennium.

Warnings about Date Setting

Although the Church will have a sense of the "times and seasons" of the coming Battle of Armageddon, the unbelievers will remain in darkness concerning the times. Jesus Christ specifically warned that "no man would know the day or the hour" of His return in glory at Armageddon. Several times the Bible declares that He will "come as a thief in the night" to the rebellious sinners of that day. Christ likens His return to the "days of Noah" and reminds them of Lot's wife who refused to believe the warnings of impending judgment.

"But concerning the times and the seasons, brethren, you have no need that I should write to you. For you yourselves know perfectly that the day of the Lord so comes as a thief in the night. For when they say, 'Peace and safety!' then sudden destruction comes upon them, as labor pains upon a pregnant woman. And they shall not escape. But you, brethren, are not in darkness, so that this Day should overtake you as a thief. You are all sons of light and sons of the day. We are not of the night nor of darkness. Therefore let us not sleep, as others do, but let us watch and be sober" (1 Thessalonians 5:1-6).

The Apostle Paul clarified Christ's message to make us understand that although Christ will come as a thief in the night to the unbeliever, the children of the night, He will not "overtake you [the Christians] as a thief" because believers are the children "of the light." In regard to understanding the timing of God's dealing with Israel and the nations, God clearly indicates that Christians will understand the approximate timing of His return to set up His Kingdom in a way that the unbelievers will never understand. Despite seven years of the fulfillment of the most detailed prophetic events involving the Antichrist, the Great Tribulation and the Mark of the Beast, Christ's glorious return will still come as a total surprise to the unbelievers. The prophet Daniel declared the same principle: "Many shall be purified, made white, and tried; but the wicked shall do wickedly: and none of the wicked shall understand, but the wise shall understand" (Daniel 12:10). No matter how many specific prophecies are fulfilled, those who lack spiritual understanding will never understand the time of His coming.

In Acts 17:31 the Apostle Paul suggests that God has set the day of His glorious victory over Satan's Antichrist from the beginning of time. "Because He has appointed a day, on which he will judge the world in righteousness by the man whom he has ordained; He has given assurance of this to all, by raising Him from the dead" (Acts 17:31).

This Generation Will Not Pass

"Now learn this parable from the fig tree: When its branch has already become tender and puts forth leaves, you know that summer is near. So you also, when you see all these things, know that it is near, at the very doors. Assuredly, I say to you, this generation will by no means pass away till all these things are fulfilled" (Matthew 24:32-34).

Jesus was asked by His disciples about the signs that would precede His Second Coming and the end of the age.

He answered with a series of very specific signs regarding wars and rumors of war, famines, earthquakes, pestilences and rising anti-semitism. One of the last prophetic signs announcing His return was the sign of the fig tree. Six times in the Old Testament the fig tree is used as a symbol of Israel (Judges 9:10-14; 1 Kings 4:25; Jeremiah 24:1; Hosea 9:10; Micah 4:4; Zechariah 3:10). The Jewish rabbis and Christ's disciples knew that the fig tree was a symbol of Israel. Jesus withered away a fig tree because it didn't bear fruit for the Messiah, indicating that Israel had failed to bear spiritual fruit for the Son of Man. A fig tree appears to die in winter and then seems to come to life again in spring when the branch "becomes tender and puts forth leaves." Two thousand years ago the exiles of Israel were taken captive into the nations. Just like the fig tree, Israel appeared to die. Many, including some Christian writers, believed that a Jewish state would never rise again. However, the prophecies of the Bible reflecting God's covenant with Israel cannot be broken. On May 15,1948, as the British Mandate ended at midnight, the new Jewish state of Israel was reborn exactly as a fig tree putting forth leaves. Christ promised that "this generation will by no means pass away till all these things are fulfilled." In the Bible a generation is sometimes forty years, seventy years, one hundred years and, in one case, one hundred and twenty years. Christ was not setting a date. His words indicate a single generation of people will witness two great prophetic events, the rebirth of Israel and the return of Jesus the Messiah. I believe the generation that witnessed the rebirth of Israel in 1948 will not die as a group until the coming of the Messiah.

The Command to be Watchful

"Watch therefore, and pray always that you may be counted worthy to escape all these things that will come to pass, and to stand before the Son of Man" (Luke 21:36). Throughout the Scriptures the Lord encourages His Church to live in earnest expectation of His soon return to take them to the Marriage Supper of the Lamb. Jesus talked to His disciples about the attitude of a faithful servant whose Master has gone away on a long journey. His words suggest the proper expectant attitude we are to hold until the glorious appearing of our Lord. "Blessed are those servants whom the master, when he comes, will find watching" (Luke 12:37). These commands to be watchful indicate that Christ could have come at any moment from the day of Pentecost until the time Antichrist appears. The Rapture has been imminent for the last two thousand years.

Why did Jesus delay His return for so long? The Apostle Peter indicates that the reason for the delay is that Christ is "long-suffering toward us, not willing that any should perish but that all should come to repentance" (2 Peter 3:9). According to church statisticians, more than eighty thousand people accept Christ as their personal Savior every single day. By delaying one more day, another eighty thousand people turn from an eternity in hell to find peace with God forever. However, while we rejoice in this marvelous growth in the Church, the world's population is increasing even faster than the Church. In light of these facts, we are called to renew our missionary and evangelistic efforts as never before.

As Christians we are called to live in a dynamic spiritual tension. We must live and witness as though Jesus could return at any moment. However, because Christ could delay His return, we must plan our life as though we have a hundred years. Additionally, we should remember that the Church is returning with Christ after the seven-year Tribulation period to set up His eternal Kingdom on earth. The study of prophecy does not lead to escapism. After the worst crisis in man's history, Jesus will return with His Church to create a government of righteousness, prosperity and peace forever. The churches will be full during the millennial Kingdom as the Gentiles born in that period will learn about salvation. As detailed in my book, *Heaven - The Last Frontier,* Christians, in their resurrection bodies, will be teaching these Gentiles and actively administering this planet for the Messiah.

Paul taught the imminency of the rapture of the Church as he advised believers "to wait for His Son from heaven, which delivered us from the wrath to come." This expression "wrath to come" refers to the wrath of God that will be poured out on the unrepentant sinners during the Tribulation period. The Bible's clear promise that Christ will "deliver us from the wrath to come" is one of the strongest proofs of the pretribulation Rapture. The very last promise of the Bible concludes with the fervently expressed hope of His soon return (Revelation 22:20). "He who testifies to these things says, 'Surely I am coming quickly.' Amen. Even so, come, Lord Jesus!"

CHAPTER FIVE

The Antichrist and False Prophet

The first mention of the coming Antichrist is found in the very first prophecy of the Bible. After the sinful rebellion of Adam and Eve, God cursed the earth because of their sin and expelled them from the Garden of Eden. Moses recorded God's promise of ultimate victory over sin and death through the coming Messiah, Jesus Christ. "I will put enmity between you and the woman, and between your seed and her Seed; He shall bruise your head, and you shall bruise His heel" (Genesis 3:15). In the same verse God prophesied that He would send "her Seed," a virgin-born Messiah-Redeemer, to defeat Satan. In addition, the Lord promised that He would defeat Satan's attempt to usurp God's power by destroying both him and "his seed," the Antichrist.

As we approach the year 2000 the world is desperately looking for a Messiah-figure to solve its huge and growing problems. The Buddhists and the Hindus are searching for the next Avatar. The Moslems are expecting the appearance of the Mahdi, a messiah-like figure mentioned by the Koran, to usher in the last days. In Israel today, there is a rising expectation of the coming Messiah. Banners in Jerusalem proclaim, "We want Messiah now!" Several Old Testament passages tell us the last great enemy of mankind will be satanically possessed in a unique way during the last days. He is identified by a number of names including: the "wicked," the "Assyrian," the "idol shepherd" and "the prince that shall come." Progressively, the prophets of the Jewish Scriptures revealed details about Satan's Prince of Darkness. The book of Daniel prophesied about the career of the Antichrist, including his meteoric rise to political and military power over the final worldwide empire. Daniel revealed that he will rise after the ten nations of the former Roman Empire confederate together into a massive political and military alliance dominating Europe and the Mediterranean. The tremendously powerful Roman Empire was prophesied by Daniel centuries before it arose from an insignificant city state in Italy. Rome dominated the known world for over a thousand years. In the last days, the Bible predicts that the nations occupying the geographical area of the ancient Roman Empire will come together once more. Initially, it will be a confederation of weak "clay" nations and strong "iron" states until the Antichrist consolidates its power under his totalitarian control (Daniel 2:42). The Scriptures described the revived Roman Empire as a "beast" with "ten horns" representing ten participating nation states. "Thus he said: 'The fourth beast shall be a fourth kingdom on earth, which shall be different from all other kingdoms, and shall devour the whole earth, trample it and break it in pieces" (Daniel 7:23).

Instead of creating the revived Roman Empire, the Antichrist will only appear on the world scene after it has come into existence. Then, as Daniel 7:24 makes clear, he will seize power over three of the ten nations during a future crisis. "The ten horns are ten kings who shall arise from this kingdom. And another shall rise after them; he shall be different from the first ones, and shall subdue three kings" (Daniel 7:24). After defeating these three nations and their leaders, the remaining seven nations of the original ten-nation alliance will submit to his tremendous power. The Antichrist will rule with absolute totalitarian power over the ten nations. He will use this power base to launch his campaign to rule the entire world. The secret to the Antichrist's power is that he will sell his soul to Satan and receive satanic power to rule the nations. The prophet Daniel describes him as an evil master of occult power who will do anything to achieve his goal of world domination. "And in the latter time of their kingdom, when the transgressors have reached their fullness, a king shall arise, having fierce features, who understands sinister schemes. His power shall be mighty, but not by his own power; he shall destroy fearfully, and shall prosper and thrive; he shall destroy the mighty, and also the holy people" (Daniel 8:23,24). In the book of Revelation, the prophet John explains that the

Antichrist and the False Prophet can only perform their satanic miracles through the direct power of the devil. Although "his power shall be mighty" it is "not by his own power." Satan will totally possess him during the last three-and-a-half years leading up to the Battle of Armageddon.

"And I looked, and behold, a white horse. He who sat on it had a bow; and a crown was given to him, and he went out conquering and to conquer" (Revelation 6:2).

The First Horseman of the Apocalypse

In the book of Revelation, John first describes the Antichrist in his vision of the Four Horsemen of the Apocalypse. The first seal judgment of the tribulation period will be the White Horseman. "And I looked, and behold, a white horse. And he who sat on it had a bow; and a crown was given to him, and he went out conquering and to conquer" (Revelation 6:2). Both the Jews and Christians are looking for the Messiah to come as the rider on "a white horse" to save humanity. The Antichrist appears in John's vision with a bow but no arrow, impersonating Christ by offering a war-sick world the false promise of peace. However, although this counterfeit Messiah will claim his crown for bringing about a false peace, he will deceive the nations as he goes out "conquering and to conquer." Using the pretense of peace, this great deceiver, as the "seed" of Satan, the "father of lies," will succeed in consolidating his supreme power over the emerging New World Order. After witnessing the massive destruction of millions of soldiers during the Russian and Arab military attack on Israel, the world will be desperate for the peace offered by the Antichrist. Daniel prophesied that "he shall destroy many in their prosperity" (and peace).

The Beast from the Sea - The Antichrist

In Revelation 13:1 John describes his terrible vision of this tyrant as he rises to world power. "Then I stood on the sand of the sea. And I saw a beast rising up out of the sea, having seven heads and ten horns, and on his horns ten crowns, and on his heads a blasphemous name." In this parallel vision to Daniel 7:23,24, the "beast" rises out of the political "sea" to rule over the revived Roman Empire represented by the "ten horns," the ten nations that will unite together. While Daniel describes his conquering the three nations, John's vision sees him at a later stage when he confidently rules his new empire, wearing "ten crowns" showing he has usurped all political power. While the "ten horns" show that all ten nations accept his rule, the "seven heads" probably indicate that only seven of the initial ten leaders survived his takeover. He may kill the three leaders or "kings" of the "three horns" (nations) when he initially seizes political and military power. Whatever his status at birth, once Satan gives him the power, the Antichrist will claim the royal prerogative of being crowned and ruling from a "throne" as the new Caesar of the Roman Empire. "And the dragon gave him his power, his throne, and great authority" (Revelation 13:2).

One of the major political moves he makes to ensure his political domination of the world is to finally solve the Middle East crisis that has defeated the best diplomats of the last century. After establishing his control over the ten nations of Europe and the Mediterranean, the Antichrist will prove his credentials as a great peacemaker by creating a false peace between Israel and her Arab neighbors. Daniel

9:27 declares: "Then he shall confirm a covenant with many for one week." This phrase indicates the Antichrist will use the power of a united Europe to guarantee Israel's security and encourage her to enter into a seven-year peace treaty with her age-old enemies. The word "week" or *shabuim* in Daniel's prophecy refers to a period of seven years. To the Jews, the word *shabuim* meant a "seven" or "week" of years, while the word for a "seven" of days was *yamim*. We in the West normally think in terms of a decimal system based on tens and therefore, we naturally count our years in decades of ten years each. The Jews of the Old Testament counted times primarily in terms of sevens or "weeks." God declared that they must rest on the Sabbath every seven days and let the land lie dormant every seven years as a Sabbath of the land. To illustrate this use of "weeks" of years, in Leviticus 25:8 God commanded Israel to calculate the time of the Jubilee: "You shall count seven weeks of years for yourself, seven times seven years; and the time of the seven weeks of years shall be to you forty-nine years." Therefore, when Daniel refers to a "week" of years, this was easily understood by his Jewish readers as a seven-year period.

The Jewish nation longs to lay down her weapons and turn to the great task of "bringing home the exiles." However, today, Israel must spend over 50 percent of her budget on defense and require every able-bodied man and woman to serve for several years in the Israel Defense Forces. Israel is currently outnumbered by the combined Arab armies more than 15 to 1 in manpower and more than 5 to 1 in almost every single area of weaponry. God's miraculous intervention together with Israel's incredible bravery and skill enabled her to survive against overwhelming military odds. Finally, the new dictator of Europe will offer the Jews a way out of this seemingly endless struggle. Israel will tragically make a seven-year treaty with the Antichrist. In Isaiah 28:18 the prophet describes the true nature of the bargain Israel will make with the "beast." "Your covenant with death will be annulled, and your agreement with Sheol will not stand; when the overflowing scourge passes through, then you will be trampled down by it" (Isaiah 28:18). Instead of providing true peace, this fateful seven-year treaty will lead Israel into her darkest hour, the "time of Jacob's trouble." Although it will be a terrible time of trial, God promised that, when the exiles return to Israel, they will never again be removed from their land. The faithful remnant of Israel who trust in Jehovah and their coming Messiah will be protected in that terrible time of persecution. "Alas! For that day is great, so that none is like it; and it is the time of Jacob's trouble, but he shall be saved out of it" (Jeremiah 30:7).

Although he claims to be a friend of Israel, after the first three-and-a-half years of the seven-year treaty, the Jewish Antichrist will betray his brethren. As Daniel declared: "But in the middle of the week he shall bring an end to sacrifice and offering" (Daniel 9:27). Although the Antichrist will be an evil man as he works his way to power behind the scenes, he will undergo a radical spiritual transformation three-and-a-half years after he signs the seven-year treaty with Israel. Revelation 12 and Daniel 12 both prophesy that Satan will be cast out of heaven by Michael the archangel after a titanic struggle at the mid-point of the seven-year treaty. After thousands of years as the "prince of the power of the air" Satan will be defeated. "And war broke out in heaven: Michael and his angels fought against the dragon; and the dragon and his angels fought, but they did not prevail, nor was a place found for them in heaven any longer. So the great dragon was cast out, that serpent of old, called the devil and Satan, who deceives the whole world; he was cast to the earth, and his angels were cast out with him" (Revelation 12:7-9).

Satan has some freedom at the present time on earth and in the heavenlies. The book of Job describes Satan appearing before God to accuse Job. Jesus also described Satan in the heavenlies accusing Christians to God. When Satan loses his freedom and is forced to the earth, it will signal the beginning of the greatest crisis in human history. The angels will announce this initial victory over the devil as the first stage in the ultimate triumph of Christ. The angels of heaven will warn the earth of its coming trial: "Woe to the inhabitants of the earth and the sea! For the devil has come down to you, having great wrath, because he knows that he has a short time" (Revelation 12:12). Satan can read the prophecies of the Scriptures as well as any human. The devil will know that he will only have three-and-a-half years to attempt to change the prophesied course of history that will lead inexorably to his defeat at the hands of Jesus Christ. The Antichrist will be totally possessed by Satan at this point as no other man in history. John's prophetic vision describes the terrible attack on Israel that will be launched by the Antichrist. "Now when the dragon saw that he had been cast to the earth, he persecuted the woman who gave birth to the male Child" (Revelation 12:13). The woman represents Israel who produced Jesus, the "male Child."

The Beast from the Earth - the False Prophet

The Antichrist will be supported by a partner in his rise to world dominance, the False Prophet. In John's visions, he described him as follows: "Then I saw another beast coming up out of the earth, and he had two horns like a lamb and spoke like a dragon. And he exercises all the authority of the first beast in his presence, and causes the earth and those who dwell in it to worship the first beast, whose deadly wound was healed" (Revelation 13:11). In this amazing prophecy John declared that the False Prophet "spoke like a dragon," indicating that his supernatural source of power will be Satan himself. His satanic power is derivative and operates only in the physical presence of the Antichrist. Because Satan's power is not omnipresent like God's, he can only project his power to the False Prophet while he is "in his presence."

Who is this False Prophet? What is his role in the events leading up to the coming of Christ? The Jews have longed for the coming of the Prophet Elijah for over two thousand years. Malachi predicted that the Prophet Elijah would appear in the last days to announce the coming of the Messiah. He will save Israel from their enemies and establish His kingdom of righteousness. "Behold, I will send you Elijah the prophet before the coming of the great and dreadful day of the Lord" (Malachi 4:5). This widespread expectation of the return of Elijah expresses itself in the annual Passover meal celebrated by Jewish families around the world for the last two and a half thousand years. Every Passover, they leave a window or door ajar for Elijah to enter and join them in anticipation of their coming Messiah. They set out an extra cup of wine for Elijah in the hope that this will be the year God fulfills His promise to Israel.

"Then I saw another beast coming up out of the earth, and he had two horns like a lamb and spoke like a dragon" (Revelation 13:11).

Satan's Counterfeit Messiah and False Prophet

The Jewish rabbis expect Elijah will "turn the hearts of the fathers to the children, and the hearts of the children to their fathers, lest I come and strike the earth with a curse" (Malachi 4:6). When the Jewish scribes and Pharisees approached John the Baptist and Jesus, their first question was: "Are you Elijah? Are you that prophet?" Their first question referred to their expectation that the prophet Elijah would appear as a forerunner of the Messiah. The second question about "that prophet" is not a repeat of the first question. The title "that prophet" was a common name for the Messiah because Moses had prophesied that God would send them the Messiah, a "prophet like unto me" (Moses). After asking if John or Jesus was Elijah, they then asked if either one was the Messiah. The expectation of the coming Messiah and His forerunner was almost universal in the first century in Judea because Daniel's prophecy of the seventy weeks (Daniel 9:24-27) indicated that the Messiah would appear at that time. Simeon and Anna were waiting in the

Temple "for the consolation of Israel" because of Daniel's prophecy. Herod's scribes were not surprised by their king's question about where the Messiah was to be born for the same reason.

John tells us about the actions of the False Prophet: "He performs great signs, so that he even makes fire come down from heaven on the earth in the sight of men" (Revelation 13:13). Of all the prophets in the Bible, the only one who brought fire down from heaven was the prophet Elijah. Furthermore, Elijah stopped the rain in the days of the wicked King Ahab for 1260 days, exactly the duration of the plagues that will be unleashed by the Two Witnesses during the Great Tribulation period. For these reasons we believe that Elijah will be one of the Two Witnesses. Satan will probably call his False Prophet by the name Elijah in an attempt to deceive Israel and the Gentiles. He will "make fire come down from heaven" in a counterfeit display of miraculous power to convince men that he is Elijah. Once men believe his claim that he is Elijah, the False Prophet will point to his partner, the Antichrist, as the promised Messiah.

Christians understand the Bible to teach that the Messiah is the Son of God -- perfect Man and perfect God. However, the Jewish rabbis have a different viewpoint. They believe the Messiah will be a man with a divine mission, not God. This expectation that the Messiah will be a normal man will help to prepare the Jews to accept the false claims of the Antichrist to be their Messiah.

The Death and Resurrection of the Antichrist

Hundreds of specific prophecies declare that Israel will rebuild the Temple in the last days and resume animal sacrifice. As indicated in my earlier book *Messiah*, over five hundred Jews from the tribe of Levi are now in training in preparation for the resumption of Temple services. Sixty-four of the vessels were recently constructed for the future Temple services. Millions of dollars have been pledged or set aside in wills and trusts for the Holy Sanctuary. Isaiah 2:2 prophesied the rebuilding of the Third Temple: "Now it shall come to pass in the latter days that the mountain of the Lord's house shall be established on the top of the mountains, and shall be exalted above the hills; and all nations shall flow to it." These dedicated Jewish scholars are not acting presumptuously. They are preparing so they will be ready for God's command to rebuild His Holy Temple.

While the first half of Daniel's seventieth week will be a time of terrible judgment, a crisis occurs at the mid-point, three-and-a-half years after the signing of the treaty. The crisis will surround the assassination and death of the Antichrist. The book of Daniel declares that the Antichrist will stop the daily sacrifice in the rebuilt Temple in Jerusalem. "Then he shall confirm a covenant with many for one week; but in the middle of the week He shall bring an end to sacrifice and offering" (Daniel 9:27). This was confirmed in Daniel 12:11: "And from the time that the daily sacrifice is taken away, and the abomination of desolation is set up, there shall be one thousand two hundred and ninety days." This period of 1290 days is thirty days longer than the three-and-a-half years(1260 days) of the last half of Daniel's seventieth week. Perhaps some Jewish priest or believer will succeed in killing the Antichrist, the defiler of their holy Temple. The prophet John clearly predicts the death of the Antichrist with a sword wound to the neck or head. "I saw one of his heads as if it had been mortally wounded, and his deadly wound was healed. And all the world marveled and followed the beast" (Revelation 13:3).

The curious reference in the middle of this passage that "he who kills by the sword must be killed by the sword" may refer to this assassination of the Antichrist who will kill millions of tribulation saints by beheading them with the sword. After his death, Satan will somehow resurrect the Antichrist with his satanic power. The False Prophet will "cause the earth and those who dwell in it to worship the first beast, whose deadly wound was healed" (Revelation 13:12). Satan has always wanted mankind to worship him as God. He will motivate the False Prophet to initiate a satanic religion in the last three-and-a-half years forcing people to worship the Antichrist. After Satan revives the Antichrist, the False Prophet will command "those who dwell on the earth to make an image [statue] to the beast who was wounded by the sword and lived." This "image to the beast" will be satanically supernatural in its creation. If it was simply a robot or a computer, the world would not be impressed and the image could not "both speak and cause as many as would not worship the image of the beast to be killed." Satan may use this "image" as a multiplier of his presence. If this satanic and supernatural "image" is tied into a two-way communication television-computer device, it could explain the curious expressions used by the prophet John that the False Prophet "gave breath [life] to the image of the beast, that the image should both speak and cause as many as would not worship the image of the beast to be killed" (Revelation 13:15).

The Mark of the Beast and the Final Persecution

Satan has always desired worship from mankind. In the horrible time known as the Great Tribulation, in the last three-and-a-half years after the resurrection of the Antichrist, the False Prophet will initiate an incredible totalitarian control system to enforce the worship of the Antichrist. "And he causes all, both small and great, rich and poor, free and slave, to receive a mark on their right hand or on their foreheads, and that no one may buy or sell except one who has the mark or the name of the beast, or the number of his name. Here is wisdom. Let him who has understanding calculate the number of the beast, for it is the number of a man: His number is 666" (Revelation 13:16). The Mark of the Beast will be given to everyone who worships the Antichrist or his image. However, if anyone refuses to publicly worship Satan and his Antichrist, they will not receive the Mark of the Beast. Without that Mark, "no one may buy or sell." Any who live in the kingdom of the Antichrist will be hopelessly caught in his trap unless they can escape to the mountains and "live off the land."

The Technology of the Mark of the Beast

Until this last decade it was impossible to understand how the 666 Mark of the Beast system could actually be implemented. Previously, under persecution and totalitarian police states, it was always possible for rebels to bribe officials with money, gold and silver. However, the totalitarian Mark of the Beast system will make it impossible to escape. The widespread introduction of the technology of the cashless society makes it possible to see how such a system would work. As I indicated in my book *Prince of Darkness*, corporations have developed invisible bar codes that can be miniaturized. Smart cards, with their tiny computer chips, are now used everywhere in security situations. They contain foolproof identification together with complete medical and financial records. In Toronto, Canada, all animals entering the Humane Society are injected in the neck with a small 1/4 inch long capsule with an induction coil and a chip containing up to forty-five billion bits of information including identification of the animal, the owner and medical records. The technology is being miniaturized so they can inject a tiny capsule beneath the skin containing a computer chip with your identification and records. The need to provide positive identification and security access will make this technology universal in Western countries within the next several years. In Europe they have a tremendous need to keep track of every farm and animal in the European Community because of their complicated Common Agricultural Policy subsidy system. They photographed every one of the nine million farms in the twelve nations from a space satellite. After assigning a digital number to each farm they are now implanting an computer identification chip beneath the skin of each cow and sheep. When completed, this system will track every single one of the more than one hundred million farm animals.

In addition, all western countries are moving toward new electronic financial transfer systems that will progressively replace cash. In Canada, all credit card holders will begin receiving debit cards next year. Even when you have cash, the banks and stores want you to use these debit cards that instantly take the money from your account and transfer it to the account of the merchant. Today most hotels and car rental agencies do not want customers to pay cash. They insist on a credit card, even when a person wants to pay in full up front in cash. The reason for this demand for credit cards is due to the identification they provide. These systems will provide a complete computer record of every transaction in your life. Your life will be an open book to the financial institutions you use and those who buy that information. The ultimate goal of the banks is to eliminate the credit and debit cards and replace them with an electronic funds transfer system that will use "smart card" technology implanted beneath the skin of the individual. The arguments will be that such a system will eliminate theft, lost credit cards, forgotten PIN numbers, and provide instantaneous identification of all citizens. The growing crime problem, missing children, and massive illegal immigration will all provide strong arguments for the government to implement this national identification and financial control system. In several European countries, including Spain, governments are proposing prison sentences for citizens who refuse to provide their national identification card to officials when asked.

An enormous and sophisticated computer system in Europe will provide the initial consolidated financial integration of the economic systems of the advanced nations. Already an eighteen digit number has been assigned to virtually every citizen in the western world. Your number includes your year of birth, sex, your current social insurance number, and a code identifying the street you live on. The cities and towns of the entire western world have been assigned digital codes for this purpose (based on satellite photo reconnaissance). The technology already exists. However, none of this is the Mark of the Beast system. These are just signs of how close we are to the Great Tribulation. The 666 system will not be introduced until the Antichrist is killed and resurrected at the mid-point of the seven-year-treaty period. The Christians will be raptured by Christ before the introduction of this diabolical Mark of the Beast system by the False Prophet.

Revelation 13:17 declares that "no one may buy or sell except one who has the mark or the name of the beast, or the number of his name." John's prophecy refers to three things: the Mark of the Beast or the name of the beast, or the number of his name." The Mark of the Beast may involve either one or all three of these. It will be visible on the right hand or forehead. A possible reason for mentioning both locations is that some people don't have a right hand and a scanner may not always be able to focus on a hand whereas the forehead is usually visible. Electrical scanners set up in public buildings and transportation centers could verify the location of individuals from their identification mark.

The Mystery of 666

There is a mystery concerning "the number of the beast" 666. "Here is wisdom. Let him who has understanding calculate the number of the beast, for it is the number of a man: His number is 666" (Revelation 13:18). The book of Revelation was written by John in Greek. As a priest (according to Eusebius) John also would have been familiar with Hebrew. Greek and Hebrew are the only true alphanumeric languages, which means that every single letter in their alphabets also has a numeric value. Each letter stands for both a letter and a number. Hence, all names in Greek or Hebrew have a numerical value. Your name or mine in Greek would be equal to some number (for example, say, 1728, or 398). The numerical value of the sum of the letters in the name of the Antichrist, in Greek or Hebrew, will be equal to 666. Writers from the first century till our day have mistakenly tried to apply the 666 formula to hundreds of different individuals using the Latin, French, German or English languages. However, the system only works in Greek or Hebrew. The 666 identification is not for Christians of the Church Age. The reason for this precise identification is to warn the tribulation believers not to accept the Mark of the Beast despite the fact that the Antichrist will look like the promised Messiah.

The Bible tells us that anyone who rejects the Mark of the Beast will be beheaded for their faith. In Revelation 7:9-11 John described a "great number" who come out of the Great Tribulation by the thousands every day as they are martyred for their faith. That is one more reason why we know that the Church will be raptured to heaven before the tribulation period. The one-world government, totalitarian police state of the Beast will be very efficient at beheading any tribulation believers who reject the worship of the Antichrist. Very few will be able to escape the Mark of the Beast system. While some tribulation believers will "endure to the end" the vast majority of those who reject the 666 mark will be beheaded as martyrs. As Revelation reveals: "It was granted to him to make war with the saints and to overcome them. And authority was given him over every tribe, tongue, and nation" (Revelation 13:7). The few tribulation believers who survive till the end of the Great Tribulation will probably be those who became followers of Christ in the final days of that terrible period. These tribulation saints will respond to Christ as a result of the witness of the Two Witnesses, the 144,000 and the three angelic messengers.

For those who choose to accept the Mark of the Beast, the Bible warns that they will be doomed for all eternity in hell. If anyone accepts the name, the mark, or the 666 number of the Beast on their forehead, they have sealed their doom. John's prophecy warns: "If anyone worships the beast and his image, and receives his mark on his forehead or on his hand, he himself shall also drink of the wine of the wrath of God, which is poured out full strength into the cup of His indignation. And he shall be tormented with fire and brimstone in the presence of the holy angels and in the presence of the Lamb" (Revelation 14:9,10). In Revelation 3:12 and 22:4 the Bible declares that God will write His name and the name "New Jerusalem" on the forehead of the believers in Christ. Our forehead and our life is reserved for the name of our Savior and Lord who paid the supreme price for our souls on Calvary.

Man's Final Crisis

The final crisis of human history is rapidly approaching. While many people watch the peace negotiations and the talk of a New World Order with anticipation, the prophecies of the Bible warn that this generation will face the greatest spiritual challenge since the creation of mankind in the Garden of Eden. A titanic struggle for this planet and the souls of mankind has been raging for almost six thousand years. Now, as we approach the final battle of this spiritual war, Christians need to put on the "whole armor of God" and prepare for the great struggle ahead. Although the Bible promises that the Church will be raptured before the Antichrist appears, we are living in the midst of a growing

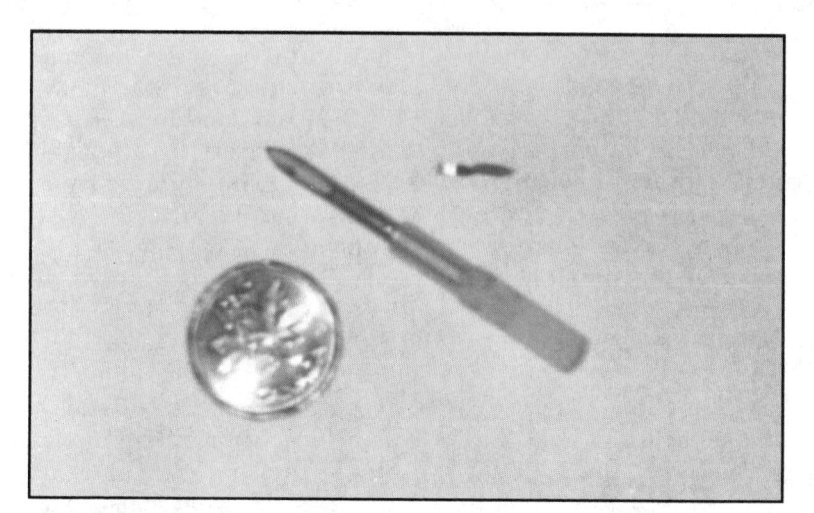

Tiny computer chip with injector needle implanted in neck of animal (with penny to show its size).

satanic assault on the believers. Satan is truly going about like a destroying "lion seeking whom he may devour." We live in a generation of rising heresies within the Church, false cults raging outside, and sustained spiritual attacks on pastors and laymen. Some Christians have misunderstood the promises of Bible prophecy to believe that we will escape all persecution or tribulation. However, we are specifically warned about growing persecution and struggle. We are promised victory in our battles if we depend on the Lord. But you cannot have a victory unless you have a war. As we rapidly approach the conclusion of this era, we should expect increasing spiritual attacks on our churches and on our own personal walk with the Lord.

We are to aggressively preach the gospel, teach the children of God, and "fight the good fight." Far from becoming passive in light of the return of Christ, this knowledge should motivate each of us to holiness in our personal spiritual lives. As 1 John 3:3 declares: "Everyone who has this hope in Him purifies himself, just as He is pure." Additionally, looking expectantly to the Lord's return at any moment, we should be motivated to witness to those around us as never before. If we truly believe the hour is late, we will share our love of Christ with our loved ones and those whom we encounter in our daily life.

CHAPTER SIX

The Opening of the Seven Sealed Scroll

The Seven Seal Judgments
The Beginning of the Wrath of God

A series of judgments will be released from heaven by Jesus Christ, the only One capable of opening the seven-sealed scroll. The seven "seal judgments" are the commencement of the wrath of God that will be poured out on the unrepentant nations after the rapture of the Church. At some point after the Rapture the Antichrist will arise in Europe to take over the ten-nation confederacy of the newly revived Roman Empire. There may be an interval of time, however small, between the Rapture and the signing of the seven-year treaty with Israel. Whether this interval occupies a few days, months or years, it must be short because God will not leave the earth without a witness to His truth. One of the Antichrist's first major acts will be the signing of a seven-year treaty between the Antichrist's confederacy and Israel. This treaty will mark the beginning of the last seven-year period, known as Daniel's seventieth week, leading up to the Battle of Armageddon.

As detailed in another chapter, the Bible clearly promises that the Church will escape the wrath of God that will characterize the seven-year tribulation period. In 1 Thessalonians 1:10 the Apostle Paul writes of God's command that we are "to wait for His Son from heaven, whom He raised from the dead, even Jesus who delivers us from the wrath to come." Later, in 1 Thessalonians 5:9, Paul promised, "For God did not appoint us to wrath, but to obtain salvation through our Lord Jesus Christ." Throughout the Bible, from Genesis to Revelation, the wrath of God has never been poured out upon the righteous. The whole focus of the Tribulation period, Daniel's seventieth week of seven years, will involve the judgment of God upon unrepentant sinners.

The Four Horsemen of the Apocalypse

The first four judgments are described prophetically in the form of Four Seals, commonly known as the Four Horsemen of the Apocalypse. These Horsemen stand as the ultimate symbol of the coming wrath of God against the evil forces of Satan. A fascinating article in the *European* newspaper, dated November 15, 1992, was entitled "Plague Joins Pale Rider of Death." The writer, Askold Krushelnycky, commented on the devastating typhoid plague gripping portions of the former Yugoslavia as a result of its civil war. "The third of the Four Horsemen of the Apocalypse, Pestilence, is now firmly in the saddle and riding alongside famine, war and the pale rider of death through this devastated country." The Four Horsemen, representing False Peace, War, Famine, and Pestilence express the worst fears of mankind for what is coming during man's last crisis.

The First Seal - The White Horseman
The Rise of Antichrist

"And I looked, and behold, a white horse. And he who sat on it had a bow; and a crown was given to him, and he went out conquering and to conquer" (Revelation 6:2).

The First Seal will be opened during the beginning days of the seven years known as Daniel's seventieth week. This period will commence with the Antichrist signing a seven-year treaty with Israel. The First Seal is also described as the White Horseman of the Apocalypse, the False Peace of the coming Antichrist. John revealed that Antichrist will impersonate Jesus Christ, the other White Horseman of Revelation 19. When Christ appears to mankind after the horrors of the seven-year tribulation, He will come as the Prince of Peace. Some writers have interpreted this first

White Horseman as Jesus Christ. However, the first horseman cannot be Christ because Jesus opens the seven-sealed scroll to reveal these Four Horsemen. The Antichrist will appear as the announcer of False Peace at the beginning of the Tribulation period. At the end of John's vision of Revelation we see Christ also riding a white horse, descending in triumph from heaven to defeat the forces of Antichrist at Armageddon. Therefore, the White Horseman of Revelation 6 is a symbol of the coming Antichrist while the White Horse of Christ in Revelation 19:11 is literal. "Then I saw heaven opened, and behold, a white horse. And He who sat on him was called Faithful and True, and in righteousness He judges and makes war." Several times, Scripture describes horses in heaven. The prophet Zechariah also had a vision of four horses. "These are the ones whom the Lord has sent to walk to and fro throughout the earth" (Zechariah 1:10). Revelation 19 tells us that the army of heaven, including the returning saints and angels, will ride white horses in the Battle of Armageddon.

The Apocalypse reveals the White Horseman going forth "conquering and to conquer" even though he carries the sign of peace and disarmament — a bow and no arrow. Daniel prophesied that the Antichrist will conquer through a false peace. "He shall magnify himself in his heart and by peace he shall destroy many." Throughout history devious leaders have often used false peace treaties to confuse their enemies and ultimately destroy them. When he rises to power, the Antichrist will conquer the first three nations and then, the remaining seven nations of the revived Roman Empire. The prophet Jeremiah warned of the false peace of the last days: "They have also healed the hurt of My people slightly, saying, 'Peace, peace!' When there is no peace" (Jeremiah 6:14). Using the huge economic, political and military power of this power base, the Antichrist will conquer nation after nation until he rules the whole world for a time.

The Second Seal - The Red Horseman
Worldwide Warfare

"When He opened the second seal, I heard the second living creature saying, 'Come and see.' And another horse, fiery red, went out. And it was granted to the one who sat on it to take peace from the earth, and that people should kill one another; and there was given to him a great sword" (Revelation 6:4,5).

The Second Seal of the Red Horseman of war will bring the earth to the edge of annihilation with the release of doomsday weapons beyond anything ever known in history. The color red has always been connected with war and bloody conflict. This symbol of a Red Horseman represents the awesome world war that will break out as the Antichrist attempts to expand from his ten-nation power base to conquer the remaining nations of the world. Note that it is Christ who opens the seven-sealed scroll and grants "to the one who sat on it [the Red Horseman] to take peace from the earth." Jesus is the only one who can take peace from the earth or bring peace to the planet. From the beginning of the seven-year tribulation period a series of wars will follow the Antichrist's tyrannical attempts to rule the world. While the world is calling for "Peace, Peace," there will be no true peace until the Prince of Peace shall come. In John's vision the "people...kill one another."

While men long for peace, the world is arming for Armageddon. Today, fourteen wars are being fought around the world. Yugoslavia is in the midst of a brutal civil war with torture, death camps and horrors that remind us of the dark days of the Nazi tyranny of World War II. Eduard Shevardnadze, the former foreign minister of the Soviet Union warns, that up to twenty civil wars may break out in the territory of the new Commonwealth of Sovereign States. Tragically, most of these flash points are based on ethnic hatreds going back hundreds of years. Unfortunately they have access to enormous supplies of conventional arms and weapons of mass destruction. While the world talks of peace, over one trillion dollars will be spent around the world this year on weapons and military forces. Despite talk of peace the nations of the world continue to arm for conflict. Around the world an enormous military build-up continues behind-the-scenes preparation for the final conflict of the ages.

The Third Seal - The Black Horseman
Worldwide Famine

"When He opened the third seal, I heard the third living creature say, 'Come and see.' And I looked, and behold, a black horse, and he who sat on it had a pair of scales in his hand. And I heard a voice in the midst of the four living creatures saying, 'A quart of wheat for a denarius, and three quarts of barley for a denarius; and do not harm the oil and the wine'" (Revelation 6:5).

Famine almost always follows the devastation of war. The First World War and the Russian Civil War produced massive famine, killing millions in Russia and the Ukraine. Farmers could not plant or reap as armies conscripted every available man as they swept through their abandoned farms. The coming disaster of a worldwide famine beyond anything ever experienced before will follow the devastating wars of the Tribulation period. John saw a "black horse" with "a pair of scales in his hand." The angelic creature explained to him that the scales reveal a terrible famine when "a denarius," the daily wage of a laborer during the first century, will only be sufficient to purchase "a quart of wheat" or "three quarts of barley," the food supply for an adult for one day. In other words, the famine will be so severe that a man's entire wage will only buy enough food for himself. It will leave nothing for his family to eat and nothing for shelter or clothing. Strangely, in the midst of worldwide famine, the angel announced "do not harm the oil and the wine." Oil and wine are products of wealth. This indicates that in the midst of famine there will still be people living with a huge collection of wealth. This strange juxtaposition of famine and wealth is a characteristic of our world as we approach the end of this century. We are witnessing the greatest accumulation of wealth in human history side by side with devastating famine and widespread depression. James warned, "Your gold and silver are corroded, and their corrosion will be a witness against you and will eat your flesh like fire. You have heaped up treasure in the last days" (James 5:3). While the rich get richer, the poor are getting poorer, just as the Bible prophesied. Today 1 percent of the American population has accumulated over 40 percent of the nation's wealth. The obscene accumulation of riches in this last decade is a sign that we are living in the last days.

One of the great horrors of the coming Great Tribulation will be the worst famine the world has ever witnessed. After decades of brilliant scientific advances in biotechnology and agriculture, many thought that the problem of hunger and famine would be eliminated from the earth. However, the specter of worldwide famine is rising in many Third World countries as pestilence and vermin destroy almost one-third of the world's food production each year. In Africa over ten million lives are at immediate risk of starvation while hundreds of millions are living without the minimum requirement of food or clean water every day. The safety margin for world food supplies is more fragile than at any other time in this century. American food reserves are at the lowest levels since the Great Depression. A great deal of our food reserves were used to provide needed aid for Los Angeles and Florida. Much of the rest was sent to Africa and Russia. Out of some 180 nations around the world, only four nations, the United States, Canada, France and Argentina, actually produce more food every year than they consume. All other nations, although they trade specific commodities, consume as much food as they produce.

Wildly fluctuating weather patterns could easily cause drought in the four countries that provide the safety net for world food supplies. In the last four years Europe has seen the greatest droughts in two hundred years. Greedy and unwise agricultural policies have eroded massive amounts of the rich topsoil that made North American agriculture the bread basket of the world. When our pioneer forefathers came to North America they discovered a treasure of rich topsoil that averaged over twelve feet deep across the continent. After two centuries of erosion the average amount of topsoil is less than two inches. It takes a hundred years for nature to produce and replenish an inch of topsoil. While modern fertilizers can produce increased agricultural returns, continued overuse of fertilizers can poison the delicate balance in the soil. Massive weather changes, such as the prophets describe in the Tribulation, will plunge the nations into a massive famine.

The Los Angeles riots gave America and the world an

unpleasant preview of things to come in our cities when the food runs out and people take to the streets. The recent hurricane in Florida rapidly overwhelmed the capacity of the nation's disaster relief organizations. It revealed how vulnerable we are to a breakdown in the food system. The U.S.A. food distribution system has less than a ten-day reserve supply. When disaster strikes, that ten-day supply will disappear in less than twenty-four hours as people buy up and horde any food they can get their hands on. A prudent person might be wise to purchase several months supply of preserved foods and supplies. The discipline and moral fiber that held America together during the Great Depression no longer exists in large sections in our population. If the Lord delays His rapture of the Church much longer we could see massive breakdowns in our countries that have never occurred before.

The Fourth Horseman - The Pale Horseman Plague and Death

"When He opened the fourth seal, I heard the voice of the fourth living creature saying, 'Come and see.' And I looked, and behold, a pale horse. And the name of him who sat on it was Death, and Hades followed with him. And power was given to them over a fourth of the earth, to kill with sword, with hunger, with death [plague], and by the beasts of the earth" (Revelation 6:7,8).

Each of the first three horsemen represented a single horrible instrument of judgment. The symbol of the final horseman, the Pale Horseman, combines the "four severe judgments" of God often seen in combination in the Old Testament. The Pale Horse is corpse-like and sickly in color, visually representing the plague he carries. The Greek word *choloros* suggests the sickly green color of plague. In Ezekiel 14:21 we read of these "four severe judgments" representing the wrath of God. "For thus says the Lord God: 'How much more it shall be when I send My four severe judgments on Jerusalem — the sword and famine and wild beasts and pestilence — to cut off man and beast from it?'" These four instruments are described together as the judgments and wrath of God in more than a dozen passages of Scripture.

While the other three horsemen were not individually named, this Fourth Horseman is called Death. The Pale Horseman will kill "over a fourth of the earth, to kill with sword, with hunger, with death [plague], and by the beasts of the earth." Just as hunger and famine inevitably follow war, the plague of the last days will devastate the population of earth.

The Aids Plague

Throughout history plagues have always reached the limits of the initial population risk group and then faded away. Until the Acquired Immune Deficiency Syndrome plague appeared in 1978, it was inconceivable how this prophecy of the Fourth Horseman killing one-quarter of mankind could ever be fulfilled. Now, with the AIDS epidemic, we know. The worst previous plague in history, the Black Plague, killed one-quarter of the population of Europe throughout the fourteenth century. Over twenty-five million people died in that horror but it finally stopped after a century. Two-thirds of the infected population survived the Black Plague. However, AIDS is the first 100 percent fatal epidemic in history. Today, as a result of homosexual and bisexual transmission, together with rampant promiscuity in Africa, Asia and South America, AIDS is set to unleash the greatest plague in history. AIDS remains primarily a homosexually and bisexually transmitted disease in North America and Europe, with some cases from blood transfusions and addicts sharing needles.

A year ago the Central Intelligence Agency gave a somber report to the president of the United States of America, warning of the projected deaths from AIDS in Africa. They gathered the best medical advice from the World Health Organization, the Center for Disease Control in Atlanta and various studies in African countries. The staggering figures revealed that up to 75 percent of the population of Africa south of the Sahara could become infected with AIDS by the year 2000. This astonishing report suggests that as many as 250 million Africans could die of AIDS over the next ten years.

While AIDS is primarily transmitted through homosexual and bisexual activity in North America and Europe, in Africa, Asia and South America it is primarily transmitted through heterosexual activity. Why would AIDS be transmitted in the Third World by normal sexual activity between men and woman while remaining primarily a homosexually transmitted disease in North America? Doctors in the Third World confirm that the average sexually active adult in those countries will have between twenty-five and one hundred different sexual partners every year. This rampant promiscuity has produced a tragic and widespread epidemic of sexually transmitted diseases (STD's). The average promiscuous adult in such countries will contract five or more sexually transmitted diseases throughout their life. Their syphilis, gonorrhoea, herpes and other sexually transmitted diseases usually remain untreated by antibiotics because of the lack of medicine and proper sanitation. These infected individuals will transmit AIDS from male to female, female to male through normal heterosexual activity through the open sores on their bodies from the previous STD's. Once a man becomes infected by a prostitute, he will then transmit the AIDS virus to his wife. She will often infect her baby during birth.

The figures for Asia and South America are equally tragic. Although AIDS started developing later in these two continents, it is spreading even more rapidly than in Africa. Figures from Dr. James Chin of the World Health Organization state that there was only one known AIDS case in Asia in 1987. Today there are more than three million. Over 96 percent of the prostitutes in Thailand are now infected with HIV. The latest study from India indicates that some 60 percent of their prostitutes are infected with AIDS. In addition, over 60 percent of the prostitutes in Paris are now infected. In Zimbabwe, two years ago 7 percent of those donating blood tested positive for AIDS. However, a year later 47 percent of the blood donors tested positive. The AIDS epidemic in Africa is so terrible that twenty-one African countries will no longer report fully on their AIDS figures. Their governments consider these terrible statistics a national security secret. In Central Africa, in village after village, only grandparents and older children remain alive to care for the babies. The parents are either dead or awaiting death in clinics. For the first time, we are looking at the prospect of the death of a whole continent. Finally, and tragically, we can understand what the prophet John was referring to when he described the Fourth Seal, the Pale Horseman, killing one-quarter of the earth.

A curious part of John's prophecy is that the Fourth Horseman will also kill men with "beasts." One of the particular horrors of the Great Tribulation is that God will remove the supernatural fear of man which He has placed within animals. When God created Adam and Eve He gave them "dominion" over the animal kingdom. After the Flood, God again supernaturally restrained the animal kingdom. This was done to protect mankind from the animals that vastly outnumber and overpower us. The Lord declared to Noah: "And the fear of you and the dread of you shall be on every beast of the earth, on every bird of the air, on all that moves on the earth, and on all the fish of the sea. They are given into your hand" (Genesis 9:2). However, during the Tribulation period, God will remove that fear of man from animals and birds. They will attack the unrepentant sinners of that day in scenes more terrible that any horror movie. The "beasts" will fight against the sinful men as they did on numerous occasions in the Old Testament judgments. God used locusts and frogs against the Egyptians. Later, during the forty years in the Wilderness, the Lord afflicted the Israelites with "fiery serpents (Numbers 21:6). The Canaanites were attacked by hornets (Joshua 24:12), while lions oppressed the Samaritans (2 Kings 17:25).

Some writers have claimed that the judgments of the Four Horsemen are not the wrath of God. They suggest that these four judgments are the actions of men upon the earth and not specifically the judgments of God. However, a careful examination of the passage will reveal that these judgments are released from heaven by Jesus Christ, who opens the seven-sealed scroll. Furthermore, the judgment of the Fourth Horseman includes the release of the animal kingdom to attack mankind. This particular judgment could only come from God, who originally restrained the animals. These judgments are therefore the wrath of God. We are promised that the Church will not endure the wrath of God. Therefore, we can have confidence that the saints of the Church will be raptured before any of the seal judgments which begin early in the seven-year Tribulation period.

"When He opened the fifth seal, I saw under the altar the souls of those who had been slain for the word of God" (Revelation 6:9)

The Fifth Seal - The Saints Under the Altar

"When He opened the fifth seal, I saw under the altar the souls of those who had been slain for the word of God and for the testimony which they held" (Revelation 6:9).

After witnessing his vision of the Four Horsemen of the Apocalypse and their devastation of the earth's population, John describes his vision of the Fifth Seal and the martyred souls of the tribulation saints. In Revelation 4:1-10, John witnessed the Rapture and the appearance of the Church in heaven represented by the twenty-four crowned elders before the Throne of God. After the Rapture the Church will experience the Bema Judgment Seat and the Marriage Supper of the Lamb. Then John saw a new group of "souls of those who had been slain for the word of God." These Jewish and Gentile tribulation martyrs will become believers after listening to the message of the Two Witnesses, the 144,000

Jewish Witnesses and the three angelic witnesses.

John described their response to their bloody death at the hands of their oppressors: "And they cried with a loud voice, saying, 'How long, O Lord, holy and true, until You judge and avenge our blood on those who dwell on the earth?'" (Revelation 6:10). We know these saints under the altar are not part of the Bride of Christ because they do not respond as Christ instructed His Church. The Apostle Paul taught believers: "Beloved, do not avenge yourselves, but rather give place to wrath; for it is written, 'Vengeance is Mine, I will repay,' says the Lord" (Romans 12:19). Hundreds of historical accounts record that Christian martyrs prayed for the salvation of their tormentors while being killed. They praised God and sang hymns rather than ask for vengeance. However, like the Old Testament patriarchs and kings, these tribulation saints will call out for vengeance upon their oppressors instead of leaving retribution to God. This is evidence that the Church will be raptured to heaven before this seal judgment. God will respond to the martyred saints' request by instructing them to wait until they are joined by "their fellow servants and their brethren, who would be killed as they were." Throughout the terrible seven-year Tribulation period, most of the believers in the gospel of the Kingdom will pay for their faith with their martyrdom.

The Sixth Seal
The Great Day of His Wrath Has Come

"I looked when He opened the sixth seal, and behold, there was a great earthquake; and the sun became black as sackcloth of hair, and the moon became like blood...For the great day of His wrath has come, and who is able to stand?" (Revelation 6:12,17).

Throughout history, massive earthquakes have often foreshadowed coming disasters and judgments of God. Many times in the Scriptures earthquakes preceded the fall of kings and kingdoms. In Zechariah 14:4,5 the prophet records that the people "fled from the earthquake in the days of Uzziah king of Judah." The Jewish historian Flavius Josephus recorded this massive quake in his *Antiquities of the Jews*

(60.10.4.) "A great earthquake shook the ground and a rent was made in the Temple...and before the city, at a place called Eroge, half the mountain broke off from the rest on the west and rolled itself four furlongs [half a mile] and stood still at the east mountain, till the roads, as well as the king's gardens, were spoiled by the obstruction." King David described an awesome earthquake in Psalm 114:3,4,7: "The sea saw it and fled; Jordan turned back. The mountains skipped like rams, The little hills like lambs...Tremble, earth, at the presence of the Lord, at the presence of the God of Jacob." This extraordinary description details exactly what occurs when a massive 6.5 magnitude earthquake creates a sudden withdrawal of the water along a sea shore, followed by a tsunami, an overwhelming returning wave. A tsunami can produce a massive tidal wave over a hundred feet high and miles wide. The inspired writer declared this historical earthquake occurred at "the presence of the Lord."

The prophet Ezekiel warns that the greatest earthquake in history will destroy the coming Russian - Arab invasion of Israel during the War of Gog and Magog. The armies will surround Israel ready to destroy the Chosen People that have returned to the Promised Land. God declares that He will intervene to save them. "For in My jealousy and in the fire of My wrath I have spoken: 'Surely in that day there shall be a great earthquake in the land of Israel'" (Ezekiel 38:19). This earthquake will manifest the wrath of God against His enemies. It will be so massive that cities and walls around the world will shake. Later, during the seven-year Tribulation period, God will unleash a series of massive earthquakes, devastating the planet. The prophet John describes the fear-stricken response of the sinners of that day as they try to hide from the wrath of God. They will say "to the mountains and rocks, 'Fall on us and hide us from the face of Him who sits on the throne and from the wrath of the Lamb!'" (Revelation 6:16). This massive earthquake of the Sixth Seal will be the first in a series of four major planet-shaking disturbances that will mark the outpouring of the wrath of God upon the unrepentant sinners in those evil days. Rather than repent, the wicked men will blaspheme God's Holy Name, torturing and killing the tribulation saints who follow the Lamb. The world will witness unparalleled horrors and tyranny as the false church of the Great Whore and the False Prophet will persecute those who follow God.

Jesus warned His disciples of massive and increasing earthquakes as one of the key signs in the generation that will witness the coming of the Son of Man. He warned of "earthquakes in various places" (Matthew 24:7). The number and severity of major earthquakes has been increasing geometrically during the last hundred years. Earth scientists calculate that a great earthquake can release more energy than one hundred thousand nuclear bombs. The tremendous earthquake that struck Alaska in 1964 registered 8.5 on the Richter scale, greater than 500 thousand nuclear bombs. Dr. Charles Richter created a logarithmic scale to measure earthquake intensity. Each number represents a quake ten times greater than the number below it. In other words, a 7.0 quake is ten times greater than a 6.0 tremor. A 6.1 quake is twice the size of a 6.0 quake.

In our generation, since the rebirth of Israel in 1948, the planet has been rocked by a series of killer earthquakes beyond anything ever experienced before. As evidence of this prophetic trend, the U.S. Geological Survey in Boulder, Colorado has tracked the major earthquakes for the last hundred years. Until 1900 the world averaged a single killer earthquake every decade for centuries. However, following the rebirth of Israel in 1948, killer earthquake activity increased dramatically. For the last forty years we have witnessed a massive increase in quakes each decade: 1950-59 -- nine killer quakes; 1960-69 -- thirteen killer quakes; 1970-79 -- fifty-six killer quakes; 1980-89 -- seventy-four killer quakes. The huge increase in the number of quakes in the last few years suggests that the total for this decade will exceed 125. Scientists have discovered that the entire crust of the planet is crisscrossed with an enormous system of fault lines and moving tectonic plates. The unprecedented earthquakes of the last days described by the prophets could set up a chain reaction throughout this interlocking grid of fault lines beneath the earth's crust. Jesus Christ warned His disciples about these prophetic signs. "Now when these things begin to happen, look up and lift up your heads, because your redemption draws near" (Luke 21:28).

During the Sixth Seal judgment, a series of seven

disasters will fall on the earth beginning with a great earthquake felt around the world. The prophet John declares that the heavens will also feel the wrath of the Lamb. "The sun became black as sackcloth of hair and the moon became as blood" (Revelation 6:12). These celestial phenomenon will terrify the inhabitants of earth. Two thousand years ago God supernaturally darkened the heavens when Jesus was crucified on Calvary. In addition to the Gospel of Luke, the pagan historian Thallus, in his *Third History*, records the miraculous darkness that overtook the Roman Empire on Passover that year. Interestingly, at Passover, the sun, moon and earth are in positions that make a natural eclipse impossible. It was an act of God. This darkening of the sun and moon under the Sixth Seal is the first of five times that God will darken the heavens during the Tribulation period. While some of these effects could be an environmental consequence of the unleashing of nuclear war, the Bible's description of the events does not suggest a natural, drawn out effect, but rather a sudden, supernatural intervention such as occurred when Christ was crucified.

The fourth event of the Sixth Seal will occur when "the stars of heaven fell to the earth." These meteors are called "stars" by the prophet John in the same manner as we call meteors "falling stars." They could not be celestial stars because they could not "fall to earth." Later, when Christ appears in glory after the Tribulation, John says the "stars will fall from heaven" as meteors will again fall to earth. Following this huge meteor shower, John says, "the sky receded as a scroll when it is rolled up, and every mountain and island was moved out of its place." The heavenly atmosphere and the earthly firmament will be shaken as never before, announcing the coming wrath of the Lamb against evil men. There are many similarities between the events of the Sixth Seal and the events that will occur at Christ's final return at Armageddon. However, there will be an interval of at least three and a half years between the Sixth Seal judgment and the final wrath of God at Armageddon. The prophetic events recorded in Revelation 7:1 through 19:10 will occur during this interval.

Jesus warned His disciples about the incredible turmoil in the heavens and on earth that will announce His return to defeat Satan's forces. "There will be signs in the sun, in the moon, and in the stars; and on the earth distress of nations, with perplexity, the sea and the waves roaring; men's hearts failing them from fear and the expectation of those things which are coming on the earth, for the powers of heaven will be shaken" (Luke 21:25,26). As the terrible hammer blows of the wrath of God are poured out on the earth during the Sixth Seal the voice from heaven will announce: "For the great day of His wrath has come, and who is able to stand?" (Revelation 6:17). When the Great Tribulation comes, none but the righteous tribulation saints will be able to stand before God. In a parallel prophecy, Isaiah describes the terror of men in the terrible days that are coming on the earth. "They shall go into the holes of the rocks, and into the caves of the earth, from the terror of the Lord and the glory of His majesty, when He arises to shake the earth mightily" (Isaiah 2:19). Even in the midst of these horrors, God promises protection for those who turn from their sin and look to Him. "He who dwells in the secret place of the Most High shall abide under the shadow of the Almighty. I will say of the Lord, 'He is my refuge and my fortress; My God, in Him I will trust.' Surely He shall deliver you from the snare of the fowler. And from the perilous pestilence... A thousand may fall at your side, And ten thousand at your right hand; But it shall not come near you" (Psalm 91:1-3,7).

The Parenthesis Between the Sixth and Seventh Seal Judgment

In the midst of John's vision of the Seven Seal judgments, there is a pause or parenthesis after the Sixth Seal before the seer describes the final Seventh Seal. During the pause, John receives a vision of two great companies of the redeemed who are saved during the Great Tribulation. These two groups include the sealed 144,000 Jewish Witnesses and "the great multitude" in heaven from every nation and tribe who come out of the Great Tribulation. In another chapter we will examine John's visions revealing the identity of these two great companies of the redeemed.

Some writers suggest that any who reject Christ's mercy before the Rapture will not be allowed to repent of their sins during the Tribulation. One speaker challenged me once by saying, "Do you think that God will give men a second chance after they have rejected Christ?" Thank God the answer to his question is, "Yes!" If Jesus never gave us a second chance, few of us would have accepted Him as our Savior. Most Christians accepted Christ after rejecting Him many times earlier in their lives. Fortunately, His mercy endures and He continues to call men to repentance. Revelation 7:9-14 describes a "great multitude which no man could number, of all nations, tribes, peoples and tongues" who "come out of the Great Tribulation." The Apocalypse reveals that millions of men and women will accept Christ as their Savior during the Tribulation period. Tragically, the persecution will be so overwhelming that most of these tribulation saints will be martyred for their faith by the false church of the Great Whore of Babylon and the Antichrist. There will be a great harvest of souls during the horrors of the Tribulation, perhaps the greatest in history. However, this will be "a harvest of blood" as the tribulation believers will pay the supreme price for their faith in Christ.

Some have questioned how men could accept Christ after the Holy Spirit is removed from the earth since the Holy Spirit is the one who calls men to salvation through His miraculous grace. They point to the fact that the Holy Spirit, the restrainer of the Antichrist, will be "taken out of the way" at the time of the Rapture to allow the Man of Sin to be "revealed." Also, the Holy Spirit, the Comforter of the Church, will be removed when the Church is raptured to heaven because Christ told us that "He will never leave you comfortless" (John 14:18).

The solution is to recognize that God, the Holy Spirit, is omnipresent, equally everywhere in the universe simultaneously. This means that the Holy Spirit, by definition, is simultaneously in all places in heaven and earth at all times. It is impossible, in the nature of things, for the Holy Spirit to remove His presence from the earth. Therefore, the Holy Spirit will be here on earth throughout the Tribulation period to draw to God all those who respond to His invitation to turn from their sinful rebellion. How can the Holy Spirit be "removed" as restrainer of Antichrist and "comforter" of the Church, while still remaining on earth?

The answer is that the Holy Spirit was always here on earth, long before He came on the day of Pentecost. This was demonstrated by John the Baptist being "filled with the Holy Spirit in his mother's womb." However, the Holy Spirit came in His new role or office as "comforter" of the Church and Restrainer of Antichrist on the day of Pentecost. It is only in these "roles" that the Holy Spirit will be removed at the Rapture. As stated earlier, the omnipresent Holy Spirit cannot be removed in totality from the earth. Therefore, the Holy Spirit will always be here to draw men back to God, even during the evil days of the Great Tribulation.

The Seventh Seal Judgment - Silence in Heaven

"When He opened the seventh seal, there was silence in heaven for about half an hour" (Revelation 8:1).

The Seventh Seal does not contain any special instrument of judgment in itself. This Seventh Seal, after the half-hour of silence, will introduce the next wave of divine wrath known as the seven trumpet judgments. The Seventh Seal begins with an ominous pause for "about half an hour" while heaven catches its breath before the rest of God's divine judgment is poured out on unrepentant sinners. The phrase "there was silence" indicates that, after the horrors of the first six seal judgments, God will pause for a little space to allow the survivors to reconsider their eternal choices and repent of their sins. While we have life we still have a choice to make. Who will we serve? Who will be the God of our life — God or ourselves? The choice is ours. The consequences are eternal.

```
                  Satan Cast
                  Down to Earth           Christ Descends
                                          Armageddon

   Seven Seals   Seven     Seven      Seven Dooms
     Four      Trumpets   Bowls                        Seven
   Horsemen                           Great Tribulation  New Things

   False Peace-War-Famine-Plague      Mark of the Beast   Millennium

            3.5 Years                    3.5 Years
  Treaty   False Babylonian Church    City of Babylon Rules
  Signed
                          Antichrist
                          Defiles Temple
```

Outline of Revelation's Visions

CHAPTER SEVEN

The Redeemed of the Great Tribulation

Why did God delay the Rapture for two thousand years? One answer is that, according to statisticians, over eighty thousand people accept Christ as their Savior every single day. Jesus Christ gave His Church the Great Commission almost two thousand years ago. For almost a thousand years during the Middle Ages the flame of evangelism almost died. However, despite many difficulties and setbacks, this generation has witnessed the greatest Church growth in history. The missionary endeavors of the last two centuries have borne precious spiritual fruit as hundreds of thousands of national pastors and millions of laymen around the world have taken the gospel "to every creature."In one province in northern China, over ten million accepted Christ in the last decade. The lowest estimate of Christians in the underground Church in communist China is eighty million souls. A thousand new churches are started every single week in Africa and Asia. There is another reason God may have delayed man's final crisis until this generation. Demographers claim that the astronomical population growth in this century has produced a situation where almost half of all the humans that ever lived are alive today. If God wanted to choose one single generation to manifest His glory and the fulfillment of Messianic prophecy to the greatest number of people, our generation would be the most appropriate.

The Apostle Peter suggested that Christ delayed the Rapture because He "is long-suffering to us, not willing that any should perish, but that all should come to repentance" (2 Peter 3:9). Justin Martyr, writing in his *First Apology* in A.D. 150, suggested that Christ may delay His second coming until the Church completes its evangelical mission of evangelizing the whole world. "God the Father of all would bring Christ to heaven after He raised Him from the dead, and would keep Him there until the number of those who are foreknown by Him as good and virtuous is complete, on whose account He has still delayed the consummation." It is an intriguing idea that Christ has delayed His Second Coming until this generation when the Church will complete the Great Commission.

However, the Bible tells us that the Rapture will come without warning to take the Church home to heaven. What will happen to the billions of men and women left on earth after the Rapture? Will God provide a means for them to hear the good news about the Messiah and be saved? The Bible's answer is, "Yes." Millions will find salvation during the dreadful persecution of the Tribulation period. Tragically, most will become martyrs for their faith in Christ. Who are the redeemed of the Tribulation period? How will they hear about Christ after the Rapture removes all born again Christians from the earth?

The 144 Thousand Witnesses

"And I heard the number of those who were sealed. One hundred and forty-four thousand of all the tribes of the children of Israel were sealed" (Revelation 7:4).

The first group of 144 thousand redeemed souls is identified in Revelation 7 as twelve thousand from every one of the twelve tribes of Israel. God will choose these Jews from each of the twelve tribes and supernaturally seal them to provide protection from the terrible persecution of Satan. If they were not "sealed" with divine protection, the Antichrist would kill them. God will not leave the earth without a witness after the rapture of the Church. He will give these 144 thousand Jewish Witnesses a special mission to preach the gospel of the Kingdom to the Jews and Gentiles. The Bible does not tell us how they become followers of the Messiah. Possibly, as God supernaturally appeared to Paul on the road to Damascus, the Lord may specially reveal Himself to these 144 thousand witnesses. Another mystery is how these individuals will learn their tribal identity. Today, the only Jews who know their tribe are those from the tribe of Levi. Some rabbis have speculated that one of the acts of Elijah may involve the identification of the tribal origins of each Jew in Israel. Somehow, God will restore the "lost tribes of Israel" allowing twelve thousand from each tribe to take their place among the 144 thousand.

John later saw these special witnesses in heaven, indicating that they will be translated from the earth after completing their special mission. "Then I looked, and behold, a Lamb standing on Mount Zion, and with Him one hundred and forty-four thousand, having His Father's name written on their foreheads" (Revelation 14:1). We know that these 144 thousand in heaven are the same group because they are identified as those "who were redeemed from the earth". Although some writers have speculated that this second group may be angels, the Apocalypse specifically identifies them as "redeemed from among men, being firstfruits to God and to the Lamb" (Revelation 14:4).

The Great Multitude

"After these things I looked, and behold, a great multitude which no one could number, of all nations, tribes, peoples, and tongues, standing before the throne and before the Lamb, clothed with white robes, with palm branches in their hands" (Revelation 7:9).

John witnessed the results of the Rapture when he described the twenty-four crowned elders before the Throne of God, representing the Church in heaven. Two chapters later, John described this "great multitude" as a new class of redeemed saints. Since John described an army of 200 million later in the Apocalypse, this "great multitude which no man could number" must be greater in size than 200 million. This will be the greatest harvest of souls in history. One of the elders asked, "Who are these arrayed in white robes, and where did they come from?" The answer is: "These are the ones who come out of the great tribulation, and washed their robes and made them white in the blood of the Lamb" (Revelation 7:13,14). The verse indicates that this group of redeemed saints are "coming out daily" as huge numbers are persecuted and beheaded each day for their faith. This "great multitude" will respond to the message of the gospel of the Kingdom that will be preached by the 144 thousand Jewish Witnesses, the Two Witnesses, and the three angelic messengers during the Tribulation period.

The Gospel of the Kingdom

Jesus Christ prophesied that "this gospel of the kingdom will be preached in all the world as a witness to all the nations, and then the end will come" (Matthew 24:14). This gospel of the Kingdom differs from the gospel of the Church that has been preached throughout the Age of Grace. Both Jesus and John the Baptist preached the gospel of the Kingdom for three and a half years until Israel rejected their Messiah. Their message was: "Behold, your King is coming to you" (Matthew 21:5). The Kingdom message declared: "I am 'the voice of one crying in the wilderness: 'make straight the way of the Lord,' as the prophet Isaiah said" (John 1:23). The message preached during the Tribulation will announce the return of the Messiah, the King of kings, coming in glory to establish His righteous government.

Israel's Final Trial

In Revelation 12 John recorded a vision of the Woman, Israel, fleeing into the wilderness prepared by God. Despite the fact that Christ created a Church composed of Jews and Gentiles to complete the Great Commission, God is not finished with Israel. His covenants are unchangeable and unbreakable. In Zechariah and many parallel passages, we are told that all those in Zion who turn to the Messiah will be saved. The Apostle Paul prophesied that "blindness in part has happened to Israel until the fullness of the Gentiles has come in. And so all Israel will be saved, as it is written: 'The Deliverer will come out of Zion, and He will turn away ungodliness from Jacob'" (Romans 11:25,26). While the Tribulation will be the "time of Jacob's trouble" the Lord will save and purify a remnant from Israel as well as the "great multitude" from the Gentiles even during the darkest days of the Great Tribulation. The deliverance of Israel will be examined in detail in a later chapter.

The Three Angelic Messengers

"Then I saw another angel flying in the midst of heaven, having the everlasting gospel to preach to those who dwell on the earth; to every nation, tribe, tongue, and people" (Revelation 14:6).

Many times, Christians have despaired at the great difficulties in reaching the whole world with the gospel of salvation. Some have wondered why God did not use His supernatural power and write the message of the gospel across the sky with the angels to convince all mankind of God's reality. Finally, during the darkest days of the Tribulation, God will unleash His supernatural power by allowing three angels to preach the message of warning through the heavens. The first angel will preach "the everlasting gospel" to the whole earth.

The second angel will announce that "Babylon is fallen, is fallen, that great city, because she has made all nations drink of the wine of the wrath of her fornication" (Revelation 14:8). The third angel will warn all men of the coming destruction of those who accept the Mark of the Beast. "Then a third angel followed them, saying with a loud voice, 'If anyone worships the beast and his image, and receives his mark on his forehead or on his hand, he himself shall also drink of the wine of the wrath of God'" (Revelation 14:9,10).

The Two Witnesses

In another chapter we will examine in detail the prophecies about the role of the Two Witnesses during their 1260 day mission. Just as Elijah stopped the rain for 1260 days during the reign of King Ahab, the Two Witnesses will supernaturally "have power to shut heaven, so that no rain falls in the days of their prophecy" (Revelation 11:6). They will use their supernatural power to authenticate their message. "Now when they finish their testimony, the beast that ascends out of the bottomless pit will make war against them, overcome them, and kill them" (Revelation 11:7). Their witness will be so effective that everyone on earth will know who they are. The wicked men throughout the whole world will rejoice when the Antichrist kills them at the end of the 1260 days. John declared that "those who dwell on the earth will rejoice over them, make merry, and send gifts to one another, because these two prophets tormented those who dwell on the earth" (Revelation 11:10). It is fascinating to realize that, despite the supernatural signs provided to mankind during the Great Tribulation, the vast majority of sinners will still refuse God's mercy. As the prophet recorded in Revelation 9:21: "They did not repent of their murders or their sorceries or their sexual immorality or their thefts." This confirms that the reason men reject the gospel message is not due to intellectual doubts about God or the Bible. Though all doubt is removed, many will still choose to reject God's offer of salvation.

The Apocalypse reveals that God will use the 144 thousand Jewish Witnesses, the Two Witnesses, and three angelic witnesses to reach the "great multitude" during the Tribulation period. The Church was given the Great Commission by Christ to reach the world with the gospel during the Age of Grace. The introduction of these three new groups during the Tribulation to evangelize the world strongly suggests that they are required because the Church will be removed by the Rapture before the Tribulation.

The Seven Trumpet Judgments

"And I saw the seven angels who stand before God, and to them were given seven trumpets" (Revelation 8:2).

Following the half-hour of silence in heaven, the Seventh Seal will introduce a series of dreadful judgments that God will unleash against the earth and unrepentant sinners. John received a vision of the coming wrath of God, as described in Revelation 8:2 through to the end of chapter 10. These judgments will be uniquely focused upon the earth and its supporting ecological system that makes human life possible. As mankind reaches the end of this era, the wrath of God will be poured out on the globe as never before in history.

The first angel will sound the First Trumpet triggering

an outpouring of "hail and fire...mingled with blood, and they were thrown to the earth." This disaster from the heavenlies will burn up one-third of the trees and the green grass. For the last century man has greedily used and abused the planet we were given to tend. The day of reckoning is at hand. The unrepentant sinners of that evil day will join in a bloody persecution of the tribulation saints. They will blaspheme the holy name of God. The second angel will sound the Second Trumpet and a huge burning meteor will be cast into the oceans. The horrific result will be witnessed by all mankind as "a third of the sea becomes blood." This judgment will turn one-third of the oceans to blood, killing one-third of marine life and destroying one-third of the ships.

The third angel will sound the Third Trumpet judgment, releasing another huge meteor, called Wormwood, meaning "Bitter." As a result, many will die because one-third of the rivers, fountains and waters will become "bitter" or poisoned. The Fourth Trumpet will affect the heavens as one-third of the sun, moon and stars are "struck so that a third" were darkened. In addition, one-third of the day and night will experience a supernatural darkness. These disasters will cause many men and women to realize that these calamities are produced by God. However, the ever present threat of the Antichrist and the False Prophet will force most of mankind to reject God and accept the 666 Mark of the Beast.

The Three Woes

The last three Trumpet judgments — the fifth, sixth and seventh — are also called the Three Woes. In recognition of the horrible judgment about to be unleashed upon the earth, the angels of heaven call out, "Woe, woe, woe to the inhabitants of the earth, because of the remaining blasts of the trumpet of the three angels who are about to sound!" (Revelation 8:13). The Fifth Trumpet is called the First Woe by the angels because of its horror. When the angel blows the Fifth Trumpet a plague of demonic locusts from the Abyss, "the bottomless pit," will be released to torment "those men who do not have the seal of God on their foreheads." The only ones who will be immune to this terrible plague are the 144 thousand Jewish Witnesses who will be "sealed on their foreheads" (Revelation 7:3). These demonic creatures are described symbolically as "locusts" as they torment sinners for "five months." These cannot be normal locusts because they arise from the Abyss and their king is Satan, named "Apollyon," the "destroyer." It is significant that the duration of the plague of demonic locusts is the same five-month (150 day) period when the waters were at the full during the earlier judgment of God, the Flood. "And the waters prevailed on the earth one hundred and fifty days" (Genesis 7:24). Though painful as a scorpion's bite, the sting of these demonic locusts will not kill the unrepentant sinners, though they will want to die.

The Sixth Trumpet, the Second Woe, will kill a third of the human race as God releases a 200-million-man army to wreak havoc throughout the earth. This judgment will set the stage for the Battle of Armageddon at the end of the seven-year tribulation period. The angel's command is: "Release the four angels who are bound at the great River Euphrates." These angels have been reserved for an exact time set by the sovereignty of God. The enormous army of the kings of the East will cross Asia from China, India and Japan to contest the supremacy of the world against the forces of the West, led by the Antichrist and the False Prophet. For thousands of years the Euphrates River served as a great military barrier to armies attacking from the East. However, the government of Turkey built the gigantic Ataturk Dam in the late 1980s to control the vast waters of the Euphrates River. For the first time in history this great river can be dammed up at the push of a button. The ancient prophecy can be fulfilled in our lifetime. Although the final battle will center on Armageddon and Jerusalem, the Antichrist will obviously attack the huge armies of the Kings of the East during the months they march across Asia. "The four angels, who had been prepared for the hour and day and month and year, were released to kill a third of mankind" (Revelation 9:15). Despite the plans and powers of great men and nations, everything is subject to the will of Almighty God. When He sets an appointment with destiny for a man or an empire, that appointment will be kept; it will not be postponed.

"There should be delay no longer...in the days of the sounding of the seventh angel, when he is about to sound, the mystery of God would be finished" (Revelation 10:6,7).

The blowing of the Seventh Trumpet, the Third Woe, will introduce a series of spectacular events that will lead inexorably to the final Battle of Armageddon. John records: "Then the seventh angel sounded: And there were loud voices in heaven, saying, 'The kingdoms of this world have become the kingdoms of our Lord and of His Christ, and He shall reign forever and ever!'" (Revelation 11:15). Even though a number of significant prophetic events must still unfold, the angels rejoice because the final countdown to victory has begun. Within the prophecy of the Seventh Trumpet the prophet describes his vision of the Woman and Man Child, Satan's persecution of Israel, the defeat of Satan and the rise of the Antichrist.

CHAPTER EIGHT

War in Heaven – Hell on Earth

Satan Will Be Cast Out of Heaven

"At that time Michael shall stand up, the great prince who stands watch over the sons of your people; and there shall be a time of trouble, such as never was since there was a nation, even to that time. And at that time your people shall be delivered, every one who is found written in the book" (Daniel 12:1).

At some point in the dateless past, before the creation of Adam and Eve, Jesus Christ created an anointed Cherubim, an angel of heaven. "You were the anointed cherub who covers; I established you; you were on the holy mountain of God; you walked back and forth in the midst of fiery stones" (Ezekiel 28:14). This Cherubim, known as Lucifer, was one of the most privileged angels involved in God's original divine administration of heaven. However, Lucifer became puffed up in his pride to the point where he believed that he could become like God. In Ezekiel 28:2 God revealed the nature of Satan's age-long rebellion against His Throne. "Son of man, say to the prince of Tyre, 'Thus says the Lord God: Because your heart is lifted up, and you say, 'I am a god, I sit in the seat of gods, in the midst of the seas,' yet you are a man, and not a god, though you set your heart as the heart of a god." In this passage Satan is addressed under the title of "Prince of Tyre." The wealthy city of Tyre in Lebanon, with its pagan worship and temples, was a center of satanic worship in the ancient world.

Many cults present a theology of an eternal contest between a good god and an evil god. This is false. Satan is not a god, nor is he eternal. He was created by Christ in the dateless past. The Scriptures describe his first sinful rebellion in the words of the Lord to Satan: "You were perfect in your ways from the day you were created, till iniquity was found in you" (Ezekiel 28:15). Many people, including Christians, have a false view of Satan the enemy of our souls. Where did this false image come from? The medieval image of Satan pictured him as an ugly red-horned devil with pitchfork and a tail. This false image serves the interests of evil because it makes Satan either unbelievable or ridiculous.

The Bible reveals that Satan was created as a beautiful angel of light. The prophet Ezekiel was given a vision of the mighty power and perfections of Satan when he was originally created by Jesus Christ, "Thus says the Lord God: 'You were the seal of perfection, full of wisdom and perfect in beauty. You were in Eden, the garden of God; every precious stone was your covering...The workmanship of your timbrels and pipes was prepared for you on the day you were created'" (Ezekiel 28:12,13). The Bible declares that spiritual pride is the source of all other sins. Sinful pride, a belief that we deserve things we have not earned, lies behind the greed that expresses itself in theft of all kinds. Pride elevates our desires above the needs of other people and the law of God. It results in immorality, murder, war and every other sin. Long before the Garden of Eden, Satan fell into that sinful indulgence called spiritual pride and tried to overthrow the Throne of God. Christ revealed the mystery of the origin of evil: "For you have said in your heart: 'I will ascend into heaven, I will exalt my throne above the stars of God; I will also sit on the mount of the congregation on the farthest sides of the north; I will ascend above the heights of the clouds, I will be like the Most High'" (Isaiah 14:13,14).

There are two errors that man falls into regarding the devil. One is to magnify him to the point where we fear and blame him for every difficulty in our life. The other error is to act as though Satan and his demons do not exist at all. The truth is that we are spiritual creatures and we dwell in a universe where a titanic spiritual war has continued for thousands of years between the forces of God and Satan. The focus of the battle is the planet earth and the object of the war is the souls of mankind. Fortunately, the final victory in this awesome spiritual warfare was described by the prophets of Israel centuries ago. Jesus Christ will defeat Satan and his fallen angels during the Great Tribulation and cast the devil into a bottomless pit to imprison him for a thousand years. Man will finally be released from the spiritual oppression that has afflicted humanity for thousands of years. Today, we live in a world that is under the occupying force of Satan and his demonic host of fallen angels.

Satan's Fall

When Satan first rebelled against God's government many of the angels of heaven joined him in an attempt to set himself up as God. The prophet Isaiah described Satan's fall from his original perfection and glory. "How you are fallen from heaven, O Lucifer, son of the morning! How you are cut down to the ground, you who weakened the nations!" (Isaiah 14:12).

In Revelation 12:4 we learn that a third of the angels joined in that first rebellion. "His tail drew a third of the stars of heaven and threw them to the earth." Centuries later, after the fall of Adam and Eve, Satan tried to eliminate forever the possibility of a Messiah Redeemer being born to a woman to save the souls of mankind. Some of those fallen angels demonically impregnated the "daughters of men." In the end, only one single family remained on earth that was uninfected by demonic possession. God mercifully unleashed the Flood to destroy the demonic races of men and cleanse the earth from violence and evil. Those fallen angels were imprisoned by God until the time when they will be judged at the Great White Throne judgment at the end of the Millennium. God created His angels with awesome powers. The fallen angels and Satan are also extremely powerful. However, a believer who stands under the protection of Christ is protected from the "fiery darts" of the devil. In one battle in the Old Testament, a single angel destroyed 185 thousand Syrian soldiers who were trying to defeat the Children of Israel.

Jesus Christ could have called "legions of angels" when He was crucified to atone for the sins of mankind. His angels had the power to destroy all of the legions of Rome's mighty empire. The only thing that held Christ upon that Cross was His overwhelming love for you and me.

Satan's Power

The Bible reveals that we are presently living in enemy-occupied territory where Satan rules as the "Prince of the power of the air." When Adam and Eve fell in sin, Satan took the dominion to rule this planet. Paul warned Christians that Satan has blinded mankind about the truth of Christ's salvation. He declares that the gospel "is veiled to those who are perishing, whose minds the god of this age has blinded" (2 Corinthians 4:4). Satan took Christ up to the Mount of Temptation and offered Him the kingdoms of this world. "And the devil said to Him, 'All this authority I will give You, and their glory; for this has been delivered to me, and I give it to whomever I wish'" (Luke 4:6). It is significant that Christ did not dispute the basic fact that the devil presently controls the kingdoms of this world, and will continue to do so until the day of his defeat at the hands of Christ.

Spiritual Warfare

The prophet Daniel revealed that fallen angels have demonic authority over nations. Daniel wrote that the angel was delayed in coming to him by a demonic angel, "the prince of the kingdom of Persia." While many people live in ignorance of this reality, we are engaged in an ongoing spiritual warfare that affects our daily lives. John, in the Apocalypse, described a group of over 100 million angelic beings surrounding the Throne of God. When we arrive in heaven we will finally understand how often angels have intervened in our lives and in the lives of our families to protect us from danger. How are we to protect ourselves in the spiritual battles of life? The Lord advises that we are to "put on the whole armor of God, that you may be able to stand against the wiles of the devil. For we do not wrestle against flesh and blood, but against principalities, against powers, against the rulers of the darkness of this age, against spiritual hosts of wickedness in the heavenly places" (Ephesians 6:11). A secret spiritual battle continues in the heavenlies but it is rapidly approaching its final crisis. Satan's freedom is about to be curtailed.

"Behold, a great, fiery red dragon having seven heads and ten horns, and seven diadems on his heads" (Revelation 12:3).

The Dragon -- Satan

Satan is described thirteen times in the Apocalypse as a "Dragon." In Revelation 12:3 Satan appears for the first time in John's Revelation in the symbol of a "a great fiery red dragon." It reveals him as the relentless, terrifying and murderous enemy of the saints of God. In other biblical passages, Satan is described as "Leviathan." Job says: "He beholds every high thing; He is king over all the children of pride" (Job 41:34). The prophet Isaiah saw a vision of the final battle between God and Satan. "In that day the Lord with His severe sword, great and strong, will punish Leviathan the fleeing serpent, Leviathan that twisted serpent; and He will slay the reptile that is in the sea" (Isaiah 27:1). In the book of Revelation (19:15) John saw a vision of Christ coming down from heaven with "a sharp sword, that with it

He should strike the nations" and defeat the host of Satan's army.

John saw Satan as "a great, fiery red dragon having seven heads and ten horns, and seven diadems on his heads" (Revelation 12:3). The thirteenth chapter of the Revelation reveals that Satan will completely possess the soul and body of the Antichrist during the last of the Tribulation period. He will enable the Antichrist to conquer the ten nations of the Revived Roman Empire that will voluntarily confederate in the last days. After they unite he will arise among them. During a future crisis, he will defeat three of the nations and probably kill their leaders. The ten horns represent the ten nations of the Revived Roman Empire, the future power base of the Antichrist. The "seven heads" and "seven diadems" represent the remaining seven leaders of the European superstate that survive Antichrist's violent takeover. They will give their power to "the beast" and "rule with him for one hour."

The "Sun-Clothed Woman" and the "Man-Child"

"Now a great sign appeared in heaven: a woman clothed with the sun, with the moon under her feet, and on her head a garland of twelve stars" (Revelation 12:1).

Many different theories about the identities of the Woman and Man-Child appear in the multitudes of commentaries on Revelation. The correct identification of the Woman and the Man-Child are critical to our understanding of the prophecies in the Apocalypse. This identification is so important that it forms a fundamental factor in our interpretation of the rest of John's visions. If you wish to understand at a glance the prophetic interpretation principles and theological position of a writer in a biblical commentary, simply examine his interpretation of Revelation 12. His interpretation of the identity of the Woman and the Man-Child will reveal his position on the rest of the prophecies.

Some writers have suggested that the Woman is Mary, the mother of Jesus. While Mary gave birth to Jesus, the rest of the prophetic description does not fit the human mother of Christ. John's vision reveals that "the woman fled into the wilderness" for 1260 days. Obviously, this prophecy fits the nation of Israel, not Mary. On the other hand, many writers believe that the Woman represents the Church and suggest that the Man-Child is Jesus Christ. While the Man-Child is certainly Christ, the Woman cannot be the Christian Church. First, the Church never gave "birth" to Christ. It is Christ whose actions and commands gave birth to the Church. As Eve was "created" out of the side of Adam, the Church was "created" out of the blood flowing from the side of Christ. Additionally, the Church is never referred to as a mother in Scripture. While the Church is often seen as the Virgin Bride, it is Israel that is described as a married woman, a mother.

The Woman Is Israel

Throughout the Old Testament Israel is represented as a "woman." The Bible always interprets its own symbols in other passages. God often used the symbol of a faithful woman or an unfaithful, adulterous woman to refer to Israel's spiritual relationship to their Lord. In the New Testament Paul speaks of Israel in these words: "My kinsmen according to the flesh, who are Israelites...from whom, according to the flesh, Christ came" (Romans 9:3,5). Here Paul clearly identified Israel as the mother of Jesus "of whom, according to the flesh, Christ came."

John described the "woman clothed with the sun, with the moon under her feet, and on her head a garland of twelve stars." The final proof of the identification of Israel as the "sun-clothed woman" is found in Genesis where Joseph received an inspired vision of Israel, the eternal Chosen People. "Then he dreamed still another dream and told it to his brothers, and said, 'Look, I have dreamed another dream. And this time, the sun, the moon, and the eleven stars bowed down to me'" (Genesis 37:9). The "eleven stars" were Joseph's eleven brothers, the heads of the eleven other tribes of Israel. Joseph and his tribe was the twelfth star. These twelve sons of Jacob became the twelve Patriarchs. "Jacob begot the twelve patriarchs" (Acts 7:8). Every Jew, who studied the five books of Moses every year in Synagogue, knew that the "sun-clothed woman" represented Israel. The "sun" stood for the light of God's glory and the "moon" indicated the reflected glory of God.

The Man-Child

The Man-Child is Jesus Christ, who was born as "the seed of promise" to Israel as their promised Messiah. When Jesus was born, Satan did everything in his power to destroy the Messiah who will someday destroy him. In John's vision he witnessed a spiritual war extending over thousands of years. First, he saw the Woman, Israel, giving birth to the Messiah, the Man-child. He witnessed that "the dragon stood before the woman who was ready to give birth, to devour her Child as soon as it was born" (Revelation 12:4). King Herod, motivated by Satan, sought to kill Jesus by ordering the murder of all children below the age of two in the town of Bethlehem. Only God's supernatural intervention, through an angel warning Joseph to escape to Egypt, saved the child from the Dragon's devouring attack. "And she bore a male Child who was to rule all nations with a rod of iron. And her Child was caught up to God and to His throne" (Revelation 12:5). As many Old Testament prophecies affirm, the destiny of Jesus the Messiah is to "rule all nations with a rod of iron" throughout His millennial Kingdom. King David was given a vision of the future rule of the Messiah when He comes to set up His Kingdom. "You shall break them with a rod of iron" (Psalm 2:9).

After Christ completed His earthly mission through His death and resurrection, He ascended to heaven to sit at the right hand of His Father. In Revelation 12:5 John described his vision that "her Child was caught up to God and to His throne." During the following two thousand years Jesus Christ gave the Church a mission to fulfill His Great Commission. "Go into all the world and preach the gospel to every creature" (Mark 16:15). Christ remains in heaven at the right hand of His Father where He will someday give the signal to launch the great war against Satan and his fallen angels.

The Army of Heaven Will Defeat Satan's Demons

"And war broke out in heaven: Michael and his angels fought against the dragon; and the dragon and his angels fought, but they did not prevail, nor was a place found for them in heaven any longer. So the great dragon was cast out, that serpent of old, called the Devil and Satan, who deceives the whole world; he was cast to the earth, and his angels were cast out with him" (Revelation 12:7-9).

When Christ declares war against Satan, the Archangel Michael will marshal the awesome military forces of heaven to attack and defeat Satan's demonic army. Although angels are spiritual beings they can take on a physical form. This war is a real battle that will result in Satan's expulsion from the heavenlies. Some have written that Satan rules today as the king of hell. However, the Scriptures tell us he won't be cast into the lake of fire until the end of the Millennium. The Bible indicates that Satan presently has access to both the earth and the heavenlies. In the book of Job Satan appeared before God with "the sons of God" to accuse Job. Later, in the New Testament Jesus declared that the devil is our accuser who accuses us before the Father, while Christ, as our advocate, defends us. This battle for the heavens is the opening military struggle of the final war that will seal the fate of Satan, the great enemy of our souls. In a parallel prophetic passage Daniel described the great war in heaven. "At that time Michael shall stand up, the great prince who stands watch over the sons of your people; and there shall be a time of trouble, such as never was since there was a nation, even to that time. and at that time your people shall be delivered, every one who is found written in the book" (Daniel 12:1).

The Bible describes a multitude of angelic beings in the heavenlies: seraphim, cherubim, *Zoa* -- living creatures, archangels, spirit horses and chariot drivers, a hundred million angels around the Throne, warrior angels, messenger angels, and the demonic fallen angels. Only a few angels are named in the Bible. The archangel Michael and Satan are two of the mighty created angelic creatures of God. The Scriptures reveal that the spiritual universe includes wicked principalities, powers, wicked spirits, demons, fallen angels, spirits in prison, and unclean spirits. The initial rebellion of Lucifer will reach its logical solution as the mighty forces of heaven engage in a climactic battle to determine who shall rule the universe. Thankfully, the outcome is not in doubt. Although God has, in His mercy, allowed Satan a measure of freedom for thousands of years to test mankind, the ultimate victory of Christ's army is assured. The angelic army, led by Michael, Israel's great defender, will succeed in driving Satan and his fallen angels out of the heavenlies. They will be cast down to this earth and restricted in their activities to this planet for the final 1260 days leading to Armageddon.

Rejoicing in Heaven's Victory Over Satan

"Then I heard a loud voice saying in heaven, 'Now salvation, and strength, and the kingdom of our God, and the power of His Christ have come, for the accuser of our brethren, who accused them before our God day and night, has been cast down'...Therefore rejoice, O heavens, and you who dwell in them!" (Revelation 12:10,12).

As a result of the battle, the inhabitants of heaven will rejoice because they have finally witnessed the victory over Lucifer, an event for which they have awaited expectantly for many millennia. The phrase "they did not prevail" describes the beginning of the end for the forces of evil in the universe. Satan, who thought he "was like god," will be "cast to the earth, and his angels were cast out with him." The heavens will resound with the triumphant victory cry, rejoicing in the defeat of evil. The angelic host will announce the victorious cleansing of the heavenlies from the pollution of sin.

A Warning to the Earth

Unfortunately, the joy in heaven over Satan's expulsion will be matched by an equal but opposite despair on earth. The descent of Lucifer's demonic army will unleash the worst horrors in history. As the devil and his powerful angelic army are cast out of heaven they will descend in anger and wrath to the earth, intent on wreaking vengeance on mankind. Satan will possess the soul of the wicked individual who rules the earth from the capital of his Revived Roman Empire. The angels will warn the unrepentant sinners about the coming Great Tribulation. "Woe to the inhabitants of the earth and the sea! For the devil has come down to you, having great wrath, because he knows that he has a short time" (Revelation 12:12). The devil can read prophecy as well as we can. He knows that the ancient prophecies tell him that he will be defeated at the Battle of Armageddon and imprisoned for a thousand years exactly 1260 days from the moment he is cast down to earth.

Satan's War against Israel

After Satan's descent to earth he will totally possess the soul and body of the Antichrist. The "Prince that shall come" will go to Jerusalem and enter the rebuilt Temple on Mount Moriah. First, he will break his covenant with Israel. Then he will stop the daily morning and evening sacrifice because he hates the sacrifice to God. As detailed in the chapter on the Antichrist, someone will kill him with a sword wound to the head. Later, the devil will satanically resurrect him to cause "the earth and those who dwell in it to worship the first beast...who was wounded by the sword and lived" (Revelation 13:12,14). Then he will enter the Holy of Holies of the Temple and defile the Holy Place. The prophet Daniel calls this the "abomination of desolation." Possibly the Ark of the Covenant will be recovered before this time and placed again in the Holy of Holies of a rebuilt Temple. If this occurs, perhaps the Antichrist will defile the Ark of the Covenant, triggering the judgment of God and the Great Tribulation. Jesus warned that the wrath of God would be poured out on the earth when this "strange act" occurred in the Holy Place. He told the Jews to "flee to the mountains" because of the coming judgments. "For then there will be great tribulation, such as has not been since the beginning of the world until this time, no, nor ever shall be. And unless those day were shortened, no flesh would be saved; but for the elect's sake those days will be shortened" (Matthew 24:21,22).

The "dragon" will attack Israel when the Jews reject his false claims to be their Messiah and "God." When the

Antichrist sits in the Holy of Holies and demands that Israel worship him as a god, the majority of the Jews will realize that he is the False Messiah. In John's vision he saw that Satan "persecuted the woman who gave birth to the male Child" (Revelation 12:13). Many Old Testament Scriptures warn that Israel will face its greatest trial of faith in the coming persecution of the last days after the Jews return to the Promised Land. The devil will use his satanic powers in an attempt to destroy Israel, who gave birth to his enemy, Jesus Christ. However, God will intervene with His miraculous power to protect her.

Divine Deliverance for the Woman

In Revelation 12:14 John says that "the woman was given two wings of a great eagle, that she might fly into the wilderness to her place, where she is nourished for a time and times and half a time, from the presence of the serpent." In some supernatural manner, God will preserve the Jewish remnant from this satanic attack by miraculously protecting Israel for three-and-a-half years. The prophet promises that food will be supernaturally provided: "She has a place prepared by God, that they should feed her there one thousand two hundred and sixty days" (Revelation 12:6). Perhaps God will once again provide manna for the Children of Israel.

A prophecy in the Psalms suggests that the ancient rock city of Petra, Jordan, will be one of the places of refuge for the Jews in that time of trial. "Who will bring me into the strong city? Who will lead me to Edom?" (Psalm 60:9). The prophet Isaiah also refers to Israel escaping to Moab (Jordan): "Let My outcasts dwell with you, O Moab; be a shelter to them from the face of the spoiler. For the extortioner is at an end, devastation ceases, the oppressors are consumed out of the land" (Isaiah 16:4). However, Petra is not large enough to hold a significant part of the population of the nation Israel. Many nations, including Africa, North America and others may be part of the "wilderness" where the Jews will flee for protection from the Antichrist. Isaiah prophesied that five cities in Egypt that will have so many Jews in the last days that the common language will be Hebrew. Christ declared in

Matthew 25 that He will judge the nations of the earth on the basis of how they treat the Jews and Gentile tribulation believers who flee the Mark of the Beast system. If the citizens of our nations provide refuge for the Jews, they will be blessed and allowed to participate in the blessings of Christ's millennial Kingdom. Sinful individuals in the nations that join in the persecution will be cast into darkness and hell.

The book of Revelation describes a satanic attack on the fleeing Jewish refugees as "the serpent spewed water out of his mouth like a flood after the woman, that he might cause her to be carried away by the flood" (Revelation 12:15). One possible scenario is that Antichrist may detonate an enormous nuclear explosion triggering an artificial tidal wave to kill the Jewish refugees. One reason for thinking the "flood" may be literal, rather than symbolic, is that God protects Israel in the following way. "But the earth helped the woman, and the earth opened its mouth and swallowed up the flood" (Revelation 12:16). Is it possible that God will supernaturally cause an earthquake that will open the ground to absorb the water to protect the Jews? Only history will reveal how each individual prophecy will be fulfilled.

The Great Multitude

When Satan realizes that the awesome power of God prevents him from succeeding in his attacks on Israel, he will turn his attention to launching a war against this "great multitude" the huge number of tribulation saints who "have the testimony of Jesus Christ." As a result of the message preached by the supernaturally protected Two Witnesses, the 144 thousand Jewish Witnesses, and the three angelic messengers, an enormous number of people will repent of their sinful rebellion and accept Christ. The prophet warns that Satan will "make war with the rest of her offspring, who keep the commandments of God and have the testimony of Jesus Christ" (Revelation 12:17). These tribulation saints will prove their faith by martyrdom during the severe persecution, first, from the Great Whore church and later, from the Antichrist. In Revelation 7:9 John saw "a great multitude which no one could number, of all nations, tribes, peoples, and tongues, standing before the throne and before the Lamb." The angel told John that these are the tribulation martyrs who will form the last great harvest of souls. They will pay the supreme price of martyrdom for their faith. "These are the ones who come out of the great tribulation, and washed their robes and made them white in the blood of the Lamb" (Revelation 7:14).

CHAPTER NINE

The Mystery of Babylon – A Tale of Two Cities

"The great city was divided into three parts and the cities of the nations fell: and great Babylon came in remembrance before God, to give unto her the cup of the wine of the fierceness of His wrath" (Revelation 16:19).

The seventh angel will pour out his vial and say: "It is done" (Revelation 16:17). The certainty of Babylon's destruction is declared in the Apocalypse. The time for mercy and repentance has passed. On the Great Day of the Lord, the threatened wrath of God will fall on the city of Babylon and those who join in her lascivious worship of Satan. Babylon's annihilation will be accompanied by the greatest earthquake in history, the fall of cities and mountains, tidal waves swamping islands and a fierce plague of hailstones "the weight of a talent" (114 pounds).

In Revelation 15 and 16 John described the terrible judgments of God that will be poured out on rebellious men by the seven angels. At the close of chapter 16 John prophesied about the final outpouring of the wrath of the seventh bowl judgment on Babylon, one of the culminating judgments of God. The final act in the heavenly drama will be the glorious return of Jesus Christ as King of kings and Lord of lords to defeat His enemies and establish His eternal kingdom. However, before recording Christ's victorious return, the prophet introduced a parenthesis, a pause, in which he revealed the nature of the final satanic religious system of the last days. In this interlude John recorded his mysterious vision of God's destruction of the two Babylons. Revelation 17 focused on the destruction of the Great Whore of Babylon religious system while Revelation 18 describes the destruction of the rebuilt city of Babylon.

The Two Babylons of Prophecy

Revelation 17 and 18 prophesied the judgment of God on the two Babylons. Unfortunately, there are more errors of identification about Babylon than any other part of prophecy. Although both entities are called Babylon, they are separate in identity. The failure to correctly identify the two Babylons has led to great confusion in interpretation. The two are obviously related by sharing the name "Babylon" and have the same satanic religious worship. However, the Great Whore of Babylon of Revelation 17 is a totally different entity than the city of Babylon of Revelation 18. The most obvious difference is that they will be destroyed at different times, according to the Word of God. The Great Whore of Babylon, the false ecumenical worship system of the Tribulation period, will be destroyed by the Antichrist and his ten allied kings at the midpoint of the seven-year treaty period. In Revelation 17:16 we read, "And the ten horns which you saw on the beast, these will hate the harlot, make her desolate and naked, eat her flesh and burn her with fire."

On the other hand, the city of Babylon will be destroyed three-and-a-half years later by God directly through His supernatural power "as Sodom and Gomorrah." This will occur on the Great Day of the Lord at the end of the seven-year treaty. In Isaiah 13:1, 6, and 19 God warned of the coming destruction of the city of Babylon. In prophesying his "burden against Babylon," Isaiah warned, "Wail, for the day of the Lord is at hand! It will come as a destruction from the Almighty." After telling us that it will happen at "the Day of the Lord," Isaiah declared that this destruction of the city of Babylon will occur through supernatural fire from heaven. "Babylon, the glory of the kingdoms, the beauty of the Chaldeans' pride, will be as when God overthrew Sodom and Gomorrah" (Isaiah 13:6,19). The seventh bowl judgment describes God's final wrath poured out on the city of Babylon. The demonic religious, commercial and social system of the last days will be centred on Babylon. This ancient wicked city was the enemy of God from its creation by Nimrod until its final destruction as one of the capital cities of the Antichrist. John's vision in Revelation 18:8 to 10 took him forward in time to the end of Daniel's seventieth week to witness the final wrath of God on Satan's counterfeit religious and commercial system which will occur on the Great Day of the Lord.

The Origin of the Mystery Religion of Babylon

The key to Babylonian worship is the exaltation of the individual "to become like god" by means of initiation, secret rituals and gnostic knowledge of god. This demonic system motivated every ancient false religion and modern New Age cult that opposed the true worship of God. The city and empire of Babylon was founded by Nimrod, the "mighty hunter" according to Genesis 10:8-10: "Cush begat Nimrod; he began to be a mighty one on the earth. He was a mighty hunter before the Lord;...And the beginning of his kingdom was Babel." The phrase "mighty hunter" was paraphrased by the ancient Jewish *Targum of Jonathan* as follows: "A mighty rebel before the Lord." The *Jerusalem Targum* described him as "mighty in sin, lying in wait to catch and overthrow men, drawing men away from the worship of the true God; as taught by Shem, to join that taught by Nimrod." The name Nimrod became a proverb for a great apostate or evil rebel against God.

Nimrod had a wife named Semiramis, according to ancient tradition. Their son, Tammuz, was killed. The occult tradition claims his mother prayed for forty days and he was revived. This story of Semiramis and Tammuz was known to the Greeks as Aphrodite and Eros, to the Romans as Venus and Cupid and to the Egyptians as Isis and Osiris. The Assyrians called her Ishtar and her son Tammuz but the Phoenicians, who inhabited Palestine, called her Astarte and her son Baal. This primeval Babylonian myth traveled to Assyria, Egypt, Greece and Rome. It became the source of many of the occult mystery religions of the ancient world. The worship of Astarte involved offering incense and weeping for forty days until they celebrated her son's resurrection by exchanging Astarte eggs.

This mysterious Babylonian cult was a continual temptation and snare for the Children of Israel. The prophet Jeremiah confronted the idol worshippers in Israel who were still burning incense to Astarte and offering a host, a wafer of bread, to honor "the mother of heaven." Later, the prophet Ezekiel was taken by God into the secret chamber of the Temple to observe the occult worship of the pagan mother Astarte and the child. "So He brought me to the door of the north gate of the Lord's house; and to my dismay, women were sitting there weeping for Tammuz [Astarte's son]" (Ezekiel 8:14).

The Rise of the City of Babylon

Throughout history, Babylon has stood as a determined enemy of God and of Israel. When her armies were not destroying Jerusalem, her false cult of the worship of the mother and child continually tempted Israel, ultimately spreading throughout the whole world. God will finally judge Babylon for her past, present and future oppression of God's Chosen People. It was no accident that Iraq's Saddam Hussein claimed that he was rebuilding the Babylonian Empire, and then fired thirty-nine SCUD missiles on Israel during the War in the Gulf. Throughout the prophecies of the Old Testament, God warned Babylon about the punishment for her sinful pride, her sexual sins and luxurious living. The worship of Babylon was always surrounded by idolatry, spiritualism, fornication and the killing of righteous believers who rejected her satanic religion. When the city of Babylon is completely rebuilt it will become one of the capital cities of the Antichrist. Once again, it will become a center of satanic witchcraft and martyrdom for the tribulation saints. The emerging false worship of the Earth Mother Goddess is a sign of the rise of Babylon's religion in the last days, just as the prophets warned.

The Final Fall of Babylon

Over the centuries many looked at Babylon's ruins in the desert and thought the biblical prophecy of her total destruction was fulfilled. However, the Bible's predictions about Babylon's destruction by fire from heaven is very different from the historical record of the final days of that ancient city. Over a thousand years ago Babylon was abandoned and gradually covered by desert sand. For centuries, an Arab village of over a thousand people existed beside the site of the ruins. However, the prophecies of Isaiah and Revelation point to a future rebuilding of this ancient city and its final destruction at the time of Armageddon by the power of God.

The current rebuilding of the city of Babylon by Saddam Hussein proves that the final destruction must still lie in our prophetic future. Revelation 18 and Isaiah 13 clearly indicate that its destruction will occur on the Great Day of the Lord. When God destroys this center of satanic worship and persecution of the tribulation saints, the voices of the heavenly host will rejoice over Christ's victory. "Rejoice over her, O heaven and you holy apostles and prophets for God has avenged you on her!" (Revelation 18:20). God hates the religion of Babylon and her horrible crimes of persecuting the righteous saints in every generation.

The Current Rebuilding of the City of Babylon

When Babylon is finally destroyed, she will never be rebuilt again. "It [Babylon] will never be inhabited. Nor will it be settled from generation to generation" (Isaiah 13:20). It appears from the prophecies that Babylon (Iraq) will participate joyfully in the Antichrist's persecution of the Chosen People during the terrible persecution of the Great Tribulation. It will become the major center of satanic demon oppression after the Church is raptured to heaven. God will destroy Babylon because it is a center of demonic witchcraft. As reported by the *Los Angeles Times*, October 12, 1990, the anti-semitic President Saddam Hussein declared in a speech that he admired the ancient emperor of Babylon, King Nebuchadnezzar, because he "was the one who brought the bound Jewish slaves from Palestine." His fondest goal would be to conquer Jerusalem as Babylon did twenty-five centuries ago.

God has never forgotten Babylon's destruction of His Temple in 587 B.C. In describing the coming destruction of the city of Babylon, Jeremiah wrote, "Come and let us declare in Zion the work of the Lord our God...For His plan is against Babylon to destroy it, because it is the vengeance of the Lord, the vengeance for His temple" (Jeremiah 51:10,11). As detailed in my earlier book *Messiah*, the Iraqi government has already spent over $600 million in rebuilding a large number of temples, palaces and amphitheatres to honor the pagan gods of ancient Babylon. Every summer a Babylonian Festival is held with over four thousand invited guests from around the world to witness the most unique rebuilding project in history. Iraq's $100 million a day oil revenue could easily be harnessed by an Iraqi government to create a wealthy new Babylonian Empire at the mouth of the Persian Gulf.

The Great Whore of Babylon -- The Harlot Church of the Last Days

John was given the vision of the future apostasy of the false church after the rapture of the Christians. He saw the final Babylonian religious system persecuting the tribulation saints. He wrote,"When I saw her, I marveled with great amazement" (Revelation 17:6). Although he had earlier observed the awesome career of the Antichrist, the Great Tribulation and the Wrath of God, he did not use the expression "I marveled with great amazement" until he saw the Great Whore of Babylon. John's experience in the first-century Church was of a small, powerless group under continual persecution by the Roman Empire. Now he saw a vision of the false church of the last days grown rich, powerful and apostate. Instead of being persecuted, the final false Babylonian church will persecute and kill the tribulation believers who reject her demonic doctrines. Over the course of a thousand years the medieval Church perverted its doctrine, lost sight of the Bible and compromised with the kings of the earth. Later, it persecuted and martyred tens of millions of believers in Christ who rejected her false Babylonian religious practices.

The Ecumenical Movement of the Last Days

Revelation 17 describes the future career and destruction of the false, ecumenical Babylonian church that will be formed after the Rapture of the saints to heaven. The true believers in Christ from every single denomination on the earth will be raptured to the Marriage Supper of the Lamb. Following the Rapture, the many religions and false cults of the world will rapidly unite in the greatest worldwide, ecumenical religious system in history. The Protestants, Roman Catholics, Greek and Russian Orthodox, the Muslims, Hindus, Buddhists and the growing New Age cults will joyfully join forces with the rising Antichrist to produce the greatest consolidation of political and religious power ever seen. In Malachi Martin's insightful book *The Keys of This Blood*, he provides evidence that Pope John Paul II and the Catholic Church are actively campaigning to establish the primacy of their church over the emerging ecumenical worldwide church. Their goal is to obtain the spiritual leadership of the New World Order. John Paul actively rejects Marxism and Capitalism as models for the emerging New World Order. His goal is to create a new spiritual-political model for Europe and Russia based on a Catholic-socialism.

A profound behind-the-scenes decision was made by the Papacy during the final days of the Vatican II sessions in 1965. This unprecedented shift in the scope of Catholic ecumenical activities resulted in the inclusion of all other Christian denominations and, for the first time, Muslims and Jews. Later, in a logical extension of this ecumenical revolution, Buddhists, American Indians, Shintoists and New Agers were also brought into the fold. The only groups that have successfully resisted these ecumenical entreaties are fundamentalist and evangelical Christians. In 1965 Pope Paul IV told Vatican II that the Catholic Church would henceforth focus on the hopes, fears and aspirations of man on this earth, rather than the biblical focus on man's spiritual condition in light of his heavenly destiny. Pope John Paul II has continued this ecumenical revolution while paving the way for a profound shift in the geo-religious systems of the planet. During the last ten years, the Pope has met with religious leaders from every Christian denomination plus Muslims, Jews, Hindus, Buddhists, Sikhs and Shintoists.

Over the last decade there have been many ecumenical discussions between the Roman Catholics, the Greek and Russian Orthodox Churches and the Church of England.

Significantly, it has been taken for granted by all sides that the ultimate spiritual and organizational leadership will be provided by Rome. No one has ever suggested that the Archbishop of Canterbury or any other religious leader will lead the worldwide ecumenical church. The Bible tells us that the false church of the last days will be centered on the ancient city of Rome. In Revelation 17:9, John declares: "Here is the mind which has wisdom: The seven heads are seven mountains on which the woman sits." The city of Rome was commonly known from ancient times as the "city of seven hills."

According to Dr. Wordsworth, "Virgil, Horace, Ovid, in short, the unanimous voice of the Roman poetry during more than five hundred years, beginning with the age of St. John, proclaimed Rome as the seven-hilled city." He also noted that "on the imperial medals of that age which are still preserved, we see Rome figured as a woman on seven hills, precisely as she is represented in the Apocalypse." In the fifth century, the Christian writer Jerome compared Rome to Babylon when he wrote, "When I dwelt in Babylon, and resided within the walls of the scarlet adulteress, and had the freedom of Rome, I undertook a work concerning the Holy Spirit." To eliminate all doubt, John concluded his vision with these words: "The woman whom you saw is that great city which reigns over the kings of the earth" (Revelation 17:18). The rebuilt Babylon will be a key power center of the Antichrist, but the Bible's prophecies in Daniel 2 and Revelation 13 make it abundantly clear that the capital of the Revived Roman Empire of the Antichrist will be Rome. This does not suggest that the Papacy and the Roman Catholic religion will be the sole participants in the coming false church of the tribulation period. As explained above, every religious group in the world will join together once the true believers in every denomination have been raptured to heaven.

Growing Ecumenical Movements

Hundreds of ecumenical groups in every nation have set a goal of creating a worldwide ecumenical church. It will be humanist, pantheistic, New Age and totally opposed to biblical Christianity. John Wright, a Cardinal of the Catholic Church, was a founding member of one of these ecumenical groups, the World Conference of Religion for Peace. Ironically, in 1988, on the isle of Patmos where John received his vision of the Great Whore of Babylon, a group of religious leaders met to plan the one world church. Buddhists, Roman Catholics and the Greek Orthodox Patriarch of Constantinople met with the World Conference of Religion for Peace to coordinate plans for the growing worldwide ecumenical movement. As an example of how far this process has proceeded, consider the following. In New York's Saint Patrick's Cathedral, Catholic Cardinals recently joined with mainline Protestants and Jewish clergy to honor the leader of the Tibetan Buddhists, supposedly the Dalai Lama's latest reincarnation.

One of the most powerful ecumenical organizations, the World Council of Churches has now changed the definition of a "church" to include people of any particular faith, Christian or non-Christian, or even people who are atheists. The ultimate goal of these ecumenical groups is to unite men together without regard to any particular religious belief system. The fascinating and frightening thing is that the only people the ecumenical groups oppose are born-again Christians who believe that there are fundamental biblical truths that cannot be compromised. There is an interesting parallel with ancient Rome which accepted all religions equally, no matter how bizarre. The only group pagan Rome attacked was the Christians, because they believed that Jesus was God and the Bible was the inspired authority about spiritual matters. The pagans, then and now, hated the Christians for their supposed "intolerance" of other religions contradictory falsehoods.

Today, television talk shows will discuss the most absurd religious views or perversions with acceptance and toleration. However, if some Christian in the audience says that Jesus is the Son of God and the Bible is true, the audience will attack the "offending" Christian. They will criticize him as an "intolerant bigot" because he dares to believe there is an absolute right and wrong. Millions have been taught that all religious beliefs are equally true and that "as long as you are sincere, God will accept you." This emerging ecumenical world church will become the perfect tool in the hands of the Antichrist and the False Prophet as they manipulate it in their rise to world power. Just as Rome hated the Christians, the rising false church will persecute the Jewish and Gentile tribulation believers who will proclaim the "testimony of Jesus" during the terrible tribulation period.

A Catholic View of Prophecy

Very few books on prophecy have been published by Catholic writers over the years. However, a fascinating Catholic commentary on the Revelation was written in 1955 called *The Book of Destiny*. It was approved by the Catholic censors with their "Nihil Obstat" and "Imprimatur." In this interesting book the writer, Bernard Leonard, interprets the language of prophecy in an unusually literal manner. He arrives at some startling conclusions for a Catholic religious writer about the identification of the Great Whore of Babylon. After carefully examining the issue, he reluctantly concludes that the Bible declares that Rome and the Roman Catholic Church will be taken over by Satan during the last days leading up to the return of Christ. Referring to Revelation 17, Leonard wrote: "Hence this great harlot is a city whose apostasy from the true faith is a monstrous thing. This may point to Rome...And the apostasy of this city, and her becoming the head of an empire that would lead all possible nations and peoples into antichrist-worship would indeed merit for her the title of THE GREAT HARLOT. The apostles called ancient Rome 'Babylon' (1 Peter V.13). So the conclusion is near that the great harlot of the future shall be Rome."

The Scarlet Woman and the Beast

"Come, I will show you the judgment of the great harlot who sits on many waters, with whom the kings of the earth committed fornication, and the inhabitants of the earth were made drunk with the wine of her fornication" (Revelation 17:1).

"The woman was arrayed in purple and scarlet, and adorned with gold and precious stones and pearls..." (Revelation 17:4)

The prophet described the Scarlet Woman: "On her forehead a name was written: MYSTERY, BABYLON THE GREAT, THE MOTHER OF HARLOTS AND OF THE ABOMINATIONS OF THE EARTH" (Revelation 17:5) The Roman writer Seneca wrote in his *Controversies 5.1* that the harlots of Rome wore a nameplate or label on their foreheads with their names. Revelation describes a future unholy alliance between the rising political power of the Antichrist's ten-nation confederacy and the ecumenical church body of the last days. The Scarlet Woman, the Great Whore of Babylon, represents the apostate church of the end times that will religiously prostitute itself to achieve its goals to rule the New World Order. This cynical union will help the Antichrist consolidate his evil totalitarian power. The role of the ecumenical church will involve the spiritual and intellectual preparation of the world's population to accept the rule of a new Caesar. However, after achieving and consolidating his world power, the Antichrist and his ten nations will turn and destroy the false harlot church. The reason is that Satan will not share his power with anyone, not even a false religion. Adolph Hitler destroyed his allies, the S.A. troops, once he gained power. Joseph Stalin destroyed all of his political comrades. The brutal logic of terror and revolution is that your allies must be killed once you obtain the supreme power because they are the only possible alternative to your power. Once Satan possesses the Antichrist at the mid-point of the tribulation period, he will destroy the false church, defile the rebuilt Temple and demand to be worshipped as "god."

There is a growing consensus among religious leaders around the world that the various nations and religions need to unite together to solve the great problems facing humanity today. This "Great Whore of Babylon" religious system will be based on the Babylonian satanic principle that "we can become like god." This is the great self-realization movement we see manifested in the New Age influence throughout religious and cultural movements today. Many of those supporting the environmental movement are seeking alliances among the world religions. The pantheistic religions of the American Indians, Buddhists and other animist belief systems are very attractive to the New Age leaders. As an example, Vice President Al Gore, in his book *Earth in the Balance* makes it clear that he admires the pantheistic vision that identifies the earth as our Mother Goddess. He quotes with approval James Lovelock's *Gaia Hypothesis* that suggests that the earth and its interlocking ecosystems are part of an enormous planet-wide living creature with intelligence and purpose. This bizarre notion is pantheism taken to an extreme. Al Gore also suggests that we must harness the religious motivations of all mankind into "a single organizing principle of civilization" to save the earth from environmental disaster. While many Christians, like myself, have been life-long conservationists, we do not believe the heresy that the earth and its life forms are actually a divine religious being that we must worship and serve spiritually.

This is a return to the kind of idolatry that the Old Testament prophets denounced thousands of years ago. In his discussion about his belief that God exists as part of the earth and all life, Vice President Gore asked the question: "Why does it feel faintly heretical to a Christian to suppose that God is in us as human beings?" The answer is that this New Age belief is heresy. It is a direct violation of the Word of God. The Scripture declares: "I am God and there is none like Me" (Isaiah 46:9). The heresy of pantheism, that believes the earth is part of God, is in total opposition to the Bible. The Apostle Paul declares that Jesus Christ is the Creator of the vast universe. He is not part of the universe; He created it out of nothing. "For by Him all things were created that are in heaven and that are on earth, visible and invisible, whether thrones or dominions or principalities or powers. All things were created through Him and for Him. And He is before all things and in Him all things consist" (Colossians 1:16-17). Yet, just as the prophets declared, idolatry, pantheism and paganism are rising everywhere in these last days.

The Difference Between Mystery Babylon and the City of Babylon

Revelation contains a series of prophetic descriptions of God's coming judgment on the false harlot church and also on the literal city of Babylon. There are many similarities between the two Babylons as follows: both commit spiritual fornication with the kings of the nations; they both martyr the saints, are clothed with scarlet and are ultimately destroyed. Both are motivated by a hatred of Israel and God. They both serve the interests of Satan. However, although they both bear the name "Babylon," there are many significant differences that prove these two Babylons, though related, are quite different entities.

If we are to understand the book of Revelation we must carefully differentiate between these two Babylons. While "Mystery Babylon" will be destroyed at the mid-point of the seven-year tribulation period by the Antichrist and his ten kings, the city of Babylon will be destroyed three-and-a-half years later by God at Armageddon, the Day of the Lord. Revelation records that John "wondered" at the false Babylonian church because it is still in our future. However, he did not wonder at the city of Babylon because he was already familiar with its role as an opponent of God. While the destruction of the city of Babylon is a major part of the Old Testament's prophecies, chapter 17 of Revelation is the only place in Scripture where we find prophecies about the end-time false church. The ecumenical church is called "the Great Harlot" and "the woman" while the city of Babylon is never described as a woman. Another difference is that the false Babylonian church makes herself rich and is "arrayed in purple and scarlet and adorned with gold and precious stones and pearls" (Revelation 17:4). On the other hand, the city of Babylon will make others rich, as Revelation declares: "The merchants of the earth have become rich through the abundance of her luxury" (Revelation 18:3).

One of the most significant differences between the two is that the Babylonian church will be destroyed by men as "the ten horns which you saw on the beast, these will hate the harlot, make her desolate and naked, eat her flesh and burn her with fire" (Revelation 17:16). However, when God destroys the city of Babylon with fire, the men of the world will lament and mourn her destruction: "The merchants of these things, who became rich by her will stand at a distance for fear of her torment, weeping and wailing" (Revelation 18:15). Unlike the end-time false Babylon religious system, the city of Babylon of Revelation 18:11-13 is described in detail as a commercial city with thirty different types of merchandise including gold, silver, pearls, cinnamon, oil, wheat and chariots. These types of merchandise have nothing to do with a false religious system. Although both Babylons are connected in their origin in the ancient demonic worship of Nimrod, Revelation 17 focuses on the career and destruction of the ecumenical church of the tribulation period. Revelation 18 deals with God's final judgment on the revived city of Babylon that will be one of the capitals of the Antichrist and a center of the terrible demonic worship of the last days.

The New Age and the Babylonian Religious System

The massive humanist and secularist movement in the early part of this century prepared hundreds of millions to accept the rising New Age religion of the last days. One of the New Age writers, John Price, claimed that today there are at least "half a billion New Age advocates on the planet at this time, working among various religious organizations."

While it draws on Theosophy, Buddhism, Baha'i, and satanic pantheism, the New Age movement was inspired by the Japanese spiritual leader, Meishu Sama's vision in the 1930s of a coming transformation in humanity. He saw a New Age of transforming illumination following a series of catastrophes that will shake the planet. He believed that the final crisis will purify the planet, its population, and end the Age of Darkness. Sama described a coming Messiah-like figure called a "Maitreya." He believed this superman will have tremendous psychic and occult abilities enabling him to establish a New Age, a global transformation of society ushering in a new type of humanity. Many apostate Christians are now secretly infiltrating their former churches and denominations in an organized New Age plan to modify and transform Christian theology to resemble the ancient Babylonian religious system. Thousands of New Age organizations are working night and day toward their goal of bringing about a New World Order by the year 2000. These New Age groups will join the growing Catholic and Protestant ecumenical groups that will ultimately fulfill the visions of the Apostle John on the isle of Patmos almost two thousand years ago.

The Mystery of the Beast with Seven Heads

"Here is the mind which has wisdom: The seven heads are seven mountains on which the woman sits. There are also seven kings. Five have fallen, one is, and the other has not yet come. And when he comes, he must continue a short time" (Revelation 17:9,10).

In the midst of John's parenthetical vision of the two Babylons, he witnessed the Babylonian harlot church riding upon the back of "a scarlet beast which was full of blasphemy, having seven heads and ten horns" (Revelation 17:3). There is a deep mystery concerning this beast. In some passages in Revelation the Beast represents the Revived Roman Empire in its various stages of rebirth, growing power, and final destruction at Armageddon. There is an allusion here to the mysterious rise and fall of the Roman Empire, the fourth Kingdom of Iron, that dominated the world for a thousand years, then ceased to rule, and will rise to rule the world again at the end of this age. From the standpoint of a reader of John's prophecy today, the Roman Empire certainly "was, is not and will be again."

However, other passages use the word "Beast" to describe the Antichrist personally and the satanic spirit that will animate this last enemy of mankind. The angel told John that "the beast that you saw was, and is not, and will ascend out of the bottomless pit and go to perdition" (17:8). Since an empire cannot "ascend out of the bottomless pit and go to perdition," a more satisfactory interpretation of Revelation 17:8 is that "the beast" describes the Antichrist personally at various positions during his rise and fall. In some mysterious way, the person of the Antichrist is spiritually connected to a spirit that will "ascend from the bottomless pit." At the mid-point of the seven-year treaty period, when Satan is cast out of heaven to the earth, the "man of sin" will be killed by a sword wound (Revelation 13:3,12,14). When the Beast, the Antichrist, miraculously rises from the dead, Satan "ascends from the bottomless pit" to demonically empower the Antichrist to declare war against the saints of God. The last three-and-a-half years leading to the Battle of Armageddon will be characterized by supernatural satanic power as the Antichrist is possessed as no other man in history. Revelation declares that Christ will destroy the Antichrist and the False Prophet on the Great Day of the Lord, sending them to perdition." As John records, "These two were cast alive into the lake of fire" (Revelation 19:20).

John's next vision is one of the most difficult passages in the book of Revelation. "Here is the mind which has wisdom: The seven heads are seven mountains on which the woman sits. There are also seven kings. Five have fallen, one is and the other has not yet come. And when he comes, he must continue a short time. The beast that was, and is not, is himself also the eighth, and is of the seven, and is going to perdition" (Revelation 17:9-11).

Failed Interpretations of "the Seven Kings"

Some writers have interpreted "the seven kings" as seven individual Roman emperors, suggesting that Emperor

Nero, will be resurrected as the future Antichrist. An early Church legend suggested that Nero might return as the Antichrist in the last days. However, more than five emperors had ruled Rome by the time of John. Beginning with Emperor Julius Caesar, the following emperors ruled in sequence until John's day: Julius Caesar, Augustus, Tiberius, Caligula, Claudius, Nero, Galba, Otho, Vitellius, Vespasian, Titus and, finally, Emperor Domitian (the twelfth). The number and sequence do not fit. Additionally, since the Antichrist must be Jewish to be accepted by the Jews as their Messiah, the Gentile Nero is an unlikely candidate for a revived Antichrist.

Another failed theory tried to identify seven specific stages or types of government of the Roman Empire as the "seven kings." One attempt identified the first "five kingdoms" as five successive forms of government that ruled Rome. These included Kings, Consuls, Dictators, Decemvirs and Military Tribunes. They suggested the sixth "kingdom" was the form of Roman emperors and the seventh, the Antichrist, a different kind of ruler of a confederated and Revived Roman Empire. The theory indicated that the eighth would be the Antichrist, revived from his death, but now ruling satanically. Aside from stretching the definition of the seven "kings" or "kingdoms," the system failed when few could agree on the specific types of governmental administration. This interpretation is unsatisfactory because the divisions between these forms of Roman government are not distinct or prophetically significant.

The Identification of the Seven Kingdoms

After many years of prayerful consideration I believe there is a solution that is consistent with the rest of Revelation's prophecies. This interpretation places this particular vision in its proper perspective in God's plan of redemption for the earth. The initial statement that the "seven heads are seven mountains on which the woman sits" suggests a two-fold interpretation as the passage indicates. First, the woman, the Great Whore religious system, is obviously identified with Rome, the "city of seven hills" (mountains). John then revealed the secondary meaning of the seven mountains by his inspired words, "There are also seven kings." In prophetic language the word "kings" can indicate individual kings or kingdoms, depending on the context. For example, in Daniel 7:17 when the prophet described the four great beasts, which he earlier identified as four empires and kingdoms, he says, "Those great beasts, which are four, are four kings, which arise out of the earth."

John's words in Revelation 17:9 declares: "There are also seven kings." This statement reveals that there are seven kingdoms or empires whose destiny is to rule the world during the thousands of years comprising the Times of the Gentiles. "Five have fallen, one is and the other has not yet come. And when he comes, he must continue a short time. The beast that was, and is not, is himself also the eighth, and is of the seven, and is going to perdition" (Revelation 17:9-11). Five empires ruled the known world in succession before John the Apostle wrote his book of Revelation. The empires of Egypt, Assyria, Babylon, Media-Persia and Greece each ruled the known world. Each empire in its turn oppressed the Children of Israel. John wrote, "One is and the other is not yet come" describing the sixth kingdom, the Roman Empire that ruled the world in John's day. Rome, the sixth kingdom, will return in the last days as the seventh kingdom, the Revived Roman Empire with its ten-nation confederacy.

Then John declared, "And when he comes, he must continue a short time" describing the death of the "prince that shall come" (Daniel 9:27) when he is killed after three-and-a-half years, "a short time." The seventh kingdom, the Revived Roman Empire of the first half of the seven-year treaty period will be wicked but human. However, the eighth kingdom will differ markedly in character from the other kingdoms because of Satan's supernatural possession of the Antichrist. After the Antichrist's death, "the Beast" will supernaturally rise from the dead through the demonic power of Satan. The Antichrist will then, for the last three-and-a-half years, oppress Israel and the Gentiles that refuse to worship him as god. Revelation describes the Antichrist in his resurrected form as the "eighth" kingdom because his final satanic three-and-a-half-year reign will be the most oppressive and demonic kingdom in history. John describes his final revived empire as follows: "The beast that was, and is not, is himself also the eighth, and is of the seven and is going to perdition." The satanic and terrifying persecution of the Mark of the Beast totalitarian system of the last three-and-a-half-years, called the Great Tribulation, will be a time of unparalleled terror for those rebellious sinners living in his kingdom.

The false religious system that originated in ancient Babylon corrupted each of the great world empires from the beginning of ancient history till today. The Babylonian religious system of the last six thousand years led untold billions of lost souls to an eternity in hell in its vain religious pretensions. Finally, both Babylons will be destroyed by the wrath of God at the appointed time during the Great Tribulation. The false worshippers and supporters of Babylon will cry, "Alas, alas, that great city Babylon, that mighty city! For in one hour your judgment has come" (Revelation 18:10). However, the verdict of the inhabitants of heaven is quite different. The heavens will ring with the joyful announcement that the great enemy of the saints has been destroyed by the righteous judgments of Almighty God. "After these things I heard a loud voice of a great multitude in heaven, saying, 'Alleluia! Salvation and glory and honor and power to the Lord our God!'" (Revelation 19:1).

The New European Currency Unit with the Symbol of a Woman Riding a Beast

In an astonishing sign of the times we live in, the European Community introduced a new currency note on January 1, 1993 to usher in the unification of the European superstate. The bill illustrated is a new ECU (European Currency Unit note). On the left side of the bill we find an engraving of a woman, riding a beast with two horns. This is the ancient mythological symbol of Europa, the woman, riding the two horned beast, a mythological god. John saw a two horned beast in his Apocalypse. Later, in another vision, he saw the woman riding the scarlet colored beast. Why would Europe choose this symbol for their new currency?

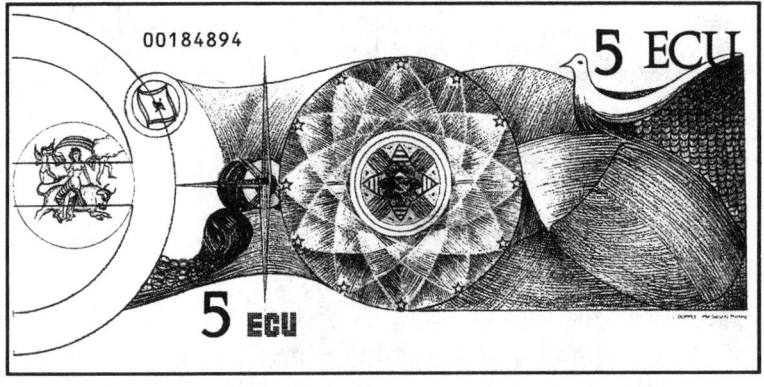

The New European Currency Unit

Enlargement of Symbol of Woman and Beast

CHAPTER TEN

The Great Day of His Wrath

"Fall on us and hide us from the face of Him who sits on the throne and from the wrath of the Lamb! For the great day of His wrath has come, and who is able to stand?" (Revelation 6:17).

One of the great mysteries is why God has allowed Satan to continue his evil reign as "prince of the power of the air" for thousands of years. Almost all thoughtful people have pondered the mystery of evil that continues unpunished century after century. Where is the justice of God that will finally punish the wicked and reward the righteous? The ancient prophets promised that the reign of evil will finally end when Satan meets his Creator at Armageddon. From the foundation of the world, God promised that He will return to destroy the reign of terror and evil that has afflicted mankind for millennia. The prophet John warned about this coming day of wrath when God will unleash the overwhelming power of heaven against the evil of unrepentant men. "For the great day of His wrath has come" (Revelation 6:17).

The Great Day of the Wrath of God

"Then I saw another sign in heaven, great and marvellous: seven angels having the seven last plagues, for in them the wrath of God is complete" (Revelation 15:1).

John saw a "great and marvelous" sign in the heavens that will introduce the final series of judgments that will seal up the wrath of God. He witnessed a "sea of glass mingled with fire" and the tribulation saints that were victorious over the Antichrist. These saints sang "the song of Moses, the servant of God, and the song of the Lamb" praising Christ for

His great and righteous works. The doors of the Temple in heaven were opened and the seven angels with "the seven golden bowls full of the wrath of God" prepared to unleash on Satan's followers the final judgment from heaven. During earth's darkest hour all decency and restraint will be removed as men openly worship Satan. One of the seven angels reminds us of the horrors of the persecution the tribulation saints will undergo at the hands of the followers of the Antichrist and False Prophet. "For they have shed the blood of saints and prophets" (Revelation 16:6).

For thousands of years evil men have tortured, abused and killed their helpless victims with seeming impunity. While billions have cried out for justice, the heavens seemed silent as if no one heard their cry for deliverance and a just sentence upon evil doers. Almost fifty years ago the German Nazis killed more than twelve million innocent victims in the death camps of the Holocaust. Less than 2 percent of these war criminals ever faced punishment. For seventy-four years the Communist Party of the U.S.S.R. killed more than fifty million innocent citizens. Red China and Cambodia have butchered more than thirty-five million men and women in the name of totalitarian Marxism. Where is the justice? The ultimate answer is that every man and woman will someday stand before God to give an account of every deed and word. God, who knows every motive and action, will be the perfect judge. He will deliver a just verdict for every sinner at the Great White Throne judgment at the end of the Millennium. However, even in this life, God promised that justice will be given out from heaven to those who oppress Israel and the Gentile saints during the terrible tribulation period. These visions of John reveal the swift judgment of God upon those who will join in the Antichrist's persecution of the saints who refuse to worship Satan.

The Seven Great Bowl Judgments on the Earth

"Then I heard a loud voice from the temple saying to the seven angels, 'Go and pour out the bowls of the wrath of God on the earth'" (Revelation 16:1).

The seven angels will pour out their frightening

judgments on all the sinners on earth. Each of these seven elements in the wrath of God is represented in John's vision as a separate golden bowl filled with that particular judgment. The first bowl will produce "a foul and loathsome sore on the men who had the mark." Perhaps God will cause skin infections to be produced in reaction to the physical Mark of the Beast implanted on the right hand or forehead. The second bowl will turn the sea into blood as Moses did in the days of the Exodus. This will be devastating as "every living creature in the sea died." The third angel's bowl will cause the rivers and fountains to turn to blood. The men who have shed the blood of the saints will discover God's just response. As the angel declares: "You have given them blood to drink. For it is their just due" (Revelation 16:6).

The fourth golden bowl will allow the sun's heat to increase until men are "scorched with great heat." Even now, environmental damage is reducing the ozone layer of protection against the sun's harmful rays. If this protective layer is damaged greatly during the Tribulation, it would produce the affect prophesied two thousand years ago. Incredibly, despite these proofs of God's power and justice, most people will choose to curse God rather than repent. The Apocalypse records that "they blasphemed the name of God who has power over these plagues; and they did not repent and give Him glory" (Revelation 16:9).

The fifth angel will produce a supernatural darkness over the kingdom of the Antichrist. The pagan historian Thallus recorded in his *Third History* that the Roman Empire was mysteriously darkened when Christ was crucified. Once again, God will darken the skies to warn men of the impending judgment of Armageddon. The sixth angel will pour out his bowl on the great Euphrates River causing it to dry up "so that the way of the kings from the east might be prepared." This action will be necessary to allow the 200-million-man army of the kings of the East to cross the Euphrates River from central Asia through Syria towards the Battle of Armageddon in northern Israel.

The Bible prophesies that "three unclean spirits" will be released from Satan, the Antichrist and the False Prophet to "perform signs" to convince the "kings of the earth and of the whole world, to gather them to the battle of that great day of God Almighty" (Revelation 16:14). These actions will prepare the nations for the titanic struggle over who shall rule the earth for the next millennium. The months leading up to Armageddon will see the greatest mobilization of military forces in history. No nation will be allowed to stand aside. As an old book's title suggested: "Only the stars will be neutral." Nations will either join with the kings of the East in their struggle to throw off the shackles of the Antichrist's tyranny or they will join the confederacy of the Antichrist.

Simultaneously with the conclusion of the Battle of Armageddon, the seventh angel will release the seventh bowl containing the judgment of a planet-shaking earthquake beyond anything ever experienced. "There was a great earthquake, such a mighty and great earthquake as had not occurred since men were on the earth" (Revelation 16:18). Although the War of Gog and Magog, before the seven-year tribulation period, will witness the greatest earthquake till that time, this final quake will devastate the whole planet. Jerusalem, "the great city was divided into three parts, and the cities of the nations fell." At the same moment "great Babylon was remembered before God," indicating that the prophecy of Isaiah 13:19 involving its destruction "as Sodom and Gomorrah" with fire from heaven, will occur at that moment. The planet will reel like a drunken man as "every island fled away, and the mountains were not found" (Revelation 16:20). These awful judgments will be accompanied with great hailstones "about the weight of a talent" (more than a hundred pounds).

The Judgment Seat of Christ

"For we must all appear before the judgment seat of Christ, that each one may receive the things done in the body, according to what he has done, whether good or bad" (2 Corinthians 5:10).

Many people look at the apparent injustice of human life and wonder when God will finally render true justice for the things that men do in their lives. Artists have often pictured one single judgment when all men, wicked and righteous, will stand before God's Throne. However, the Bible clearly shows that the Christians will "appear before the judgment seat of Christ" in heaven before the Millennium, while all the wicked dead will be raised to stand before the Great White Throne for judgment at the end of the first thousand years of Christ's reign.

The Word of God declares that our salvation depends solely on Christ's completed work on the Cross when He paid the price for our salvation. Our presence at the rapture of the Church and in heaven itself is not a reward for good service. In the eyes of a Holy God, "All our righteousnesses are like filthy rags" (Isaiah 64:6). The only qualification for living in heaven in the presence of the Living God is the righteousness of Jesus Christ applied to our lives through our faith in Him. Some may ask: "If all Christians equally go to heaven, regardless of the works they have done, where is the justice of God?" The Apostle Paul gave us the answer to that question in his revelation of the *Bema* Judgment Seat of Christ. The name "Bema" comes from the name of the judge's throne or bench where they judged athletic contests and handed out laurel wreaths as rewards for the winners. Paul used this expression to reveal that all Christians will be judged and rewarded by a just God on the basis of how well we have served Him since we became believers.

The New Testament reveals Jesus Christ as the great "foundation stone." Our spiritual life and ultimate rewards are built on the sole foundation of Jesus Christ and His completed work on the Cross. "Now if anyone builds on this foundation with gold, silver, precious stones, wood, hay, straw, each one's work will become manifest; for the Day will declare it, because it will be revealed by fire; and the fire will test each one's work, of what sort it is" (1 Corinthians 3:12,13). The "gold, silver and precious stones" represent the truly valuable spiritual works of our lives when God "works" through us to accomplish His purpose. However, the "wood, hay and straw" represent the less valuable and temporary things in a life that is not focused on Christ. The "wood, hay and straw" also suggests works that are done in our own strength, not Christ's. Finally, at the end of our life on earth, God will judge our every action and motive. His purpose is not to punish believers, but rather to reward us for faithful

190

service to our Lord. Some will receive rewards and crowns at the Bema Judgment Seat while some believers will receive none. Though they will be saved and raptured because of their faith in Christ, some Christians will not receive any rewards because their "works" were only "hay and stubble." God evaluates our life's activities in light of eternity. "If anyone's work which he has built on it endures, he will receive a reward. If anyone's work is burned, he will suffer loss; but he himself will be saved, yet so as through fire" (1 Corinthians 3:14,15).

Rewards and Crowns

The Bible does not describe all of the rewards that Christ will give to His faithful servants. Many of the details will not be known until we arrive in heaven. However, the nature of Christ assures us that He will judge correctly and fairly, giving the true and proper reward every soul deserves. While many good deeds are done in secret, in heaven all such actions will be proclaimed and rewarded. Even in this earthly life it is wonderful to receive a reward and a thank you from an employer or a parent. Can you imagine the joy we will have when we see Jesus Christ face to face and hear His praise? He will say to the victorious saint: "Well done, good and faithful servant." Regardless of the sacrifice or cost, it will be worth it all to receive praise from our Messiah. Unlike every earthly reward that tarnishes and becomes old, our heavenly rewards will still gleam as brightly a million years into eternity as the first day we arrived. Our Lord encorages us to "lay up for yourselves treasures in heaven, where neither moth nor rust destroys" (Matthew 6:20).

Among the rewards that are promised to faithful saints are "mansions" and "crowns." Jesus specifically promised us: "In My Father's house are many mansions; if it were not so, I would have told you. I go to prepare a place for you. And if I go and prepare a place for you, I will come again, and receive you to Myself; that where I am, there you may be also" (John 14:2,3). In my book *Heaven - The Last Frontier* I explored in detail the incredible promises that await believers in the New Jerusalem, the City of God.

The crowns will be given to us for our faithful service and actions on behalf of our Lord and Savior. We are told that among these precious crowns there is a Crown of Life -- the martyr's crown for those who have paid the supreme price for their faith by laying down their lives for Christ. The second is a Crown of Glory for those elders and pastors who have faithfully served in the Church. There is a Crown of Rejoicing for those who are soul winners. This crown is called "Rejoicing" because we are told that "there is joy in the presence of the angels of God over one sinner who repents" (Luke 15:10). Victorious saints who live in purity will receive the Crown Incorruptible. Finally there will be a Crown of Righteousness for those who "love His appearing." The doctrine of the second coming of Christ is vital for the Church in every age, but especially in this last generation. The hope of the imminent return of Christ motivates us to walk in purity as never before. The "love of His appearing" encourages us to witness to a lost world that there is hope for every man, woman and child in our Savior Jesus Christ.

Destined for a Throne

The destiny of the saints of the Church is to rule with Christ forever. While we will enjoy the New Jerusalem as our home in eternity, many Christians have forgotten the explicit promises of the Bible that we shall also rule with Christ on this earth forever. The Apostle Paul declared: "If we suffer, we shall also reign with him" (2 Timothy 2:12). This promise is not limited to martyrs only, we have additional passages in Revelation that indicate that the promise is extended to all the saints of the Church. John wrote about the ultimate destiny of the believers: "They shall reign forever and ever" (Revelation 22:5). Some writers suggest that only the tribulation martyrs will rule on earth during the millennial Kingdom. The prophet John wrote about the special rewards that will be given to those who died under the persecution of the Antichrist. While these martyrs will receive a special privilege of ruling over the nations during the Millennium, this rule will not be limited solely to martyrs. Revelation 20:6 declares that all believers will share in the privilege of reigning with Christ. The prophet wrote: "Blessed and holy is he who has part in the first resurrection: over such the second death has no power, but they shall be priests of God and of Christ, and shall reign with Him a thousand years."

Jesus indicated that our faithful actions in this life will determine the degree of responsibility and authority that we will receive throughout eternity. He spoke to His disciples about the eternal consequences of our actions. Speaking in His parable about the nobleman and his servants, Christ said: "And he said unto him, Well done, good servant: because you were faithful in a very little, have authority over ten cities" (Luke 19:17).

The Marriage Supper of the Lamb

"'Let us be glad and rejoice and give Him glory, for the marriage of the Lamb has come, and His wife has made herself ready.' And to her it was granted to be arrayed in fine linen, clean and bright, for the fine linen is the righteous acts of the saints. Then he said to me, 'Write: "Blessed are those who are called to the marriage supper of the Lamb!"'" (Revelation 19:7-9).

Jesus Christ constantly used the symbol of a virgin Bride to describe His faithful Church. It is significant that the image of marriage appears often in the Scriptures as a symbol of the eternal spiritual union of God with man. The faithful Bride stands in stark contrast to the symbol of an adulterous woman of the Old Testament and the Great Whore of Babylon in the Apocalypse. While the saints of Israel live with us in the New Jerusalem, the capital city of heaven, they are not the Bride of Christ. Though we are all saved through the blood of Christ shed on the Cross, the saints of the Old Testament are not part of the Bride of Christ. Paul showed that the mystery of the Church was not revealed in the Old Testament. The Apostle referred to "Him who is able to establish you according to my gospel and the preaching of Jesus Christ, according to the revelation of the mystery which was kept secret since the world began" (Romans 16:25).

In Revelation 19 John witnessed a vision of the glorious marriage supper of the Lamb which will occur in heaven during the time the earth is enduring the Tribulation period.

After the Bema Judgment Seat, when all Christians have received their just rewards for their righteous works, we will enjoy the final consummation of the spiritual marriage between Jesus Christ and the Church as His faithful Bride. The place of the marriage supper is definitely in heaven, the home of the Bride. Some posttribulationists have suggested that the marriage supper will take place "in the air" allowing the Church to rise at the Rapture and immediately return from the marriage supper to participate in the Battle of Armageddon. However, this position is in total contradiction to the clear words of John's prophecy. This marriage supper takes place in heaven as seen by John. Furthermore, John's Gospel reveals that, when Christ returns, He will take the Church to heaven. "And if I go and prepare a place for you, I will come again and receive you to Myself; that where I am, there you may be also" (John 14:3). This passage eliminates the possibility of the marriage occurring "in the air."

In regard to the timing of the marriage of the Lamb, it must take place between Christ's coming "in the air" for His Church and His coming "with the saints" at Armageddon. Consider the language that John used. He wrote: "For the marriage of the Lamb is come." He used the Greek word *elthen* which is translated "come." John chose the aorist tense of the word *elthen* which signifies an act that was completed. This indicates that the marriage will be spiritually consummated by this point in time. According to Revelation 19:7, the marriage will clearly precede the second coming of Christ. After describing the marriage supper, John then recorded his vision of the second coming. A normal reading of the passage shows that the marriage supper must occur prior to Christ's glorious Advent with the heavenly armies at Armageddon.

John described the garments of the Bride as follows: "And to her it was granted to be arrayed in fine linen, clean and bright, for the fine linen is the righteous acts of the saints" (Revelation 19:8). This description reveals the complete cleansing of the spirits of the saints through the atonement of Christ's completed work on the Cross. Some have suggested that the Church must go through the Tribulation to cleanse and purify her in preparation for the marriage of the Lamb. They have forgotten that we are not purified by tribulation. We are purified and qualified for the Rapture solely by Christ's righteousness applied to our hearts through faith in Him as our Lord and Savior. The Bride is seen at the marriage supper clothed with the "fine linen which is the righteous acts of the saints." This proves that the Church has already participated in the Bema Judgment Seat where rewards were given for faithful works. It is significant that John later describes the Christian saints "clothed with fine linen, white and clean" returning from heaven to join battle at Armageddon. "And the armies in heaven, clothed in fine linen, white and clean, followed Him on white horses" (Revelation 19:14). This passage confirms the order of prophetic events: first the Rapture, then the Bema Judgment Seat granting us rewards, including righteous garments, next, the marriage supper and finally, returning to earth at Armageddon.

There were three basic stages in a marriage in ancient Israel. The first stage was the betrothal, a legally binding agreement. When we accept Christ as our Savior we are spiritually "betrothed" to Him. The second stage is the coming of the bridegroom to meet his bride. This is equivalent to Christ "coming in the air" to meet His Bride. The third and last stage is the marriage supper that celebrates the marriage in the home of the groom. Following the Rapture, the complete Bride of Christ, including all departed saints and the living believers, will celebrate the marriage supper with Jesus in the presence of the assembled angelic host of heaven.

The marriage supper in the Heavenly City will be attended by guests just as any other wedding. "Blessed are those who are called to the marriage supper of the Lamb!" (Revelation 19:9). Guests are the ones who are "called"or invited to weddings. The Bride is not a guest at her own wedding. Who are these guests at the marriage supper in heaven? They are the souls of the Tribulation martyrs and the Old Testament saints who are already in heaven because they were raptured when Christ ascended to heaven forty days after His resurrection. Matthew 27:52,53 recorded that "the graves were opened; and many bodies of the saints who had fallen asleep were raised." These souls are now in heaven enjoying the presence of the Lord. In John 3:29 we find John the Baptist, the greatest of the Old Testament prophets, comparing himself to a wedding guest. "He who has the bride is the bridegroom; but the friend of the bridegroom, who stands and hears him, rejoices greatly because of the bridegroom's voice."

The final judgment of the earth will occur in "the valley of decision" when God gathers all the nations of the world together for the Battle of Armageddon. In another chapter we will explore the incredible prophecies that will be fulfilled when the nations meet their Judge, the returning Messiah, the King of kings.

CHAPTER ELEVEN

Judgment of the Nations

The psalmist David described the rage of the Gentile leaders against the rule of God. "Why do the nations rage, and the people plot a vain thing? The kings of the earth set themselves, and the rulers take counsel together, against the Lord and against His Anointed, saying, 'Let us break Their bonds in pieces And cast away Their cords from us.' He who sits in the heavens shall laugh; the Lord shall hold them in derision" (Psalm 2:1-4). The nations are full of vain and arrogant pride in their military prowess and power. But God's verdict on their pretensions is that their power is nothing.

The prophet Isaiah rendered the Lord's evaluations of the power of the world's great empires. "Behold, the nations are as a drop in a bucket, and are counted as the small dust on the balance; look, He lifts up the isles as a very little thing...All nations before Him are as nothing, and they are counted by Him less than nothing and worthless" (Isaiah 40:15-17). Today the nations are joining in huge confederacies to bolster their power. Ultimately all of the countries will unite together in a New World Order. The final form of the one world government will arise when the Revived Roman Empire is taken over by the Antichrist, the planet's last dictator.

The Origin of the Nations

Before the Flood there were no nations, languages or tribes. After the devastation of the Flood, Noah's sons and grandsons resettled the Middle East and, ultimately, the rest of the earth. Moses recorded the original genealogy of mankind. "Now this is the genealogy of the sons of Noah: Shem, Ham, and Japheth. And sons were born to them after the flood" (Genesis 10:1). All the tribes and races of the earth can be traced back to these three great divisions. The nations originated from the dozens of sub-tribes that gradually migrated from the Middle East until they found their ultimate place of settlement. Mankind possessed a common language from the time of Adam until the Tower of Babel. "There the Lord confused the language of all the earth; and from there the Lord scattered them abroad over the face of all the earth" (Genesis 11:9). The nation state serves a fundamental purpose in providing a common identity and natural organizing principle for the natural groupings of mankind.

The arrogance of the sinful leaders of the last days will motivate them to rebel against God's coming Messiah. Revelation declares that the nations of the world will bring their armies against Israel and each other in a titanic struggle to determine who shall rule the world. "And they gathered them together to the place called in Hebrew, Armageddon" (Revelation 16:16). When they mobilize the huge armies of their nations, they will march toward the Holy Land to do battle. Despite all the talk of peace and over seven thousand disarmament talks, the armories of the nations contain at least one military weapon for every man, woman and child on earth. The prophetic warning was given by Joel: "Proclaim this among the nations: 'Prepare for war! Wake up the mighty men, let all the men of war draw near, let them come up'" (Joel 3:9). God has set an appointment to judge the nations in the Promised Land where they rejected the Messiah two thousand years ago.

Multitudes in the Valley of Decision

"Let the nations be wakened, and come up to the Valley of Jehoshaphat; for there I will sit to judge all the surrounding nations...Multitudes, multitudes in the valley of decision! For the day of the Lord is near in the valley of decision" (Joel 3:12,14).

The Battle of Armageddon will focus on the enormous valley that extends south for two hundred miles from northern Israel to Jerusalem. It will become "a valley of decision" because the great deciding issue of life and death for the nations will be determined there. Initially the Antichrist will use his ten-nation power base to consolidate his power over the nations until he rules the entire globe. After he is killed he will be resurrected by satanic power at the mid-point of the seven-year tribulation period. "And authority was given him over every tribe, tongue, and nation. And all who dwell on the earth will worship him, whose names have not been written in the Book of Life" (Revelation 13:7-8).

The Battle of Armageddon will commence with a climactic struggle between the forces of the Western nations under the leadership of the Antichrist fighting against the immense armies of the kings of the East. Israel is the natural battleground because of its vital geostrategic position. Whoever controls the Middle East will control the world. Their goal is to destroy each other's armies and Israel. Twenty five centuries ago the prophet Joel recorded his vision of the gathering of the nations for this final conflict. The Lord declared: "I will also gather all nations, and bring them down to the Valley of Jehoshaphat; and I will enter into judgment with them there on account of My people, My heritage Israel" (Joel 3:2). The name Jehoshaphat means "where Jehovah judges."

These armed forces will unleash all of the horrors of the modern weapons of mass destruction. The chemical, biological and nuclear weapons will create devastation beyond anything ever experienced in history. The sophisticated armaments laboratories of the West and Russia have produced doomsday weapons during the last two decades that can devastate whole cities. Particle beam weapons and massive laser weapons can reflect off a satellite's mirrors and destroy entire army battalions. Experiments have proven that weather warfare is possible. Some of my sources have told me that certain weather disasters during the last decade were caused by climactic experiments.

The Battle of Armageddon
The Winepress of the Wrath of God

The armies of the world will gather to destroy Israel but Christ will suddenly descend from His heavenly throne to defeat the forces of evil. "Then the sign of the Son of Man will appear in heaven, and then all the tribes of the earth will mourn, and they will see the Son of Man coming on the clouds of heaven with power and great glory" (Matthew 24:30). After the Rapture and marriage supper of the Lamb, the armies of heaven, robed in white linen, will marshal their forces to conquer the earth with Christ. John saw Christ's ultimate victory in his vision. "And the armies in heaven, clothed in fine linen, white and clean, followed Him on white horses. Now out of His mouth goes a sharp sword, that with it He should strike the nations. And He Himself will rule them with a rod of iron. He Himself treads the winepress of the fierceness and wrath of Almighty God" (Revelation 19:14,15). This image of the treading of the winepress appears frequently in the prophecies of Isaiah and Joel in connection with the ultimate conflict of the ages. The prophet Isaiah described His awesome vision of the Messiah coming in wrath to destroy the huge armies that will attempt to wipe out His Chosen People. "I have trodden the winepress alone" (Isaiah 63:3). The slaughter will be beyond the powers of description as the combined armies of the world meet their fate at the hand of Christ. Although the battle will begin in the north of Israel, the conflict will rage throughout the length and breadth of the Promised Land until it reaches the walls of Jerusalem. "And the winepress was trampled outside the city, and blood came out of the winepress, up to the horses' bridles, for one thousand six hundred furlongs" (Revelation 14:20). The carnage over the whole area will be so awful that men and horses will sink in the bloody mud up "to the horses' bridles."

Once before, the horrific slaughter caused the blood to flow in the streets of Jerusalem. Flavius Josephus described the destruction of Jerusalem by the Roman armies of Titus in his *Wars of the Jews* (6.8.5). He wrote that the Roman soldiers killed all they encountered "and obstructed the very lanes with their dead bodies, and made the whole city run down with blood, to such a degree indeed that the fire of many of the houses was quenched with these men's blood." The Bible does not indicate how many horses will be involved in this final conflict. Revelation 9:16 declares, "Now the number of the army of the horsemen was two hundred million." The "horsemen" in this passage are the Four Horsemen of the Apocalypse who will symbolically lead these armies to their appointment with destiny. The vast majority of the armies will be infantry but there will be some horses used according to the prophets. Interestingly, Russia, China, Pakistan and India still use limited numbers of horses and mules to bring supplies into impassable mountainous terrain.

"So the four angels, who have been prepared for the hour and day and month and year, were released to kill a third of mankind. Now the number of the army of the horsemen was two hundred million" (Revelation 9:15).

Although hundreds of millions of saints will return from heaven at Armageddon, it will be Jesus Christ alone as the Lord of the heavenly hosts who will utterly destroy the Antichrist and False Prophet. The Apostle Paul described the supernatural nature of the death of the Antichrist. "The lawless one will be revealed, whom the Lord will consume with the breath of His mouth and destroy with the brightness of His coming" (2 Thessalonians 2:8). While the Antichrist

201

and False Prophet will be cast into the lake of fire, some surviving remnants of their army will conquer Jerusalem several days later. The prophet Zechariah prophesied that the Lord will save the Jewish people who turn to Him in their final crisis. He described Jerusalem in the hands of the satanically inspired armies of Antichrist. "Jerusalem; the city shall be taken, the houses rifled, and the women ravished. Half of the city shall go into captivity, but the remnant of the people shall not be cut off from the city" (Zechariah 14:2). At the point when all seems lost, Christ will descend on the Mount of Olives, splitting it asunder. He will annihilate those who dare to touch the "apple of His eye," destroying the attacking armies with an incredible plague. "And this shall be the plague with which the Lord will strike all the people who fought against Jerusalem: Their flesh shall dissolve while they stand on their feet, their eyes shall dissolve in their sockets, and their tongues shall dissolve in their mouths" (Zechariah 14:12).

The Golden Gate

One of the most familiar views of Jerusalem includes the famous "sealed" Golden Gate along the eastern wall of the Temple Mount. After descending to the Mount of Olives the Lord will cross the Kidron Valley between the mountain and the city entering through the sealed Eastern Gate into the rebuilt Temple. This Golden Gate, sealed for twelve centuries, will finally open for Jesus Christ, the King of kings. Ezekiel prophesied that "the glory of the Lord came into the temple by way of the gate which faces toward the east" (Ezekiel 43:4). When Christ predicted that Israel would reject its Messiah, He also promised that someday they will acknowledge Him as their King. "You shall not see Me until the time comes when you say, 'Blessed is He who comes in the name of the Lord!'" (Luke 13:35). Jesus, as our great High Priest, will announce the Great Jubilee, the restitution of all things and the cancellation of all debts. He will "proclaim liberty to the captives" and bring in the everlasting kingdom of righteousness. Unlike every earthly empire which flourished and passed away, the Kingdom of Christ will endure forever. The prophet Daniel received a glorious vision of the coming Kingdom of the Messiah. "Then to Him was given dominion and glory and a kingdom, that all peoples, nations, and languages should serve Him. His dominion is an everlasting dominion, which shall not pass away, and His kingdom the one which shall not be destroyed" (Daniel 7:14).

The Judgment of the Nations

"When the Son of Man comes in His glory, and all the holy angels with Him, then He will sit on the throne of His glory. All the nations will be gathered before Him, and He will separate them one from another, as a shepherd divides his sheep from the goats" (Matthew 25:31,32).

In the Bible the symbol of the sheep represents the Gentiles that will provide sanctuary to the Jewish and Gentile believers of the Tribulation period who flee the power of the Antichrist. The goats represent the unrighteous Gentiles that choose to serve the Antichrist and persecute Christ's servants. "And He will set the sheep on His right hand, but the goats on the left" (Matthew 25:33). The right hand stands for righteousness and salvation while the left hand indicates destruction. This judgment will occur in the Valley of Jehoshaphat, the Kidron Valley below the Eastern Gate, following the Battle of Armageddon. It is ironic that Christ will judge the nations in the very spot where He was betrayed in the Garden of Gethsemane.

This judgment is called the Judgment of the Nations but a more correct designation would be the Judgment of the Gentiles. Those judged will be individuals from each nation on earth, not the national governments. Christ's words in Matthew 25:41 can apply only to individuals, not nations. "Then He will also say to those on the left hand, 'Depart from Me, you cursed, into the everlasting fire prepared for the devil and his angels'" (Matthew 25:41). All living Gentiles that survive the horrors of the Tribulation period will appear before the conquering Messiah to give an account of how they treated His servants during the terrible persecution of that time. In the *Apocalypse of Baruch* (72), a non-canonical writing, the writer describes the Judgment of the Nations in which the Messiah will judge individuals on the basis of their treatment of His servants. "Every people which knows not Israel, and has not trodden down the seed of Jacob, he shall live; and this because men of every nation shall be subject to thy people. But all those who ruled over you or knew you, they shall be delivered to the sword."

The purpose of this judgment is to deal justly with the inhabitants of the earth that survive Armageddon. While most of those who reject the Antichrist will be martyred during the Great Tribulation, some will survive. According to the prophecies, perhaps a third of humanity will survive. Thus some two billion or more people, mostly unrepentant sinners, will appear before Christ to be judged. These righteous Gentiles, the "sheep," are not saved because they acted properly toward the Tribulation saints. Rather, they acted kindly towards Christ's servants because they accepted the testimony of Christ during the Tribulation period. These righteous ones will enter the millennial Kingdom of Christ and will inherit all of the blessings of the Kingdom of heaven on earth. These blessed individuals will continue to work, live and have children under the benevolent rule of the Messiah and the saints of the Church. These saved Gentiles and the children of Israel will multiply their generations filling the whole earth with praise.

The Nations in the Millennium

Some Christians believe that nations will disappear after Christ returns to establish His eternal Kingdom. However, the Bible describes the continuation of the nations throughout the millennial Kingdom and Christ's eternal Kingdom on the New Earth. The prophet Zechariah prophesied that the nations and their leaders would come to Jerusalem forever to worship the Messiah. "And it shall come to pass, that every one who is left of all the nations which came against Jerusalem shall even go up from year to year to worship the King, the Lord of hosts, and to keep the Feast of Tabernacles" (Zechariah 14:16).

The New Earth

The nations will flourish throughout eternity in the New Earth. "And the nations of those who are saved shall walk in its light, and the kings of the earth bring their glory and honor into it. Its gates shall not be shut at all by day (there shall be no night there). And they shall bring the glory and the honor of the nations into it" (Revelation 21:24-26). This prophecy indicates that these nations will continue to have "kings" and leaders throughout the millennial Kingdom. Zechariah foretold that the representatives of every nation will come to Jerusalem "from year to year" forever to celebrate the Feast of Tabernacles. The saints of the Church are promised the privilege of ruling and reigning with Christ forever on the restored earth. God promised Abraham that he would have children "as the stars of the heavens." Moses recorded another promise: "And I will make your descendants as the dust of the earth; so that if a man could number the dust of the earth, then your descendants also could be numbered" (Genesis 13:16). The nations, composed of the descendants of these saved Gentiles and Jews, will sanctify the Holy Name of Christ forever.

CHAPTER TWELVE

Israel in the
Valley of Decision

If we wish to understand where we are in the prophetic countdown to Armageddon we must keep our eyes on the nation of Israel. The greatest miracle in history is the survival of the Jewish people against all odds during two thousand years of unremitting persecution. Finally after millennia of exile the captives have returned to Zion in fulfillment of the ancient prophecies of the Bible. God's covenant with His Chosen People continues to be fulfilled in the survival and prosperity of the Jewish people in their Promised Land today. The prophet Joel received a tremendous vision of the final conflict between the nations and Israel at the end of this generation. "Multitudes, multitudes in the valley of decision! For the day of the Lord is near in the valley of decision" (Joel 3:14). As detailed in another chapter, God will bring all of the nations on earth to meet their judgment in the titanic battle of Armageddon.

Although Israel rejected her Messiah, God has not revoked His promise to Abraham and his descendants. "For the gifts and the calling of God are irrevocable" (Romans 11:29). The Lord has not changed His mind concerning His gift of Palestine to Israel. God promised that Abraham's seed should bless the whole world. We have witnessed more fulfillment of prophecy in our lifetime than any other generation in history. The most significant of the prophecies concerns the rebirth of the nation Israel in the land of their forefathers. Beginning with the Balfour Declaration of 1917, the process culminated in Israel's declaration of independence at midnight on May 15, 1948. While over five million Jews now live in Israel, the Arabs are determined to wipe out the memory of the Jewish state. The eyes of the world will increasingly focus on the startling events transpiring in the Middle East as the conflict moves inexorably towards the climactic struggle known as the Battle of Armageddon.

Who Owns the Promised Land?

Around the world political pressure continues to mount on Israel to withdraw from the West Bank, Gaza and East Jerusalem to allow the Palestinian Liberation Organization (PLO) to establish their own state. The irony is that a genuine Palestinian state already exists on the East Bank of the Jordan River. When Britain conquered the Turkish Ottoman Empire at the end of World War I, she allocated five million square miles of Ottoman territory to the local inhabitants. Britain gave 99.8 percent of the conquered land to the Arabs. Only one-fifth of one percent of the land was reserved by Britain to establish a Jewish National Home to allow the Jews of the world to return to their Promised Land after two thousand years of exile. The Balfour Declaration of November 2, 1917, declared that the whole of the British Mandate territory, including both sides of the Jordan River, was to be given to the Jews for their homeland. They were to establish a sovereign Jewish state including a Jewish majority and an Arab minority. The Balfour Declaration became international law when it was confirmed on July 24, 1922, by the League of Nations, the predecessor of the United Nations. The United States and Canada both officially endorsed this arrangement.

However, in response to Arab pressure and British anti-semitism, the United Kingdom reneged on her pledge to the Jews. In 1921 England gave 80 percent of the British Mandate territory to a Saudi Arabian prince named Abdullah, creating the state of Transjordan. Abdullah had previously been offered the kingdom of Iraq, but that proved to be impossible. As a result, he received this new nation carved out of the Jewish National Home. All of the Jewish National Home territory east of the Jordan River was ceded to the Arabs, creating a "Arab Palestinian" state out of what had legally been given to the Jews. Today, over 70 percent of the population of Jordan is Palestinian Arab. Before the 1967 Six Day War, both King Hussein of Jordan and Yassir Arafat of the PLO declared in speeches that "Jordan is Palestine." However, after the Six Day War and the loss of the territories, the PLO insisted for the first time that they wanted to create a second Palestinian Arab state between Jordan and Israel. They also began to claim that Arab Palestinians had lived there in their own state for millennia. Most Palestinians in the West Bank still retain their Jordanian citizenship and passports.

The creation of a second Palestinian state on the West Bank and Gaza would represent a dangerous threat to both Israel and Jordan. The PLO's official charter declares that their non-negotiable goal is the establishment of a Palestinian state occupying the complete territory of both Israel and Jordan. No Jews will be allowed to live in such a state. In illustration of this attitude, today no Jew can live or travel in Saudi Arabia, Iraq or Jordan. Fewer than a thousand older Jews are allowed to live in Egypt, despite the Camp David peace treaty. If the PLO ever succeeded, a small Palestinian state created out of the West Bank and Gaza would not be economically viable. The Palestinian leadership wants this mini-state as a initial stepping stone to a better strategic position from which it will launch a fatal attack on a weakened Israel. The repeated wars, unceasing terrorism and speeches of Arab leaders make it clear that the Jewish population would be totally wiped out if the Arab armies ever succeeded in occupying Israel.

The Peace Talks

For more than a year the Arab states and Israel have negotiated to resolve their differences. Unfortunately, the Middle East Peace Talks seem no closer to a solution than when they started. Initially, it was believed the demise of the Soviet Union as the great adversary to the West might change the dynamics of the Arab-Israeli conflict. Many hoped that new talks would lead to a real peace between these ancient peoples. There are two words for peace in the Arab vocabulary. The true peace we enjoy between Canada and the U.S.A. is one type of "peace." However, in hundreds of speeches, the Palestinians and the Arab nations have made it abundantly clear that their goal in the Middle East Peace talks is a "peace of Saladin." During the Crusades, Saladin, the great Muslim Kurdish general, offered a "peace" treaty to Richard the Lion-Hearted, the English general. However, this was not a true offer of peace, but simply an armed truce which the Muslim armies used to re-arm for their final, successful assault on King Richard's forces. Significantly, the Arabs use this word for an armed truce, not a true peace when they offer Israel "peace for land." Israel is being asked to give up real land in return for a false peace, a mere piece of paper. These "territories" were originally given to Israel by God as part of the Abrahamic Covenant. No other people can truly claim such an unbroken historical link with this land. The Promised Land was settled by the Jews thousands of years ago and ruled by Israel's kings for over fifteen centuries. Since the destruction of Jerusalem in A.D. 70, the Romans, Persians Saudi Arabians, Egyptians and Turks have in turn ruled the land. However, none of those empires ever established a separate country, nor did they ever make Jerusalem a capital. God preserved the Promised Land as a desolate place until the return of the Chosen People in the last hundred years. It is significant that during the following two thousand years, despite continual oppression, a Jewish remnant continued to live in the land as well as in Jerusalem itself. As indicated in my book *MESSIAH*, the Jews have formed the majority of the population of Jerusalem for the last few centuries.

Can Israel Safely Surrender the Territories?

Can Israel, as a militarily strong nation, safely give up the Golan Heights, the West Bank and Gaza to their implacable Arab enemies? Many studies by independent military experts from Britain and the United States concluded that Israel cannot surrender these conquered territories and retain her strategic security. Sir Basil Liddell Hart, the greatest military strategist in this century, strongly recommended that Israel retain every single inch of the territories captured during the 1967 Six Day War. Several detailed studies were completed by the Joint Chiefs of Staff on the orders of President Johnson to determine the minimum territory Israel needed to retain to survive a military invasion by the vastly larger Arab armies. The strong and unanimous recommendation of these military officers was that Israel must retain virtually all of the land it captured when the Arabs invaded their country in the 1967 Six Day War. The only part of the territory that could be safely returned in the event of peace was a portion of the Sinai Peninsula.

The Arab nations always refer to the 1967 war as if Israel launched an unprovoked attack against them. However, the Arab armies launched several acts of war against Israel, including closing the Suez Canal, that forced the Jews to respond to these attempts to destroy them. Following the Yom Kippur War in 1974, Israel agreed to return all of the strategic high ground in the Golan Heights that Syria used in four previous wars to attack northern Israel. Secondly, Israel returned all of the Sinai Peninsula to Egypt in return for a piece of paper, the Camp David Accord. Israel gave up all of the vital strategic depth of the vast Sinai desert while Egypt still refuses to enter into a real peace with Israel. No one doubts that a future Arab invasion of Israel will find the massive Egyptian army attacking from the Sinai territory which Israel relinquished to her.

Today Syria demands that Israel return the rest of the Golan Heights she lost in the last days of the Yom Kippur War. Thousand of young Israelis gave their lives to capture this vital territory that Syria repeatedly used for nineteen years to attack villages in northern Israel. Syria argues that Israel's retention of this small territory is part of a plan to create a "Greater Israel." However, the Golan, though militarily vital, is only 1190 square kilometers in size. This represents a tiny sliver (one-half of one percent) of Syria's 184,030 square kilometers. Syria, the most brutal regime in the Middle East, is more than eight times the size of Israel. The Golan is the high ground militarily dominating the villages of northern Israel. Prior to 1974, Syria created a military fortress on the Golan with underground bunkers and bases. The land slopes down from the present border and represents a difficult terrain for Israel to reconquer, fighting uphill the whole way. If Israel surrenders this, she will have to reconquer it in another bloody war, if she can. The loss of the Golan Heights may mean the difference between survival and defeat in a future war. The Jews remember the tender mercies of Hafez Assad, the president of Syria, who killed twenty thousand of his own innocent men, women and children in the town of Hom in February, 1982, because they belonged to the wrong clan.

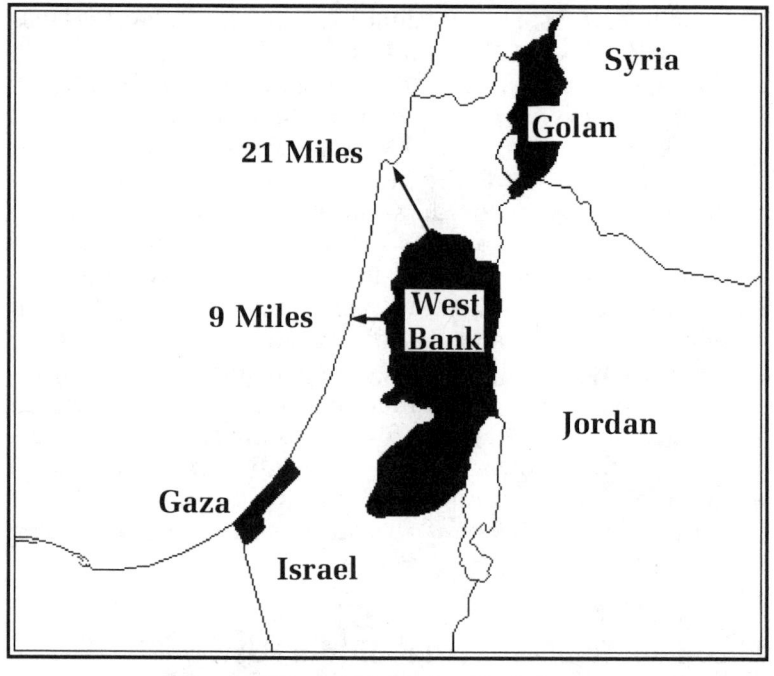

The Military Risk of a PLO State

As my map illustrates, if Israel returns the West Bank to the Arabs, she will be less than nine miles wide in the vital center of the country where 80 percent of her population lives. Relinquishing the West Bank and Gaza would eliminate Israel's strategic depth, leaving her vulnerable to a lightning attack by Arab armor and tanks across its narrow width.

American Policy Toward Israel

We find it fascinating and ominous that the declared policy of all American administrations is that Israel must surrender to her enemies all of the territories captured in 1967. This policy stands in stark contradiction to her own strategic studies that Israel will be at the mercy of overwhelming Arab armies in a future war if she gives up these small but vital territories. In 1988 the United States military completed a critical study, by more than a hundred retired generals and admirals, of the question of Israel's defensible borders. On November 7, 1992, the *Jerusalem Post* reported the text of this study in an article by the retired American colonel, Irving Kett. He was sent to complete a military analysis of Israel's defensible borders for the U.S. Army College in 1974. "Defensible borders are not impregnable borders. Rather, they are borders that give early warning time and provide some strategic depth...Having repelled continued attacks on its population from this territory, and having acquired it in a defensive war in 1967, Israel has no legal, political or moral obligation to relinquish it...Missiles, artillery and aircraft can cause devastation. They cannot occupy. Only infantry and armor can overrun a country -- and those are vulnerable to natural boundaries... With the Arab armies at least four times the size they were 20 years ago, this assessment is even more valid today. To expect that Israel can repeat the miraculous military feat it performed in 1967, when it was attacked from those borders, is to tempt fate."

European Interest in the Middle East

Despite the fact that the best military experts of Israel and the West recommend retaining the territories, the nations of the world are placing enormous pressure on Israel's leaders to give up its strategic depth. The Bible tells us that the leader of a ten-nation European superstate will arise in the last days that will guarantee Israel's security for a period of seven years. For forty-five years, Europe has abandoned the Middle East to the Americans and the Russians. However, in the last few months, the European Community (E.C.) has requested involvement in the ongoing Middle East Peace talks and has asked to co-sponsor them. For the first time, Europe wants to play a significant role in the peace negotiations. Israel and Egypt became associate members of the European Community Economic Zone several years ago. The E.C. is now offering Israel special economic assistance and trade concessions if she will encourage the other nations to allow Europe to become involved in the peace process. These motives and events are setting the stage for the next major fulfillment in Bible prophecy. During the coming War of Gog and Magog against Israel, God will intervene causing the supernatural destruction of the Arab-Russian armies. This will create a military power vacuum allowing the rise of the Antichrist and the ten-nation confederacy. The Antichrist will make a seven-year treaty with Israel guaranteeing her security. However, the prophet Isaiah warned the Jews against this "covenant with death."

Despite his promises to secure their borders and give them peace, the Antichrist will betray the Jews and lead them to disaster. In Daniel 9:27 we read of his false peace treaty. "Then he shall confirm a covenant with many for one week; but in the middle of the week he shall bring an end to sacrifice and offering." Rather than trust in the God who saved them from the exile among the nations, Israel will trust in a man-made treaty of paper. "Therefore hear the word of the Lord, you scornful men, who rule this people who are in Jerusalem, because you have said, 'We have made a covenant with death, and with Sheol [Hell] we are in agreement. When the overflowing scourge passes through, it will not come to us, for we have made lies our refuge, and under falsehood we have hidden ourselves'" (Isaiah 28:14,15). After an initial period of false peace the Antichrist will be revealed as the worst tyrant the world has ever seen. In Revelation 6 the prophet John saw a vision of the Antichrist riding a white horse, in imitation of the Messiah, the Prince of Peace. He carries a bow but no arrow, as he goes out "conquering and to conquer" (Revelation 6:2). This indicates his promises of disarmament and peace are false. God's verdict on this peace treaty is final."Your covenant with death will be annulled, and your agreement with Sheol will not stand; when the overflowing scourge passes through, then you will be trampled down by it" (Isaiah 28:18).

God's Eternal Covenant of the Promised Land

The ultimate question of ownership and sovereignty of the Promised Land relates back to the original Abrahamic Covenant given by God thousands of years ago. A careful

213

study of Israel's right to the land reveals that it is based on God's sovereign covenant. The promise that Israel would return to the land did not depend on their actions, but rather upon God's unchangeable choice. If it were otherwise, Israel would have disappeared and become extinct like all other ancient peoples. The purpose of God does not change. "For the gifts and calling of God are irrevocable" (Romans 11:29). The Scriptures declare that God chose Israel because of His sovereign choice, not because of their size, significance or actions. "For you are a holy people to the Lord your God; the Lord your God has chosen you to be a people for Himself, a special treasure above all the peoples on the face of the earth" (Deuteronomy 7:6). While some will acknowledge that God originally chose Israel, they suggest that Israel's promises and covenants were rescinded when Christ was rejected two thousand years ago. Some writers believe that the Church has somehow replaced Israel in God's plans to redeem the earth. They allegorize God's promises to Israel and apply them spiritually to the Church. This position is totally at odds with the clear and repeated promises and covenants of God. After referring to His creation of the sun, moon and stars to provide day and night, the Lord declared, "'If those ordinances depart from before Me,' says the Lord, 'then the seed of Israel shall also cease from being a nation before Me forever.' Thus says the Lord: 'If heaven above can be measured, and the foundations of the earth searched out beneath, I will also cast off all the seed of Israel for all that they have done,' says the Lord" (Jeremiah 31:36,37).

God has promised to preserve the nation of Israel forever in the Holy Land where the ancient prophets walked. The prophet Isaiah declared that Israel's seed will remain forever. "For as the new heavens and the new earth which I will make shall remain before Me," says the Lord, "so shall your descendants and your name remain" (Isaiah 66:22). Jesus promised that the generation that saw the rebirth of Israel will live to witness the coming of the Son of Man. King David also prophesied that the generation that would live to see Israel rebuilt will also see God "appear in His glory." "You will arise and have mercy on Zion; For the time to favor her, Yes, the set time, has come... For the Lord shall build up Zion; He shall appear in His glory" (Psalm 102:13,16).

In Search of the Ten Lost Tribes of Israel

Two thousand and seven hundred years ago the ten tribes of Israel were taken captive by their enemies to northern Assyria. Although God promised Abraham that all his children would inherit the Promised Land, these ten tribes and their innumerable descendants never returned from the provinces of Assyria where they were taken in captivity in 721 B.C. These tribes of Israel, scattered to the winds, will someday return to join their brothers from Judah and become a united nation in their ancient homeland. God originally promised Abraham that He would create a great nation through Isaac, his miraculously conceived son. Later, Isaac, the "seed of promise," had a son named Jacob. God changed his name from Jacob to "Israel." The Lord promised him, "'Your name is Jacob; your name shall not be called Jacob anymore, but Israel shall be your name.' So He called his name Israel" (Genesis 35:10). The name Israel means, "Prince with God." Ultimately Jacob fathered twelve sons from whom came the twelve tribes of Israel. Ten of these tribes are today called the "Ten Lost Tribes of Israel" because they have disappeared from history.

What happened to the ten lost tribes of Israel? Do they still exist in some forgotten part of the world? Or, are they just a legend from the distant past? Do they still have a role to play in the prophecies that will be fulfilled in the last days according to the Bible? One of the great mysteries of the Bible is the location and future role of the ten lost tribes of Israel. Somehow, all twelve of the tribes, representing the whole nation of Israel, will be restored to the Promised Land in fulfillment of the Bible's prophecies. An anticipation of this restoration is provided by the fact that sacrifices were offered for the twelve tribes of Israel when the Jewish exiles returned from Babylon (Ezra 6:16,17 and 8:35).

One night after Jacob left his father Isaac, he slept at a place called Bethel (House of God). The Lord gave him an amazing vision of a ladder reaching from earth to heaven with angels ascending and descending on it. "And behold, the Lord stood above it and said: 'I am the Lord God of Abraham your father and the God of Isaac; the land on which you lie I will give to you and your descendants. Also your descendants shall be as the dust of the earth; you shall spread abroad to the west and the east, to the north and the south; and in you and in your seed all the families of the earth shall be blessed. Behold, I am with you and will keep you wherever you go, and will bring you back to this land; for I will not leave you until I have done what I have spoken to you'" (Genesis 28:13-15).

God made an unbreakable and unconditional covenant with Jacob and his descendants. It did not depend on Israel's subsequent obedience for its prophesied fulfillment. Later, when Jacob obeyed the command of God and journeyed to Egypt to escape the serious famine in Canaan the Lord reaffirmed the promise to Jacob's descendants. "And He said, 'I am God, the God of your father; do not fear to go down to Egypt, for I will make of you a great nation there. I will go down with you to Egypt, and I will also surely bring you up again; and Joseph will put his hand on your eyes'" (Genesis 46:3,4). In this promise God affirmed that He would fulfill His covenant to create a great nation out of Jacob's seed. The prophecy of Genesis 49:1-28 lists the twelve sons of Jacob whose descendants formed the twelve tribes of the future nation that were to partake of the covenant promises of God.

The Twelve Sons and Twelve Tribes of Israel

1.	Reuben	7.	Dan
2.	Simeon	8.	Gad
3.	Levi	9.	Asher
4.	Judah	10.	Naphtali
5.	Zebulun	11.	Joseph
6.	Issachar	12.	Benjamin

Jacob's final prophecy about the future of his twelve sons and their tribes is recorded in Genesis 49:1-28. In this extensive prophecy given just before he died Jacob was inspired to describe the nature of his sons, their individual characteristics and their prophetic future. After he completed his prophecy, the Bible records the statement "All these are the twelve tribes of Israel." The subsequent history of Israel's captivity in Egypt, the forty years in the Wilderness, the conquest of the Holy Land and the establishment of the monarchy in Jerusalem involved all twelve of the tribes of Israel.

Israel Shall Dwell Alone

The pagan prophet Balaam prophesied about the unique nature of the tribes of Israel. Despite the Moabite King Balak's order to curse Israel, God forced Balaam to prophesy as follows: "How shall I curse whom God has not cursed? And how shall I denounce whom the Lord has not denounced? For from the top of the rocks I see him, and from the hills I behold him; There! A people dwelling alone, not reckoning itself among the nations. Who can count the dust of Jacob, or number one-fourth of Israel?" (Numbers 23:8-10).

The Division Between Judah and Israel

King Solomon ruled the twelve tribes of the united kingdom of Israel for forty years. It was a golden age of trade, prosperity and peace as Israel expanded its borders from Egypt to the Euphrates River. Solomon died after building the beautiful Temple in Jerusalem to house the Ark of the Covenant. The glorious united Kingdom of Israel died with its great king. The nation of Israel was violently split into two nations that have never yet been reconciled. God warned Solomon that he would ultimately lose the united kingdom of Israel because of his persistent idolatry against God. "So the Lord became angry with Solomon, because his heart had turned from the Lord God of Israel, who had appeared to him twice, and had commanded him concerning this thing, that he should not go after other gods; but he did not keep what the Lord had commanded" (1 Kings. 11:9,10). As a result of

King Solomon's arrogant idolatry, God warned, "I will surely tear the kingdom away from you and give it to your servant" (v. 11). However, God promised He would delay the dissolution of the nation until after the death of King Solomon, because of His love of Solomon's father, King David.

After the death of King Solomon, his son, King Rehoboam, arrogantly tried to increase his dictatorial rule with huge taxes and manpower levies. The ten northern tribes rebelled against this harsh authoritarianism and gave their allegiance to a man named Jeroboam, making him their king. The Scriptures declare, "So Israel [the ten tribes] has been in rebellion against the house of David to this day" (I Kings 12:19). The two southern tribes, Judah and Benjamin, with their tribal lands close to Jerusalem, remained loyal to King Solomon's descendants due to their close family ties. These two tribes retained Jerusalem as the capital of their reduced kingdom. The ten northern tribes called themselves Israel and made Samaria their capital. A continuous series of wars, raids and political maneuvering between the two rival kingdoms continued for the next three centuries. However, the sacred Temple in Jerusalem in the area of Judah remained a potent attraction for the true lovers of God among the ten tribes. As a result, the leadership of the ten tribes of Israel established an alternative temple in Samaria to encourage their people to ignore God's command to worship in Jerusalem on the three great annual festivals. They set up the golden calves in Dan and Bethel to prevent their people from traveling south to Judah to worship in the true Temple in Jerusalem.

The Ten Tribes of the Northern Kingdom of Israel

1.	Reuben	6.	Dan
2.	Simeon	7.	Gad
3.	Levi	8.	Asher
4.	Zebulun	9.	Naphtali
5.	Issachar	10.	Joseph

The history of Israel after the division of the kingdom is one of tragedy and rebellion against God. Centuries of religious apostasy and a long series of evil kings followed. When God raised up a series of prophets to warn Israel to turn from their sins, Israel persisted in rebellion against God. They sought protection in military alliances with Egypt and Assyria rather than relying on God's Divine protection.

The Assyrian Captivity of the Ten Tribes of Israel

"And it came to pass in the fourth year of king Hezekiah, which was the seventh year of Hoshea son of Elah king of Israel, that Shalmaneser king of Assyria came up against Samaria, and besieged it. And at the end of three years they took it: even in the sixth year of Hezekiah, that is the ninth year of Hoshea king of Israel, Samaria was taken. And the king of Assyria did carry away Israel unto Assyria, and put them in Halah and in Habor by the river of Gozan, and in the cities of the Medes" (2 Kings 18:9-11).

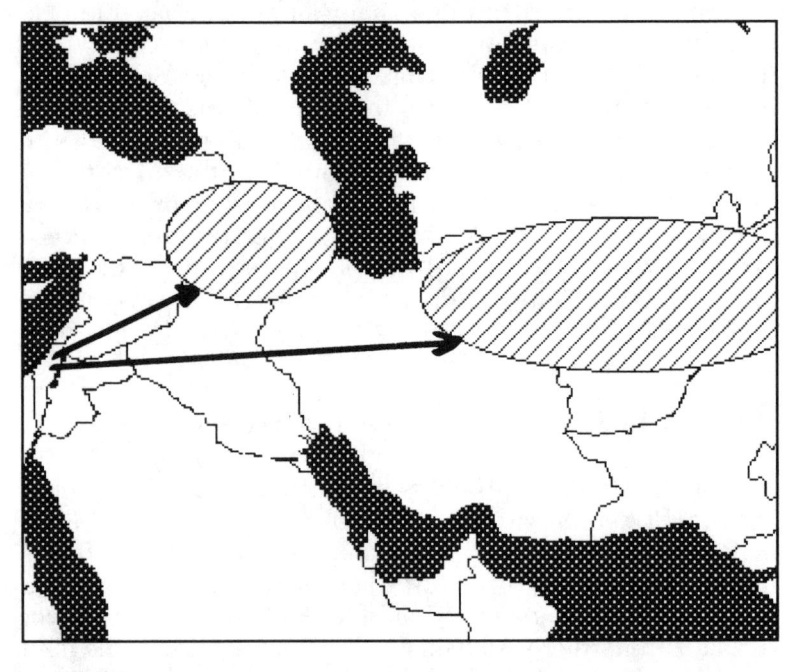

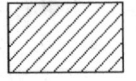 **The Ten Tribes of Israel Taken To Assyria**

The Assyrian Captivity

Finally, after centuries of pagan worship, violence and open idolatry, God sent the powerful army of Assyria to attack the unrepentant nation of Northern Israel. Initially, the enemy was turned back. The tribes of Israel east of the Jordan River, Reuben, Gad and the half-tribe of Manasseh were taken captive to Assyria. However, two decades later, in 721 B.C., the armies of Assyria successfully completed a three-year siege of Israel's capital, Samaria. King Sargon captured King Hosea and the entire nation of Northern Israel. Then they took 90 percent of Israel's population back to northern Assyria as captives in chains. Later, the remaining tribes west of the Jordan River were taken as slaves. The Assyrians replaced the original population of the conquered territory of Israel with the Samaritans, another captive race they moved from the northern part of their far flung empire. The policy was intended to make sure that the new inhabitants would have no motivation to rebel against the Assyrian Empire. Joseph Stalin used the same policy after World War II to transfer millions of Lithuanians, Latvians and Estonians from their conquered Baltic nations to Soviet Siberia. Then Stalin replaced them with millions of immigrant Russians. Israelite captives from the ten tribes were settled in the areas to the north of ancient Nineveh and Babylon (in present day northern Iraq and Iran). Gradually, over the years, these Israelites settled as colonists throughout northern Mesopotamia. They became merchants, farmers and tradesmen.

Where Did Assyria Exile the Ten Tribes ?

The Israelite captives were settled into the area the ancient Greeks called "Adiabene." This area was depopulated during the earlier conquests of Assyria. It lies north-east of Nineveh; south-east of Lake Van covering present-day northern Iraq, Iran and Afghanistan. The River Gozan is in northern Afghanistan. This large area, in the land north of ancient Assyria, was the major location for the settlement of the Israelite captives. It may well have ultimately extended to Georgia, Azerbaijan and possibly Kashmir on the present Indian-Pakistan border. The

Scriptures tell us that a second group of Jewish captives, taken by Nebuchadnezzar to Babylon in 606 B.C. may also have migrated northward into Afghanistan, Kurdistan and Khazastan in central Asia during the following centuries. In Flavius Josephus' *Antiquities of the Jews* (11.5.2.133) he described the location of the ten tribes as follows: "The entire body of the people of Israel remained in that country [Persia]; wherefore there are but two tribes in Asia and Europe subject to the Romans, while the ten tribes are beyond Euphrates till now, and are an immense multitude, and not to be estimated by numbers."

The ancient traditions of the Jews as recorded by Ginzberg's *Legends of the Jews* declare that the king of Assyria first invaded Israel in 747 B.C. and "captured the golden calf at Dan" that the Israelites worshipped. The Assyrians then "led the tribes on east side of the Jordan away into exile." In a second invasion in 721 B.C., "The Assyrians, in the reign of Hoshea, carried off the second golden calf together with the tribes of Asher, Issachar, Zebulun and Naphtali, leaving but one-eighth of the Israelites in their own land."

The Captivity of Judah

Many of the rabbis describe the division of the united kingdom of King David and Solomon into the two kingdoms of Judah and Israel as the greatest disaster in the long history of the Chosen People. One rabbi wrote, "With the exile of the ten tribes, real joy passed out of existence." Despite the continued violent attacks by Assyria against Judah, the Lord intervened to preserve and protect Jerusalem and the Southern Kingdom against the devastation delivered on Israel. While Judah's kings indulged in sinful, immoral behavior, the Southern Kingdom had not yet fallen to the terrible level of evil idolatry that prevailed in the Northern Kingdom of Israel. Twenty years later, when the Assyrian King Sennacherib attacked Jerusalem and Judah in 701 B.C., God miraculously saved the Jews by destroying the Assyrian armies with a supernatural pestilence.

The newly ascendant Babylonian Empire successfully

conquered Assyria 113 years after the destruction of northern Israel. Babylon was a province of the Assyrian Empire but it succeeded in defeating the demoralized Assyrian army in 608 B.C. However, the idolatry and immorality of Judah mounted up until God sent the brilliant Babylonian Prince Nebuchadnezzar and his armies to invade the Southern Kingdom of Judah. In 606 B.C. he conquered the city of Jerusalem. During a series of conquests, Nebuchadnezzar took huge numbers of Jewish captives back to Babylon, including the prophets Daniel and Ezekiel. God commanded Israel to obey the Babylonians because He had transferred the sovereignty of the earth to the Gentiles until the completion of the Times of the Gentiles at the return of Christ. The Jewish King Zedekiah rebelled against this command of God and against Babylon. Finally, after a brutal siege, the armies of Babylon destroyed the city of Jerusalem and the beautiful Temple on the ninth day of Av in 587 B.C.

The Captives of Judah Returned From Babylon

When the seventy-year captivity in Babylon ended in 536 B.C. (prophesied in Jeremiah 25:11), the new Media-Persian conqueror, King Cyrus, issued a decree allowing the Jews to return in freedom to their homeland (Ezra 1:1,2). However, only forty-two thousand of the Jews chose to return home to Jerusalem and Judah in response to this decree. Scholars estimate that less than 5 percent of the Jewish captives from the Southern Kingdom of Judah returned from Babylon in 536 B.C. By the time of Christ the descendants of these people were numbered in the millions. Some scholars estimate that as many as ten million descendants of the captives lived in Mesopotamia, the same number as lived throughout the Roman Empire. This well established community produced the Babylonian Talmud during a five hundred year period from 100 B.C. to approximately A.D. 400.

Of the millions from the ten tribes of Israel taken captive to the same area by Assyria in 721 B.C., it is estimated that less than 1 percent of these captives from Israel returned. By 536 B.C. the northern Israelites had been settlers in Mesopotamia for four generations (185 years). Their close ties to the Holy Land had been broken. The vast majority of the Israelites from the ten tribes remained in the Babylonian Empire and were lost to history. Those Jews who returned from Babylon contained very few individuals from each of the other ten tribes of Israel, according to the books of Ezra and Nehemiah. The great majority of the 42,700 Jews returning from Babylon were from the tribes of Judah and Benjamin with a small scattering of Levites.

The Jews from Judah and Benjamin who returned from Babylon rebuilt their country over a period of five centuries until their people fell again into terrible apostasy from God's laws. The Roman armies attacked and destroyed Jerusalem and the Temple on the ninth day of Av, A.D. 70, the same day of the year that the Babylonians destroyed Solomon's Temple some 656 years earlier. This tragic anniversary has become known as *Tisha Be-Av*, a fast of mourning for the Jews.

In my book *Armageddon - Appointment With Destiny* I examined the fascinating phenomenon of biblical anniversaries. On this exact day, the ninth of Av (in August) Israel has suffered eight terrible national tragedies:

1. The Exodus generation was condemned to 40 years in the wilderness when the 12 spies returned

2. The burning of Solomon's Temple in 587 B.C.

3. The burning of the Second Temple in A.D. 70

4. The Romans plowed Jerusalem with salt to eradicate its memory in A.D. 71

5. The destruction of 1.5 million Jews by the Romans in A.D. 135;

6. The expulsion of Jews from England in 1290;

7. The expulsion of Jews from Spain in 1492

8. The killing of 100,000 Jews in eastern Russia as World War I began in 1914

For the last three and a half thousand years every major disaster for the Jews from the Exodus to World War I occurred on this exact day of the year, the ninth day of Av. The mathematical probability of this occurring by chance is one chance in 863 zillion (863,078,009,300,000,000). Forty events in the history of Israel have occurred on exact anniversaries of their divinely ordained festivals. The hand of God is revealed in this strange phenomenon of biblical anniversaries.

Once again the Jews were dispersed as exiles among the nations. This time the national captivity of the Jews was to last almost two thousand years, ending on midnight, May 15, 1948, with the rebirth of the state of Israel. In my book *Armageddon - Appointment With Destiny* I showed how the prophet Ezekiel predicted the rebirth of Israel to the precise day. But the question remains: What happened to the ten tribes of Israel that never returned from Central Asia? Do they still exist? Or, have they simply disappeared through intermarrying and assimilation? Do they have a role to play in the biblical prophecies that will be fulfilled in the last days?

Old Testament Prophecies About the Ten Tribes

The prophecies of the Bible clearly declare that all of the twelve tribes will survive and play their significant roles in the events of the last days. Virtually every major Old Testament prophet received a vision concerning the ultimate return of the ten tribes of Israel.

Ezekiel and the Division of Land to the Twelve Tribes

The ultimate restoration and reconciliation of the ten tribes of Israel and the two tribes of Judah was prophesied by the prophet Ezekiel while he was a captive in Babylon. "Say to them, 'Thus says the Lord God: "Surely I will take the stick of Joseph, which is in the hand of Ephraim, and the tribes of Israel, his companions; and I will join them with it, with the stick of Judah, and make them one stick, and they will be one in My hand." And the sticks on which you write will be in your hand before their eyes. Then say to them, 'Thus says the Lord God: "Surely I will take the children of Israel from among the nations, wherever they have gone, and will gather them from every side and bring them into their own land; and I will make them one nation in the land, on the mountains of Israel; and one king shall be king over them all; they shall no longer be two nations, nor shall they ever be divided into two kingdoms again""" (Ezekiel 37:19-22). In this prophecy, God clearly promised that He would restore the whole nation from death in "the valley of dry bones." Yet God also prophesied that He would restore the ten lost tribes of Israel in the last days and unite them with the two tribes of Judah forever. For twenty-five centuries this prophecy has remained unfulfilled.

The prophet Ezekiel also declared that God will allocate the land of Israel between the twelve tribes after the Messiah appears. He provided a detailed description of the allotment of the land as follows: "Thus says the Lord God: 'These are the [borders] by which you shall divide the land as an inheritance among the twelve tribes of Israel'" (Ezekiel 47:13). How could the land be divided among the twelve tribes unless the ten tribes return to take their allotted place in the final division of the land during the millennial Kingdom. "Now these are the names of the tribes:...there shall be one portion for Dan...one portion for Asher...one portion for Naphtali...one portion for Manasseh...one portion for Ephraim...one portion for Reuben...one portion for Judah...Benjamin shall have one portion...Simeon shall have one portion...Issachar shall have one portion...Zebulun shall have one portion...Gad shall have one portion" (Ezekiel 48:1-27). Since God's promises are unbreakable, He will somehow preserve the ten tribes until He will reveal and restore them to the Holy Land in the final days.

Dan
Asher
Naphtali
Manasseh
Ephraim
Reuben
Judah
The Holy Portion for the Prince
Benjamin
Simeon
Issachar
Zebulun
Gad

The Tribal Division in the Millennium

Jeremiah

Another prophecy about the restoration of the ten tribes of Israel is found in the words of the prophet Jeremiah. In his description of the coming kingdom of the Messiah he declared, "At that time Jerusalem shall be called The Throne of the Lord, and all the nations shall be gathered to it, to the name of the Lord, to Jerusalem; they shall walk no more after the stubbornness of their evil heart. In those days the house of Judah shall walk with the house of Israel, and they shall come together out of the land of the north to the land that I have given as an inheritance to your fathers" (Jeremiah 3:17,18). The prophet Jeremiah foresaw the future restoration of all twelve of the tribes, including "the house of Judah" and "the house of Israel." Significantly, he predicts that they will both come out of "the land of the north."

Isaiah

The prophet Isaiah also saw a vision of the final restoration of the twelve tribes together. In his prophecy of Israel's final return to the Holy Land, he declared, "You will be gathered one by one, O you children of Israel. So it shall be in that day, that the great trumpet will be blown; they will come, who are about to perish in the land of Assyria, and they who are outcasts in the land of Egypt, and shall worship the Lord in the holy mount at Jerusalem" (Isaiah 27:12,13). In another prophecy he wrote, "He will set up a banner for the nations, and will assemble the outcasts of Israel, and gather together the dispersed of Judah from the four corners of the earth" (Isaiah 11:12). The prophet clearly differentiates in this prophecy between two different groups, the "outcasts of Israel" and the "dispersed of Judah." He also prophesied about the identity of the ten missing tribes when he declared, "Doubtless You are our Father, though Abraham was ignorant of us, and Israel does not acknowledge us. You, O Lord, are our Father; our Redeemer from Everlasting is Your name. O Lord, why have You made us stray from Your ways, and hardened our heart from Your fear? Return for Your servants' sake, the tribes of Your inheritance. Your holy people have possessed it but a little while; our adversaries have trodden down Your sanctuary. We have become like those of old, over whom You never ruled, those who were never called by Your name" (Isaiah 63:16-19). This remarkable prophecy may refer to the lost tribes of Israel. Consider these strange phrases: "Israel does not acknowledge us," "the tribes of Your inheritance," and "those who were never called by Your name." Could these veiled messages refer to the missing tribes?

Zechariah

The prophet Zechariah also foretold the return of the tribes to join their brothers in the Holy Land. "I will strengthen the house of Judah, and I will save the house of Joseph. I will bring them back, because I have mercy on them...I will sow them among the peoples, and they shall remember Me in far countries; they shall live, together with their children, and they shall return. I will also bring them back from the land of Egypt, and gather them from Assyria" (Zechariah 10:6,9,10). This extraordinary prophecy actually declares that the Lord will "gather them from Assyria," the very place where they were taken thousands of years ago. These Old Testament prophecies reveal that the ten tribes must still exist. Somehow, God will supernaturally identify the tribal identities of these Israelites at the appropriate time.

New Testament Testimonies About the Ten Tribes

Is there any direct evidence from the testimony of the New Testament that the ten tribes continued a separate existence in the centuries after their initial captivity?

The book of Acts

In the book of Acts, God addressed a promise to the twelve tribes of Israel which affirms that the ten tribes still exist. "And now I stand and am judged for the hope of the promise made by God to our fathers: To this promise our twelve tribes, earnestly serving God night and day, hope to attain" (Acts 26:6-7). If these tribes still existed as separate entities during the middle of the first century, over seven hundred and fifty years after the Assyrian Captivity, then God must still preserve them somewhere for an ultimate restoration in the last days.

The Epistle of James

In the Epistle of James, the Apostle begins his letter with these words: "James, a servant of God and of the Lord Jesus Christ, to the twelve tribes which are scattered abroad: greetings" (James 1:1). This salutation by James, the brother of Christ, was inspired by the Holy Spirit. Therefore, the ten tribes still existed in the decades following the resurrection of our Lord.

The Book of Revelation

In addition, the prophet John, in his book of Revelation, prophesied that God would seal 144 thousand Jews for divine protection during the terrible period of the Great Tribulation. He specifically named the twelve tribes of Israel, including the ten lost tribes. John declared, "And I heard the number of those who were sealed. One hundred and forty-four thousand of all the tribes of the children of Israel were sealed: of the tribe of Judah twelve thousand were sealed; of the tribe of Reuben twelve thousand were sealed; of the tribe of Gad twelve thousand were sealed; of the tribe of Asher twelve thousand were sealed; of the tribe of Naphtali twelve thousand were sealed; of the tribe of Manasseh twelve thousand were sealed; of the tribe of Simeon twelve thousand were sealed; of the tribe of Levi twelve thousand were sealed; of the tribe of Issachar twelve thousand were sealed; of the tribe of Zebulun twelve thousand were sealed; of the tribe of Joseph twelve thousand were sealed; of the tribe of Benjamin twelve thousand were sealed" (Revelation 7:4-8). John specifically foretells that each of the twelve tribes will be sealed, including naming the ten lost tribes. As mentioned earlier, the prophet Ezekiel also predicted that the ten tribes will receive their allotted inheritance during the tribal division of the land when the Messiah establishes His kingdom. We must conclude from these various prophecies that God has preserved these ten tribes over the last twenty-seven centuries until He will return them to the Promised Land in the last days.

Various Theories

If the ten lost tribes still exist as the Bible's prophecies affirm, then where have they been during the last several thousand years? Various cults and odd religious groups have tried to identify these lost tribes as (1) the British-Israelite movement, or (2) the American Indian tribes, or other equally fanciful guesses. The evidence offered by these cults for identifying the ten tribes with these groups is totally without scholarly foundation. There is no historical evidence that credibly connects the lost tribes with either Britain or the American Indians. The prophet Hosea declared: "For the children of Israel shall abide many days without king or prince, without sacrifice or sacred pillar, without ephod or teraphim. Afterward the children of Israel shall return, seek the Lord their God and David their king, and fear the Lord and His goodness in the latter days" (Hosea 3:4,5). The Jewish *Targums*, or paraphrases, on this prophecy interpret Hosea's words "David their king" as referring to the "Messiah, the Son of David." In the Middle Ages a famous Jewish commentator, Rabbi David Kimchi, wrote about Hosea's prophecy and his people Israel: "And these are the days of our present captivity, for we have neither king nor prince of Israel, but are under the rule of the nations, even under the rule of their kings and their princes." This prediction that Israel will "abide many days without king or prince" positively excludes Britain and the Anglo-Saxons because they were ruled for more than a thousand years by kings and princes.

In addition, the British Israel position is impossible because they existed for thousands of years without the distinguishing mark of circumcision. The Word of God is clear that those of Israel who refuse circumcision are removed forever from God's Chosen People. When God first commanded Abraham to circumcise all Israelite males He declared that this mark was an essential part of God's covenant with Israel. Without circumcision, they would be "cut off" from the covenant relationship with the Lord. "He who is born in your house and he who is bought with your money must be circumcised, and My covenant shall be in your flesh for an everlasting covenant. And the uncircumcised male child, who is not circumcised in the flesh of his foreskin, that person shall be cut off from his people; he has broken My covenant" (Genesis 17:13,14). The only groups who could possibly belong to the missing ten tribes must be circumcised. This biblical requirement for circumcision eliminates the American Indians and the other possibilities suggested by cult groups over the years.

Many Bible scholars claim that the ten lost tribes do not exist at all. They believe that the tribes of Israelites intermarried with the pagans in the surrounding area during the succeeding years after their exile to Assyria. These scholars believe the ten tribes must have been assimilated and subsequently disappeared from history. Others believe that some of the ten tribes joined with the forty-two thousand exiles from the tribes of Judah and Benjamin that returned to Jerusalem under Cyrus's decree in 536 B.C. They believe that this "re-absorbtion" of a few members of the ten tribes into the two tribes eliminated the existence of the ten tribes of Israel as a distinct entity. However, these opinions are contradicted by the inspired declarations in the first century books of James and Acts that the twelve tribes still existed hundreds of years later as distinct entities. Additionally, Jeremiah, Ezekiel, Isaiah and Revelation tell us that all twelve tribes still have a role to play in the prophesied events leading to the coming of the Messiah.

Evidence from the Jewish Talmud

The Jewish rabbis often speculated about the fate of the ten tribes. The *Jerusalem Sanhedrin* (10) states, "One part of Israel [the northern ten tribes] was exiled beyond the river Sambation, one part to Daphne near Antiochia, and the third part was covered by a cloud [lost]. When the time of redemption will come, all the exiles from the three diasporas will return." Some rabbis wrote about the ten tribes living beyond the River Sambation, a mysterious river said to exist north of ancient Assyria (in Afghanistan). Strong differences of opinion appear in the Talmud about the future role of the ten lost tribes. Rabbi Akiba (A.D. 135) taught that "the ten tribes will not return to Palestine for it is said 'cast them into another land.'" However, most of the other rabbis, including Rabbi Eliezer, disagreed with Rabbi Akiba and declared that they would ultimately return, "Just as the day darkens and then becomes light again, so the Ten Tribes -- even as it went dark for them, so will it become light for them."

Jewish Apocalyptic Evidence

Jewish apocalyptic writing, including the *Tobit* and the *Testament of the Twelve Patriarchs,* indicate that the hope for the ultimate return of the lost tribes of Israel and the salvation of "all Israel" continued for many centuries. The *Fourth Book of Ezra* records a somewhat mystical view of the ten tribes. "These are the ten tribes which were led away from their own land into captivity in the days of King Hoshea whom Shalmaneser the king of the Assyrians led captive; he took them across the river, and they were taken into another land. But they formed this plan for themselves, that they would leave the multitude of the nations and go to a more distant region, where mankind had never lived, that there they might keep their statutes which they had not kept in their own land...that country is called Arzareth. Then they dwelt there until the last times; and now, when they are about to come again..." (The *Fourth Book of Ezra* 13:40-47).

Flavius Josephus

The great Jewish historian, Flavius Josephus, in his *Antiquities of the Jews*, described the ten tribes as still existing as a separate people during his lifetime (A.D. 37 to 100). Writing about the decree of Cyrus to allow the Jews to return to Jerusalem, he said, "When these Jews had understood what piety the king had towards God, and what kindness he had for Esdras, they were all greatly pleased; nay, many of them took all their effects with them, and came to Babylon, as very desirous of going down to Jerusalem; but then the entire body of the people of Israel remained in that country; wherefore there are but two tribes in Asia and Europe subject to the Romans, while the ten tribes are beyond Euphrates till now, and are an immense multitude, and not to be estimated by numbers" (11.5.2.132-133). In another book Josephus describes the speech of King Agrippa that acknowledged the existence of the ten tribes located in northern Persia. "All that are under the habitable earth are (under the power of) Romans; unless any of you extend his hopes as far as beyond the Euphrates, and suppose that those of your own nation that dwell in Adiabene will come to your assistance" (*Wars of the Jews* 2.16.4.388).

Jerome

The respected Christian writer Jerome, who translated the Bible into Latin in the fifth century after Christ, wrote about the existence of the ten tribes of Israel. "Unto this day the ten tribes are subject to the kings of Persians, nor has their captivity ever been loosed" (*Notes on Hosea* 6.7). On page 80 he wrote, "The ten tribes inhabit at this day the cities and mountains of the Medes."

The Black Jews of Ethiopia

Despite the tremendous persecution against the tribes of Israel over many centuries by a series of pagan empires, God's Chosen People were never destroyed. Though many Jews were forced to convert to Islam or Christianity, these Jews often secretly retained their faith and their identity. There are tens of thousand of Black Jews in Ethiopia whose parents converted to Catholicism in the last century to avoid persecution and discrimination. Even in today's Commonwealth of Independent States, there are many former Soviet citizens, whose Jewish parents secretly hid their children's Jewish identity to minimize discrimination. In my book, *Armageddon - Appointment With Destiny*, I wrote about the tens of thousands of Black Jews, the Falashas, who had lived in Ethiopia, separated from their brethren, for over three thousand years. My research, including interviews with an Ethiopian prince, convinced me that a group of Jews travelled to Ethiopia in the days of King Solomon around 1000 B.C. with the Ark of the Covenant. Some people expressed reservations about my material on this Jewish remnant in Ethiopia because it was not widely known at that time. However, when over 55 thousand Black Jews miraculously flew home to Israel, this information became universally accepted. This return of the Jews from the south is a significant fulfillment of end time prophecy.

Since my research came out on the Ethiopians and the possible location of the lost Ark of the Covenant, several new books by secular journalists have come to the same conclusion that the Ark has been guarded in an underground Temple in northern Ethiopia for the last three thousand years. When European Jews discovered these Ethiopian Falashas during the last century, they were astonished to find that these Jews knew nothing about the Talmud or rabbis. Additionally, while they celebrated all the ancient festivals from the book of Leviticus, the Ethiopian Jews had never heard of the festival of Purim. The Talmud and rabbinic Judaism were created between 200 B.C. and A.D. 400 . The festival of Purim was initiated five centuries before Christ. These Black Jews of Ethiopia were totally unaware of these practices because they had been separated from Israel centuries before the introduction of rabbis, the Talmud or Purim. The existence and rediscovery of a large group of Ethiopian Jews, cut off and forgotten for thousands of years, strongly suggests that the ten lost tribes could also still exist in some part of Asia.

Lost Groups of Jews in India and Saudi Arabia

There are also groups of black Jews near Bombay, India, that trace their ancestry back before the Christian era. They call themselves *Ben-i-Israel* -- "the House of Israel." There are dozens of reports of ancient Jewish settlements in the trading ports along the coast of India. Many of the Jews of Yemen, at the southern tip of Saudi Arabia, claim that their community has lived there from the time of the Assyrian Captivity in 721 B.C. Deep in the "Empty Quarter" of Saudi Arabia, north of Yemen, explorers located a tribe of Jews in the last century who claim descent from the ancient clan of Rechabites. The prophet Jeremiah described God's promise that this tribal clan would continue forever. The Rechabites were descended from Jonadab who refuse to partake of any strong drink. "Therefore thus says the Lord of hosts, the God of Israel: Jonadab the son of Rechab shall not lack a man to stand before Me forever" (Jeremiah 35:19). An explorer named Wolff recorded his unique experiences with this desert tribe of many thousand Arabian Jews in *Smith's Dictionary*. They live like the nomadic Bedouins among whom they dwell. These Rechabites claimed an unbroken descent from their ancestor Jonadab. Some state that other Jews from the tribe of Dan also survive in the deep deserts of that desolate area that remains off-limits to this day. Due to Saudi Arabian government restrictions, almost no one from the West has explored the Empty Quarter for the last eighty years.

The Jews of Ancient China

The writer John Fraser, in his book *The Conquering Jew*, tells us of the Jewish synagogue discovered in Kai Fung Fu, the capital of Honan, China. This synagogue contained ancient records of Jewish settlements going back before the time of Christ. A small community of three hundred Chinese Jews, called *Beni Israel*, existed in southwest China as late as 1918. They claimed they were descended from Israelite vassals of the Media-Persian kings who invaded southern China in the fourth century before Christ. The definitive study, *Jews in Old China* by Sidney Shapiro, provides a fascinating insight into this little-known element of the history of the tribes of Israel. The stone tablets and records of the Jews of Kaifeng, China, recorded their origins, history and their beliefs. They claim their ancestors moved into China during the Zhou dynasty (1056 B.C. to 256 B.C.). From the ninth century on, various travelers explored the ancient Asian trade routes between Persia and China and often reported encounters with Jewish descendants.

A fascinating individual named Manasseh ben Israel, the Chief Rabbi of Amsterdam in A.D. 1651, wrote a book called *The Hope of Israel*. He declared that these Chinese Jews were part of the ten lost tribes who had fled to China from the area of Afghanistan to escape successive waves of Tartar invaders. Jewish synagogues dating back more than a thousand years old still existed in Kaifeng in northern China in the first part of this century. Ancient monuments and letters in the Hebrew language indicate a Jewish presence extending back before the time of Christ. Several Chinese history specialists referred to the prophecy of Isaiah 49:12 for a clue to the timing of these Jews' entrance into China. "Surely, these shall come from far; look! Those from the north and the west; and these from the land of Sinim" (Isaiah 49:12). Since Isaiah wrote in the eighth century before Christ about these Jews returning from Sinim (China), these scholars suggest that he must have been aware that these Chinese Jews went to China during his lifetime. Interestingly, these Chinese Jews identified themselves as Israelites. They were unaware of the name "Jew." This designation became widespread only after the division of the united nation into the two kingdoms of Israel and Judah. Although these Chinese Jews followed the basic festivals and feasts, they had never heard of the Feast of Dedication, Hanukkah, which celebrates the victory over the Syrians in 165 B.C. This suggests that this group of Jews was separated from the rest of Judaism before this event occurred, possibly following the Assyrian or Babylonian Captivities.

The Ten Tribes and Afghanistan

During my last research trip to Israel, I encountered several rabbis and scholars who have completed some interesting research on the history of the Jewish and Israelite captivities in ancient Assyria and Babylon. Their tentative conclusions are just that — tentative. However, their line of inquiry is so fascinating that I decided to share this information with my readers for your consideration. Obviously, at this point, any definite conclusions must await the fulfillment of the Bible's prophecies of the ultimate restoration of the ten tribes to the Holy Land. When these prophecies are finally fulfilled, hopefully in our lifetime, then we shall find the definitive answers to these curious questions. The best place to search for something that is lost is to begin searching where you last saw it. The biblical record indicates that the ten tribes of Israel were sent by their enemies into the area north of ancient Assyria. This area is now occupied by the nations of Afghanistan and Pakistan.

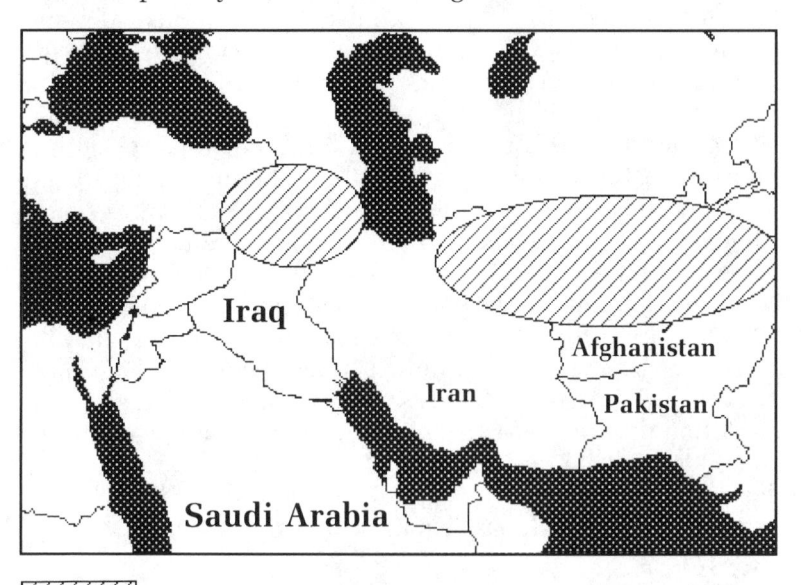

The Ten Tribes Were Exiled To These Areas

Possible Locations of the Ten Tribes of Israel

Rabbi Eliahu Amihail, in his book *The Lost Tribes in Assyria,* discussed in detail his research into the origins of the Pathan tribes of Afghanistan and Western Pakistan. These tribes are locally known as *Pashtu*. While surrounded by diverse Asiatic peoples, they differ markedly in their characteristics from their Turkish, Mongolian, Persian and Indo-Iranian neighbors. Incredibly, these thirteen million Pathan tribesmen call themselves the "Sons of Israel." Rabbi Avihail claims that these Pathans have both oral traditions and genealogical scrolls reaching back thousands of years that verify their connection with the ten tribes of Israel who were taken as captives to Assyria in 721 B.C. A curious feature of the appearance of these Pathan tribesmen is the fact that many have a Jewish appearance including wearing sidelocks and beards. The Pathan tradition holds that the royal family of Afghanistan was descended from the tribe of Benjamin and the family of King Saul.

Pan Guandan, a Chinese scholar, wrote a definitive study called *The Jews in Ancient China - A Historical Survey* in 1983. He traced how the Jews of China arrived there, concluding that many of them moved into China after first settling in the area of present-day Afghanistan and Pakistan. "The Durani in Afghanistan, who call themselves Ben-i-Israel, or Children of Israel; the Kashmiri, who Bernier de Nevilles guessed in the 13th century were descendants of the Lost Tribes; the people in the Habor River area where Jews of Israel were exiled by the Assyrian emperor in the 8th century B.C.; and the Jews in the Bombay area who also call themselves *Ben-i-Israel*, were all plainly from Israel, not Judah, and therefore descendants of the Ten Lost Tribes."

A fascinating book called *The Way of the Afghans* by Khan Rasbam Khan tells us that the Israelites came to Khorasan (Afghanistan) from Babylon and Persia. He mentions that many of these "Sons of Israel" chose to accept the laws of Islam under threat of force and became Muslims in the eighth century. These Israelites are known under the following names, "Solami, Pashtuni, Afghani, and Pathan." Evidence suggests that Muslim missionaries were sent to the area of Afghanistan after the rapid expansion of Islam following the life of Mohammed in the period A.D. 622 to A.D. 690. An article in the *Encyclopedia Britannica* describes the similarity between the Pathan laws and the Laws of Moses. Some of the Kashmir tribes of the Kashmir area between India and Pakistan also claim descent as the "Sons of Israel."

The Mysterious Pathan Tribesmen of Afghanistan

My earlier research on the mysterious Ezekiel Tablets for my book *Heaven - The Last Frontier* led me to examine the research work of the Ben Zvi Institute in Jerusalem that currently houses these marble tablets. This institute was founded by Yitzhak-Ben Zvi, the second president of Israel, and focuses its research on the history of the Jewish captives in the Diaspora (among the nations). In his report President Ben Zvi said, "The tribes of Afghanistan, among whom dwelt the Jews of Afghanistan for many generations, are Moslem tribes which kept, and still keep, the wondrous tradition regarding their origin from the Ten Lost Tribes. This tradition, which circulates amongst people of the Afghan tribes, is an ancient one and has historical backing. Some researchers and travellers, Jews and non-Jews, who visited these places, dealt with it, as did researchers of Afghanistan and its population from literary sources alone. Only a few facts have been published on this matter in books and encyclopaedias either in the European language or in Hebrew."

In the twelfth century of this era the great Jewish explorer and traveler Benjamin of Tudela returned to Spain declaring that he had located the ten lost tribes of Israel in Central Asia. He met with more than twenty-five thousand Jews in the city of Halah in present-day Afghanistan. "This congregation forms part of those who live in the mountains of Chaphton, which amount to more than 100, extending to the frontiers of Media. These Jews are descendants of those who were originally led into captivity by King Shalmaneser. They speak the Syriac language, and among them are many excellent Jewish scholars" (*The Itinerary of Rabbi Benjamin of Tudela*, Edited by A. Asher, Berlin, 1840).

There is an amazing correspondence between the names of the major tribal groupings of the Pathan tribesmen of Afghanistan and Pakistan and the ancient tribes of Israel. As examples: The Lowani tribe are judges related to the Levites. The Unramand tribe claims descent from Manasseh. The Daftani and Zai-Kan tribes claim to descend from Naphtali. The tribe of Yusef relates to Joseph's tribe. The Rabani tribe is connected to Reuben. The overall rulers of the main Pathan tribal groups are called the Yunini tribe. In addition, there is a startling similarity between some of the characteristics of these Pathan tribesmen and the ancient tribes of Israel. A list of the features in common between these Pathans and Israel is quite interesting.

The Common Characteristics of the Pathan Tribesmen and the Ancient Israelites

1. Circumcision on the eighth day following birth. Arabs and Moslems circumcise in the thirteenth year of life

2. Marriage customs including a marriage canopy, special wedding rings and the "sale" of the bride to the groom with a marriage contract

3. Religious use of a four-cornered garment with Tallit -- Prayer shawls

4. Sexual laws regarding purification and ritual baths -- mikvah

5. Leverite marriage laws -- a childless widow must marry her husband's brother to raise up children for his name

6. Levitical-type food laws with forbidden foods, including horse meat and its Kosher laws

7. Sabbath customs include total rest, refraining from labor, and the use of twelve breads (just like the Table of Shewbread) and Sabbath candles

8. The Fast of Yom Kippur and the use of Mezuzot on the sides of doors

9. While they are Muslims, many Pathans pray toward Jerusalem instead of Mecca

10. They read the Psalms of David when their family is sick

11. They use amulets with the Shema "Behold O Israel, the Lord your God is One"

12. The ancient legal principle of "an eye for an eye, a tooth for a tooth"

13. The sign of David appears on a shield in both cultures

14. During plagues they slaughter a sheep and sprinkle its blood on the lintel and door posts exactly as the ancient Jews did during the Exodus from Egypt

15. There are similarities in the Pashtu language to the Semitic languages in their common use of two- and three-letter roots. Some of the thirty-four letters in the Pashtu language appear to be of Hebrew origin

16. Many names from the history of Israel appear in the language of the Pathan tribesmen:

Hebrew	Pashtu
Aba	Aba (father)
Adam	Adam
Ibrahim	Abraham
Ishak	Isaac
Musa	Moses
Yahub	Jacob
Yusef	Joseph
Yusha	Joshua

(From *The Lost Tribes in Assyria* by Rabbi Eliahu Amihail.)

These Pathans are fierce warriors who were often enlisted to guard the Khyber Pass for the king of Afghanistan. A Canadian journalist, Eric Margolis, often traveled from Peshawar, Pakistan, north into the rugged Khyber Pass of Afghanistan to research these amazing Pathans. He points out that they are known as the most fierce and rugged fighters in the world. "North from Peshawar, the last outpost of the British Raj, marched the troops of the Queen Empress to conquer the wild Pathan tribes of Afghanistan (19th Century). The British launched 47 major expeditions into Afghan territory. All failed. In the most infamous, a British army (of 20,000) marched on Kabul. Only one man returned. British, and later, Russian, soldiers quickly learned to save their last bullet for themselves rather than fall into the hands of the ferocious Afghans...When they're not fighting one another, these tall, gaunt, fiercely bearded tribesmen love to attack outsiders...I've been huddling with mujahedin leaders, steeping myself in the most arcane Afghan political intrigue. Majestic, hawk-nosed, in long turbans or their little, round caps, they look like Old Testament companions of Abraham. No wonder the English used to believe the Afghans were the lost tribes of Israel" (*Toronto Sun*, April 9, 1992). These Pathan fighters form the basic military strength of the Afghan resistance army, the *mujahedin* guerrilla fighters that have successfully defeated every army that has ever had the misfortune to fight them. After ten years the Russian army was forced to confess defeat just as the brave British army did a century earlier. In thousands of years, no government has ever been able to collect taxes from these Pathans.

Could these Pathan tribesmen be connected to the lost tribes of Israel? It is possible but certainly not conclusive. Other groups in central Asia, in Khazastan, Georgia, Russia and Pakistan, are also possibly connected. Whether or not any of these groups turn out to be part of the ten tribes, we can rely on the prophecies of the Bible that God knows where the "tribes of His inheritance" are located. For thousands of years, the Lord protected and preserved the Jews in over seventy different countries. The God of Israel will preserve them, wherever they are, until the time for their final return arrives.

When Will the Ten Tribes Return?

The prophet Jeremiah spoke of the days when God will finally restore the tribes to their ancient homeland. His prophecy declared that the ten tribes will return in the same period as the promised Messiah. "'Behold, the days are coming,' says the Lord, 'That I will raise to David a Branch of righteousness; a King shall reign and prosper, and execute judgment and righteousness in the earth. In His days Judah will be saved, and Israel will dwell safely; now this is His name by which He will be called: The Lord Our Righteousness. Therefore, behold, the days are coming,' says the Lord, 'that they shall no longer say, 'As the Lord lives who brought up the children of Israel from the land of Egypt,' but, 'As the Lord lives who brought up and led the descendants of the house of Israel from the north country and from all the countries where I had driven them,' And they shall dwell in their own land" (Jeremiah 23:5-8). This incredible prophecy confirms that, in the last days, God will miraculously return the exiles from "the house of Israel from the north country and from all the countries where I had driven them." For thousands of years the Jews have celebrated the Feast of Passover on the 14th day of Nisan by remembering their supernatural deliverance from Egypt by the hand of God. However, Jeremiah prophesied that, in the future, they will celebrate Passover by remembering the exodus of the house of Israel "from the north country," not the exodus from Egypt. Since God commanded Israel to celebrate Passover forever "in their generations" this prophecy suggests that the future supernatural deliverance "from the north country" will also occur on the 14th day of Nisan, the day of Passover.

Many of the Old Testament prophets spoke of the coming Battle of Armageddon that is discussed further by John in the Apocalypse. The prophet Hosea indicated that the ten tribes will return at the time of Armageddon which will occur in the Valley of Jezreel during the great Day of the Lord. "Then the children of Judah and the children of Israel shall be gathered together, and appoint for themselves one head; and they shall come up out of the land, for great will be the day of Jezreel!" (Hosea 1:11).

The Conclusion of Our Search

Ultimately, only God knows the true identity and location of the ten lost tribes that disappeared into the depths of Central Asia almost twenty-seven centuries ago. Yet the ancient prophecies about the restoration of the house of Israel must be fulfilled. The promise of God cannot be broken. The Lord will return the ten tribes of His inheritance to their ancient Promised Land. Wherever they are, the Good Shepherd knows the sheep of His pasture and will fulfill the words of His prophecy. Ezekiel said, "'I will seek what was lost and bring back what was driven away...I will establish one shepherd over them, and he shall feed them; My servant David....Thus they shall know that I, the Lord their God, am with them, and that they, the house of Israel, are My people,' says the Lord God" (Ezekiel 34:22-24).

CHAPTER FOURTEEN

The Millennial Kingdom

"Thy Kingdom Come" - The Final Goal of History

Jesus taught His disciples to pray, "Thy Kingdom come, Thy will be done on earth as it is in heaven." Christ's eternal Kingdom will be realized on this planet as well as in heaven. In His Sermon on the Mount Jesus promised that the meek "shall inherit the earth" (Matthew 5:5). These promises will be fulfilled during the Kingdom of God on earth. Daniel was given a tremendous vision of the final victory of the Messiah. He declared that Christ will defeat the Antichrist and give the saints the kingdoms of earth. "Then the kingdom and dominion and the greatness of the kingdoms under the whole heaven, shall be given to the people, the saints of the Most High" (Daniel 7:27).

The early Christians longed for the return of Christ to take His Church home to glory. Living under the brutal persecution of the Roman pagans, they, like Abraham, looked "for the city which has foundations, whose builder and maker is God" (Hebrews 11:10). They knew that their Messiah would come to defeat the Antichrist to establish His millennial Kingdom. As an example, Cyril, in the second century wrote, "He [Antichrist] will be annihilated by the Second Glorious Coming from heaven of the truly begotten Son of God, who is our Lord and Savior, Jesus the true Messiah; who, having destroyed Antichrist by the spirit of His mouth, will deliver him to the fire Gehenna" (*Ante Nicene Fathers*).

We are moving inexorably toward the last great crisis of history described by ancient prophets. The final goal of history is the establishment of Christ's kingdom of righteousness and justice on both the earth and in the heavens. Strangely, some writers suggest that our belief in a literal Kingdom of God on earth is "carnal" and "unspiritual." Some claim that our belief in a literal fulfillment of Scriptural prophecies is an error. They feel we are missing the "higher spiritual realities" by taking the Bible's promises at face value. Their problem is not that they misunderstand the meaning of Scripture's prophecies. The problem is their unbelief in these promises of God. The Bible clearly promised that we shall rule with Christ in this world throughout His eternal Kingdom.

The book of Revelation (1:5) introduces Christ as "the ruler over the kings of the earth" and promises that He will make His servants "kings and priests." When John was lifted up to heaven in his vision, he saw the twenty-four elders and the four Cherubim fall down in worship before Jesus, the Lamb of God. These heavenly beings sang a new song of worship to Christ. "You are worthy to take the scroll, and to open its seals...and have made us kings and priests to our God; and we shall reign on the earth" (Revelation 5:9-10). The Lord promised the martyrs that they will "live and reign with Christ for a thousand years" (Revelation 20:4). After describing the final tremendous victory of Christ over Satan, the Bible tells us that John "saw the holy city, New Jerusalem, coming down out of heaven from God." Then a voice from heaven announced, "Behold, the tabernacle of God is with men and He will dwell with them, and they shall be His people and God Himself will be with them and be their God" (Revelation 21:2,3). The Scriptures declare that the nations will be blessed when the New Jerusalem descends from heaven. "The nations of those who are saved shall walk in its light and the kings of the earth bring their glory and honor into it" (Revelation 21:24).

Despite these clear and detailed scriptural promises, many Christians still believe that a discussion of Christ's millennial Kingdom is "too materialistic." They criticize us for believing in the literal promises of Scripture. The prophets of both the Old and the New Testaments tell us that God will establish His Kingdom on this planet. Why are so many writers reluctant to accept the literal reality of these promises of God? Jesus Christ said to them, "O foolish ones, and slow of heart to believe in all that the prophets have spoken!" (Luke 24:25). He explained why many people refuse to believe the words of the prophecies: (1) They are "foolish" about the things of God and (2) show a lack of faith demonstrated by their "slowness of heart" to believe. In the same manner, despite His many prophecies about His resurrection, Christ's own disciples could hardly grasp that He was standing in the Upper Room in His resurrected body. Today, many Christians think of heaven and the millennial Kingdom as unreal and immaterial. When they contemplate the second coming of Christ their minds cannot conceive of the reality of life during the Millennium. However, the Bible teaches that the Millennium will be as real and practical as our present life today.

From the moment of Adam and Eve's fall from grace in Paradise, the earth became a battleground between Satan and Christ for the souls of men and for the dominion of this planet. When Satan's Antichrist is defeated at Armageddon Christ will finally redeem our world from the curse of sin. Pain, suffering and the reign of evil were not part of God's original plan for mankind. It entered the universe when our parents, Adam and Eve, chose to rebel against God and listen to the temptations of Satan. Someday soon the curse of sin will be lifted from this planet. Man will live in the glorious presence of our Lord Jesus Christ ruling from the throne of David in Jerusalem.

The Millennial Kingdom According to the Jewish Sages

Although the word "Millennium" is not found in the Bible, the concept is clearly taught throughout Scripture. It is derived from the Latin words *mille* for one thousand and *annus* for years from Revelation 20. The early Christian writers in the western Roman Empire, writing in Latin, described the one-thousand-year period taught by Revelation 20 as the Millennium. Six times in Revelation 20 the expression "one thousand years" is revealed as the duration between the Battle of Armageddon and the final rebellion of Satan. Although the exact duration of the Millennium was not revealed by God until John wrote the book of Revelation, the ancient Jewish rabbis understood that the Messiah would establish a Sabbath consisting of a one-thousand-year rest for mankind. Rabbi Kattina discussed this concept as follows: "The world endures six thousand years and one thousand it shall be laid waste (that is the enemies of God shall be destroyed) whereof it is said, 'The Lord alone shall be exalted in that day'" (Isaiah 2:11). The Jewish *Gemara*, a gloss on the Talmud, also attributes these comments on the Law of the Sabbath of the Land to Rabbi Kattina. "As out of seven years every seventh is the year of remission, so out of the seven thousand years of the world the seventh millennium shall be the millennium of remission, that God alone may be exalted in that day."

Another Jewish tradition held that a Rabbi Elias, who lived some two hundred years before Christ, wrote, "The world endures six thousand years, two thousand before the Law, two thousand under the Law, and two thousand under the Messiah." These Talmudic passages clearly reveal that Jews as well as Christians believed in a literal one-thousand-year Millennium.

The Early Church's Belief in the Millennium

Even the opponents of a literal Millennium are forced by the historical evidence to acknowledge that the early Church was clearly looking for Christ to return and set up His one thousand year kingdom. As an example of the literalness of their understanding of the prophecies, we should read *The Divine Institutes* by Lactantius (A.D. 260 to 330). He taught that Christ will resurrect the rest of the Old Testament saints when He comes in glory. "But He, when He shall have destroyed unrighteousness, and executed His great judgment, and shall have recalled to life the righteous, who have lived from the beginning, will be engaged among men a thousand years and will rule them with most just command." Lactantius also wrote about those who survived Armageddon and will live as citizens in the millennial Kingdom, ruled by the resurrected saints of the Church. "Then they who shall be alive in their bodies shall not die, but during those thousand years shall produce an infinite multitude and their offspring shall be holy, and beloved by God; but they who shall be raised from the dead shall preside over the living as judges." He also described the imprisoning of Satan. "The prince of the devils, who is the contriver of all evils, shall be bound with chains, and shall be imprisoned during the thousand years of the heavenly rule in which righteousness shall reign in the world" (*The Divine Institutes*, 24). In another manuscript Lactantius described his belief in the six thousand years of history leading to the Millennium. "For six thousand years have not yet been completed, and when this number shall be made up, then at length all evil will be taken away, that justice alone may reign" (*Epitome of the Divine Institutes*, 70).

Papias, a writer who lived from A.D. 70 to 155, was taught by Polycarp, a student of John, who wrote the Apocalypse. He discussed the beliefs of the saints in the coming kingdom of the Messiah. "There will be a millennium after the resurrection from the dead, when the personal reign of Christ will be established on this earth." Another key leader of the Church, Justin Martyr (A.D. 110 to 165) acknowledged this millennial hope as the true teaching of the Scriptures throughout his teaching and writing. "But I and others, who are right-minded Christians on all points, are assured that there will be a resurrection of the dead, and a thousand years in Jerusalem, which will then be built, adorned, and enlarged, as the prophets Ezekiel and Isaiah and others declare" (*Dialogue With Trypho*, 80). In this fascinating passage he wrote about "each day being equal to one thousand years." Justin suggests that Adam died at the age of 930 because he violated God's decree that "in the day that you eat of it you shall surely die" (Genesis 2:17). "For as Adam was told that in the day he ate of the tree he would die, we know that he did not complete a thousand years." Another important Christian writer, Irenaeus in his *Against Heresies,* wrote extensively about the millennial hope of the early Church. "For in as many days as this world was made, in so many thousand years shall it be concluded...For the Day of the Lord is a thousand years; and in six days created things were completed : it is evident, therefore, that they will come to an end at the sixth thousand year" (*Against Heresies*, 28). This belief that Christ would return to establish His Kingdom at the end of six thousand years from the creation of Adam was almost universal in the first few centuries following Christ. Irenaeus rejected the allegorical method of interpreting the prophecies. "If, however, any shall endeavor to allegorize prophecies of this kind, they shall not be found consistent with themselves in all points, and shall be confuted by the teaching of the very expressions in question"(*Against Heresies*, 35).

Why Did the Church Abandon the Hope of the Millennial Kingdom?

This hope of a premillennial return of Christ and a literal one-thousand-year reign of Christ was the universal view of the Christian Church for the first two hundred and fifty years following Christ's resurrection. The official Church abandoned this biblical belief only after it began to allegorize all prophetic passages of Scripture. Unfortunately, some enthusiastic writers in the first two centuries wrote fanciful and exaggerated descriptions of the Millennium that bore no resemblance to the prophecies. These fables included statements that "vines shall grow, having each ten thousand branches, and in each branch ten thousand twigs...and on every one of the clusters ten thousand grapes" (*Fragments - Ante-Nicene Fathers*). Unfortunately, these exaggerations caused a backlash that influenced many in the Church to abandon teaching about the millennial Kingdom altogether. Rather than simply reject the false teaching, many rejected the concept of a literal reign of Christ from the throne of David. Additionally, rising anti-Semitism in the Church led some Gentile writers to reject the promises of a millennial Kingdom because it was too closely connected with the Jewish hopes for an earthly restoration of their nation. However, the whole Bible was inspired by God and written by Jewish believers initially for Jewish readers. It is only natural that the promises of a millennial Kingdom in the Apocalypse will relate closely to the prophecies of the Old Testament prophets about the coming Kingdom of God when the Messiah will rule.

The Duration of Christ's Kingdom on Earth

The Bible does not limit the duration of Christ's millennial Kingdom to a single one-thousand-year period.

The Millennium is simply "Chapter One" of the eternal Kingdom of Christ. Unfortunately, the exclusive focus on the Millennium has caused many Christians to imagine that we shall rule with Christ on earth for only one thousand years. All of the biblical promises indicate that His rule will begin at the Battle of Armageddon and continue forever into eternity. John revealed in Revelation 20 that there will be a one-thousand-year period when the saints will reign with Christ. At the end of the Millennium there will be a final test of mankind's obedience to the Messiah. This test will be Satan's final temptation of the mortals born during the Millennium. The final rebellion is described as the War of Gog and Magog. This battle is quite different from the war described in Ezekiel 38 and 39 which will occur before the Tribulation period. It differs in every area including: weapons, nations involved, purpose, leadership and outcome. The only similarity is that the name "Gog and Magog" appears in both passages. This simply indicates that the nations represented by "Gog and Magog" will participate in these two key battles that will occur over one thousand years apart. Later in this chapter we will examine the Bible's prophecies about the final battle between Satan and Christ.

In the chapter on the New Heavens and New Earth we will examine the Bible's prophecies about Christ's eternal kingdom on the New Earth. The revelation of His eternal kingdom on this planet changes our perception of the spiritual history of the earth. Many view man's history as six thousand years of continuous evil that will be followed by a mere one thousand years of peace and righteousness. However, with a correct understanding of Scripture, we can, appreciate that the six thousand years of satanic domination will be replaced by an eternal and glorious Kingdom of righteousness and justice under the Messiah. The previous six thousand years of satanic domination will then be seen as a mere prologue leading to the glorious and everlasting Kingdom of Christ.

The Bride of Christ Will Rule the Earth with Jesus

The Scriptures reveal that the destiny of the Church is to rule with Christ throughout the Millennium and forever on the New Earth. It is significant that the first sight to meet John's eyes when he was lifted up to heaven was the vision of "twenty-four thrones, and on the thrones I saw twenty-four elders sitting, clothed in white robes; and they had crowns of gold on their heads" (Revelation 4:4). The twenty-four elders are the crowned representatives of the Church sitting on thrones as rulers under their Messiah-King. The Apostle Paul endured stonings, imprisonment, hatred and flogging for his faithful witness to Christ. Yet Paul felt that these sufferings were almost nothing in comparison to the glory and honor that Christ will give to us when we rule with Him in His Kingdom. "For I consider that the sufferings of this present time are not worthy to be compared with the glory which shall be revealed in us" (Romans 8:18).

In His teaching, Christ often held out the prospect of participating in the governing of this world as a reward for those who were faithful. Christ commands His servants to be faithful so that He can say to us: "Well done, good and faithful servant; you have been faithful over a few things, I will make you ruler over many things. Enter into the joy of your lord" (Matthew 25:23). The Gospel of Luke records the parable of the nobleman and his servants. The most faithful servant is commended by Christ as follows: "Well done, good servant; because you were faithful in a very little, have authority over ten cities" (Luke 19:17). In this parable Christ indicates that our faithful service in this life will qualify us for the degree of authority and responsibility that will be given to us in His millennial Kingdom.

Those who have paid the price of suffering or martyrdom will be given special honor in Christ's government. In Paul's letter to Timothy he promised: "If we endure, we shall also reign with Him. If we deny Him, He also will deny us" (2 Timothy 2:12). In the book of Revelation John revealed that God has provided special honors in His Kingdom for those tribulation saints who pay the supreme price of martyrdom for their rejection of the Mark of the Beast. "I saw thrones, and they sat on them, and judgment was committed to them. And I saw the souls of those who had been beheaded for their witness to Jesus and for the word of God, who had not worshipped the beast or his image, and had not received his mark on their foreheads or on their hands. And they lived and reigned with Christ for a thousand years" (Revelation 20:4). God's justice and equity will be demonstrated by this coming reign of the saints on the earth. It is significant that the very place that has witnessed the persecution of the believers for two thousand years will also witness the elevation of the saints of Jesus Christ to rule the nations forever. It is a wonderful example of God's justice that the disciples of Christ will rule forever in the very place where they were despised by sinners because they were poor and needy. Where they once suffered, they shall reign triumphantly with their Savior and Lord, Jesus Christ. Where they were martyred in tears, they shall gloriously praise their exalted Lord.

The Restoration of All Things

"That He may send Jesus Christ, who was preached to you before, whom heaven must receive until the times of restoration of all things, which God has spoken by the mouth of all His holy prophets since the world began" (Acts 3:20,21).

In the beginning man was given dominion over this world to tend it as a garden for God. Man has failed miserably in this trust and the earth's ecosystems are breaking down as a result of unbridled greed and destructive pollution. The evidence is overwhelming that man has totally failed as the steward of this planet. The Aral Sea in Russia, one of the world's largest bodies of fresh water, has deteriorated to become a "dead" sea. The daily burning of huge portions of the Amazon rain forests is wiping out the "lungs" of the planet that produce the oxygen we desperately require. Poor weather and erosion have rapidly expanded deserts of the Sahara, devastating northern Africa. The planet has suffered for thousands of years because of this curse of selfishness and sin. In addition, the industrial pollution during the last two centuries has caused a tragic amount of damage to the surface of the planet. The ravages of the Antichrist's wars during the Great Tribulation will further devastate the world's fragile ecological systems. In Revelation 11:18 God declares that He will judge and "destroy those who destroy the earth" (Revelation 11:18).

The Renewal of Paradise

The curse of sin will be lifted from the earth when Satan is finally bound for a thousand years after he is defeated by Christ at the Battle of Armageddon. Christ will heal the planet's wounds when He establishes His millennial Kingdom. In Ezekiel's great vision of the Millennium he described the restoration of the planet beginning with Israel. When the Lord brought him into the Temple he recorded: "There was water, flowing from under the threshold of the temple toward the east" (Ezekiel 47:1). This stream grew larger and deeper as it made its way eastward toward the Dead Sea. In an area that has been desolate for thousands of years, Ezekiel described the miraculous restoration of the land produced by the miraculous river of living water flowing from the throne of God.

Ezekiel received an astonishing preview of the restoration of the land that will occur during Christ's millennial Kingdom. "This water flows toward the eastern region, goes down into the valley, and enters the sea. When it reaches the sea, its waters are healed. And it shall be that every living thing that moves, wherever the rivers go, will live. There will be a very great multitude of fish, because these waters go there; for they will be healed, and everything will live wherever the river goes" (Ezekiel 47:9). The Dead Sea is the perfect symbol of the desolation brought about by the curse of sin. When Christ heals the waters of the Dead Sea, this will signal the beginning of the redemption of the earth from the results of sin. To illustrate the reality of life in the Kingdom of God, Ezekiel described fishing in the Millennium. "Fishermen will stand by it from En Gedi to En Eglaim; there will be places for spreading their nets. Their fish will be of the same kinds as the fish of the Great Sea, exceedingly many" (Ezekiel 47:10). Life will be a lot more real and interesting during the Millennium than most have ever dreamed. Ezekiel saw a vision of a fertile and productive Paradise restored where they "will grow all kinds of trees used for food; their leaves will not wither, and their fruit will not fail. They will bear fruit every month, because their water flows from the sanctuary. Their fruit will be for food, and their leaves for medicine" (Ezekiel 47:12).

Millennial Splendor of Christ's Kingdom

"The wolf also shall dwell with the lamb, the leopard shall lie down with the young goat, the calf and the young lion and the fatling together; and a little child shall lead them. The cow and the bear shall graze; their young ones shall lie down together; and the lion shall eat straw like the ox" (Isaiah 11:6,7).

The world will become young again as it was in the Garden of Eden. It will never grow old. All that reminds us of death and sin will be removed forever. As Isaiah revealed, the biology of carnivorous animals will be transformed by the Creator, Jesus Christ, to enable them to live as vegetarians without killing for food. Peace will return to the animal kingdom as it will to mankind. It is hard to imagine what life will be like when we will live with no locks, police or soldiers.

In the Millennium, Christ will rule as absolute Monarch. Isaiah 11:2-4 described His righteous government. "The Spirit of the Lord shall rest upon Him, the Spirit of wisdom and understanding, the Spirit of counsel and might, the Spirit of knowledge and of the fear of the Lord. His delight is in the fear of the Lord, and He shall not judge by the sight of His eyes, nor decide by the hearing of His ears; but with righteousness He shall judge the poor, and decide with equity for the meek of the earth; He shall strike the earth with the rod of His mouth, and with the breath of His lips He shall slay the wicked." The cry of the people around the world today is for righteous government. All that we have longed for throughout the generations will finally be realized under the righteous rule of the Messiah. During the first thousand years of Christ's government there will still be some limited expression of sin. Evil actions will be dealt with immediately by Christ ruling with a "rod of iron" as "He shall slay the wicked." However, once Satan is cast into hell at the end of the Millennium, sin will never exist in the New Earth and Heaven throughout eternity. Even the possibility of sin and temptation will be removed from the universe. Finally, there will be no need for "a rod of iron." God will transform the inner hearts of all the men and women to naturally follow His Law forever.

Israel Redeemed - A Light to the Gentiles

"I will keep You and give You as a covenant to the people, as a light to the Gentiles" (Isaiah 42:6).

Israel will enter into the blessings of the Promised Land that have been denied to her for thousands of years. Instead of living in an armed truce among her enemies, Israel will live in a true peace in the midst of her brothers, the Arabs. All of the children of Abraham will dwell in peace. The prophet Isaiah (11:16) described this future time of millennial peace. "There will be a highway for the remnant of His people who will be left from Assyria, as it was for Israel in the day that he came up from the land of Egypt." The armies of the Middle East will finally put down their weapons. Then, "He shall judge between the nations, and shall rebuke many people; they shall beat their swords into plowshares, and their spears into pruning hooks; nation shall not lift up sword against nation, neither shall they learn war anymore" (Isaiah 2:4). For nations like Syria, Israel and Egypt, who have lived in perpetual warfare for thousands of years, the peace of Christ's millennial Kingdom will be the realization of the dreams of many generations.

Israel will become the preeminent nation on the planet and will bless all of the Gentile nations. Their role from the time of Abraham has been to be "a light to the Gentiles." The Chosen People faithfully transmitted the commands of God in the Old Testament by carefully preserving every "jot and tittle" of the original Scriptures. Our Messiah and Savior was born a Jew as were all the Apostles. The scientific, literary and cultural contributions of the Jews to Western culture has been tremendous. Although the Jewish people comprise less than one-sixteenth of 1 percent of the world's population, their religious and intellectual contributions to humanity exceed that of any other race in history. Four thousand years ago God made a covenant of blessing with Israel that will finally be fulfilled in the Millennium and beyond. "I will make you a great nation; I will bless you and make your name great; and you shall be a blessing. I will bless those who bless you, and I will curse him who curses you; and in you all the families of the earth shall be blessed" (Genesis 12:2,3). God promised Abraham that He would bless those nations that blessed the Jews and curse those who cursed Israel. The rise and fall of many empires can be traced to the inexorable fulfillment of this ancient biblical prophecy.

After centuries of exile the Jews will return to their Promised Land to enjoy the blessings of the Messiah's reign. The prophet Isaiah was given a vision of the exaltation of Israel in that glorious day. "The Gentiles shall see your righteousness, and all kings your glory. You shall be called by a new name, which the mouth of the Lord will name...You shall no longer be termed Forsaken, nor shall your land any more be termed Desolate; but you shall be called Hephzibah, and your land Beulah; for the Lord delights in you, and your land shall be married" (Isaiah 62:2,4. Israel's new name "Hephzibah" means "My Delight is in Her" and the land will be called "Beulah" which means "Married." Thousands of years ago God divorced Israel because of her continued sinful rebellion. The prophet Hosea recorded God's terrible decree of divorcement from His Chosen People. "Then God said: 'Call his name Lo-Ammi, for you are not My people, and I will not be your God'" (Hosea 1:9). Thankfully, God's prophecy did not stop there but promised an ultimate spiritual and physical restoration of Israel as His people. When Israel returns to the Promised Land under the rule of her beloved Messiah, the words of the prophet Hosea will finally be fulfilled. "Yet the number of the children of Israel shall be as the sand of the sea, which cannot be measured or numbered. And it shall come to pass in the place where it was said to them, 'You are not My people,' there it shall be said to them, 'You are the sons of the living God'" (Hosea 1:10).

The prophet was given a clue to the time of the final restoration of the people. Remember the biblical principle that "a thousand years are equal to a day in the sight of God." Consider these provocative words prophesied to Israel. "Come, and let us return to the Lord; for He has torn, but He will heal us; He has stricken, but He will bind us up. After two days He will revive us; on the third day He will raise us up, that we may live in His sight" (Hosea 6:1,2). The two days may equal the two thousand years of Israel's exile from the land. The prophecy may represent the "raising up of Israel" at the commencement of the "third day," the new

256

Millennium. Whether or not they were correct, most of the writers during the first three centuries of the Christian Church believed that the Lord would come to set up His kingdom at the end of six thousand years from the creation of Adam. As an example, Victorinus, Bishop of Petau, wrote a *Commentary on the Apocalypse* around A.D. 270. He wrote that "the true and just Sabbath should be observed in the seventh millennium of years. Wherefore to those seven days the Lord attributed to each a thousand years...Wherefore as I have narrated, that true Sabbath will be in the seventh millennium of years, when Christ with His elect shall reign" (*On the Creation of the World*).

Methodius (A.D. 260 to 312) wrote a fascinating treatise called the *Banquet of the Ten Virgins* in which he commented on the Millennium. In his ninth discourse he wrote: "We shall celebrate the great feast of true Tabernacles in the new and indissoluble creation,...God resting from the works of creation...By a figure in the seventh month, when the fruits of the earth have been gathered in, we are commanded to keep the feast to the Lord, which signifies that, when this world shall be terminated at the seventh thousand years, when God shall have completed the world, He shall rejoice in us."

The Gentile Nations Will Be Blessed Forever

The "seed of promise," Israel, will finally inherit the total amount of land promised to their fathers by God. However, their brothers, the Arabs, the "seed of Ishmael," will also live with them in peace in the Promised Land in fulfillment of prophecy. Following the birth of Ishmael to Abraham, God promised that Ishmael would become the father of a great nation. Additionally, God said that "he shall dwell in the presence of all his brethren" (Genesis 16:12). This promise confirmed that the Arabs will find their place of blessing, living in peace with their Jewish brothers in the millennial Kingdom.

The Final War of Gog and Magog

While many writers have assumed that the Gentile nations will cease to exist when Christ returns, the Bible clearly teaches the continuation of the nations. In Revelation 20:8 John described Satan's final rebellion when he is released from the bottomless pit to tempt the men and women born during the Millennium. We read that Satan will gather "the nations" led by the countries identified as "Gog and Magog" to do battle against the beloved City of God. Satan "will go out to deceive the nations which are in the four corners of the earth, Gog and Magog, to gather them together to battle, whose number is as the sand of the sea" (Revelation 20:8). This verse teaches that nations will still exist during the Millennium. Other verses reveal that they will flourish in the New Earth forever.

The final spiritual test of man's obedience to God will occur when Satan is released to tempt the men and women born during the first one thousand years of Paradise under the rule of the Messiah. Hundreds of millions born in the Millennium will choose to accept Christ as their Savior and Lord. They will hear the message of salvation preached by the saints and will gladly accept Him as their Lord. There will be little open sin during the Millennium because Christ "will rule with a rod of iron." Any open rebellion and sin will be dealt with instantly by Christ, the Righteous Judge. Through this final test the Lord will demonstrate that, even under the ideal conditions of Paradise under the Messiah's rule in Jerusalem, a great portion of mankind will still harbor rebellious resentment in their hearts.

The End of the Millennium -- The Final Victory

When the Millennium nears its completion, Satan will be released from the abyss to actively tempt men. These sinners will manifest their rebellion by joining in Satan's attack on the City of God. "Now when the thousand years have expired, Satan will be released from his prison and will go out to deceive the nations which are in the four corners of the earth, Gog and Magog, to gather them together to battle, whose number is as the sand of the sea" (Revelation 20:7).

First, the enemies of God will have "surrounded the camp of the saints and the beloved city." Then, Christ will suddenly destroy His enemies and cast them into hell forever. "And fire came down from God out of heaven and devoured them" (Revelation 20:9). This last attempt by Satan to destroy the saints will mark the conclusion of seven thousand years of spiritual warfare which Satan and his fallen angels have waged against Christ and His heavenly army throughout the universe. In his prophecy John saw that, when the battle ended, "the devil, who deceived them, was cast into the lake of fire and brimstone where the beast and the false prophet are" (Revelation 20:10).

The *Epistle of Barnabas*, written by someone by this name during the first century, wrote of the early Churches expectation of the coming Millennium. "'And He rested on the seventh day.' This meaneth: when His Son, coming again, shall destroy the time of the wicked man, and judge the ungodly, and change the sun and the moon, and the stars, then shall He truly rest on the seventh day...when giving rest to all things, I shall make a beginning of the eighth day, that is, a beginning of another world. Wherefore, also, we keep the eighth day [Sunday] with joyfullness, the day also on which Jesus rose again from the dead" (*Epistle of Barnabas*, 15).

The ultimate victory of Christ over Satan and the rebellious nations will mark the end of the earth's first seven-thousand-year history and the beginning of the eighth day, which will last forever. The close of the Millennium will usher in the eternal Kingdom of God of the New Earth. As detailed in another chapter, the saints will rule with Christ forever on the New Earth. The prophet Daniel was given an exalted vision of God's final triumph. In his vision of Christ's glorious victory, Daniel saw Jesus, the "Son of Man, coming with the clouds of heaven!...Then to Him was given dominion and glory and a kingdom, that all peoples, nations, and languages should serve Him. His dominion is an everlasting dominion, which shall not pass away, and His kingdom the one which shall not be destroyed" (Daniel 7:13,14).

CHAPTER FIFTEEN

The Great White Throne Judgment

The Final Judgment of the Souls of Sinners

"Then I saw a great white throne and Him who sat on it, from whose face the earth and the heaven fled away. And there was found no place for them. And I saw the dead, small and great, standing before God, and books were opened. And another book was opened, which is the Book of Life. And the dead were judged according to their works, by the things which were written in the books. The sea gave up the dead who were in it, and Death and Hades delivered up the dead who were in them. And they were judged, each one according to his works" (Revelation 20:11-13).

John received an awesome vision of the final judgment of the souls of sinners before the Great White Throne of God. He described this throne as white, representing the absolute holiness and purity of God, just as the robes of the saints are white, representing their righteousness and purity. The Judge on the Great White Throne is Jesus Christ to whom the Father has given all judgment.

Many hold a perception that the souls of all believers and non-believers will appear together at one final judgment before the White Throne to determine who goes to hell and who goes to heaven. Many paintings and descriptions depict a single final judgment at the end of this age for all mankind. However, the Bible does not teach this concept. The only ones who will appear before the Great White Throne to be judged eternally are unrepentant sinners who have rejected God's salvation. Those who accept Christ as their Savior will be judged before the Judgment Seat of Christ in heaven over a thousand years earlier, at the conclusion of the Rapture. This earlier judgment of believers will determine the rewards they will receive for their faithful service to God. No punishment will be handed out to the believers. Part of the confusion about these judgments arose because of the words of Daniel 12:2: "And many of those who sleep in the dust of the earth shall awake, some to everlasting life, some to shame and everlasting contempt." Some felt that Daniel was referring to a single final judgment. If this was the only passage in Scripture referring to these last judgments we might mistakenly assume that both groups rise to be judged at the same time. A careful reading of this passage shows that Daniel does not declare that the two resurrections take place simultaneously. He simply records the fact that two different groups are resurrected, "some to everlasting life" and "some to shame and everlasting contempt."

The First and Second Resurrections

In Revelation 20:4-11 the prophet John reveals that an interval of a thousand years will separate the resurrection to spiritual life in heaven from the resurrection to spiritual death in hell. "I saw the souls of those who had been beheaded for their witness to Jesus and for the word of God...And they lived and reigned with Christ for a thousand years. But the rest of the dead did not live again until the thousand years were finished. This is the first resurrection. Blessed and holy is he who has part in the first resurrection. Over such the second death has no power, but they shall be priests of God and of Christ, and shall reign with Him a thousand years" (Revelation 20:4-6). After describing the events of the one-thousand-year Millennium, John writes, "Then I saw a great white throne" (Revelation 20:11). John records, "Then Death and Hades were cast into the lake of fire. This is the second death" (Revelation 20:14). The Bible declares that the sea, Death, and Hades will each yield up their wicked dead to be judged by God. "The sea gave up the dead who were in it, and Death and Hades delivered up the dead who were in them" (Revelation 20:13). The "sea" and "Death" refers to the fact that the bodies of those who died in the seas as well as those in "Death," the grave, will give up the bodies of the dead sinners to be resurrected by God to stand in judgment. The expression that "Hades" will give up wicked dead refers to the fact that the souls of the wicked sinners will be delivered from Hades to the throne of God for final judgment. The wicked dead will stand before God in their resurrected bodies that cannot die.

Jesus reveals that those who reject God's mercy will possess both their soul and body in hell forever. "And do not fear those who kill the body but cannot kill the soul. But rather fear Him who is able to destroy both soul and body in hell" (Matthew 10:28). The word "destroy" refers to unending punishment, not annihilation, because a number of passages clearly teach that the souls of unrepentant sinners will suffer in hell forever. In Matthew 25:46 Jesus warned that the choices we make in this life will, in time, lead to eternal consequences. "And these will go away into everlasting punishment, but the righteous into eternal life" (Matthew 25:46). All the wicked sinners who have waited in torment for thousands of years, will finally be judged at the end of the Millennium. Hades itself, the temporary place of waiting for wicked souls, will be "cast into the lake of fire."

What Happens to a Soul When Someone Dies?

There is a great deal of confusion in the minds of people about the temporary destiny and location of the souls of both believers and non-believers from the moment of death until they reach their final destination of heaven or hell. The Bible reveals that the experience of the sinners and the saints is quite different even before the final judgment before God. The Old Testament speaks of "Hades" and the "Grave" as the destination of departed souls. Some scholars have suggested that the truth of the resurrection was not known to the Hebrews of the Old Testament. This is simply untrue. From the first book of the Bible, Genesis, until the book of Malachi we find numerous inspired statements proving that the Old Testament taught the truth of a resurrection and a final judgment. This judgment will take place before God and will be based on each person's actions and beliefs. We repeatedly find the statement in Genesis that the Patriarchs were each "gathered to his people" (Genesis 25:8, 17). This is true even in the case of Jacob, whose body was not buried with his ancestors for many years. This inspired statement proves that they knew their souls would join the souls of God's people who had died before them. Job, possibly the oldest book in the Bible, reveals his hope for the physical resurrection of his body in the last days. "For I know that my Redeemer lives, and He shall stand at last on the earth; and after my skin is destroyed, this I know, that in my flesh I shall see God" (Job 19:25,26). Later, Daniel the prophet described both resurrections as "many of those who sleep in the dust of the earth shall awake, some to everlasting life, some to shame and everlasting contempt" (Daniel 12:2).

Hades - The Place of Waiting for Lost Souls

Many people speak as though wicked sinners immediately go to hell once they die. However, the Bible declares that the souls of unrepentant sinners descend into Hades, the place of torment, to await the final Great White Throne judgment at the end of the Millennium. Christ described the state of the wicked dead when He told about the sinful rich man who went to Hades. "So it was that the beggar died, and was carried by the angels to Abraham's bosom. The rich man also died and was buried. And being in torments in Hades, he lifted up his eyes and saw Abraham afar off, and Lazarus in his bosom. Then he cried and said, 'Father Abraham, have mercy on me, and send Lazarus that he may dip the tip of his finger in water and cool my tongue; for I am tormented in this flame'" (Luke 16:22-24). From this passage and others, the Bible reveals that sinners descend into Hades and remain there in torment until the final Great White Throne judgment that will send them to an eternity without Christ in hell.

Abraham's Bosom

The words of Christ reveal that the souls of those who died as believers in God before Christ's resurrection went to a place of waiting and comfort known as Abraham's bosom. Although Christ's words reveal that people in both areas were aware of each other, it was impossible for anyone to cross from one place to the other. Abraham declared: "Between us and you there is a great gulf fixed, so that those who want to pass from here to you cannot, nor can those from there pass to us" (Luke 16:26). All Old Testament believers went to Abraham's bosom to wait for their resurrection to heaven. However, the Gospel of Matthew declared that, when Christ arose from the empty tomb, "the graves were opened; and many bodies of the saints who had fallen asleep were raised; and coming out of the graves after His resurrection, they went into the holy city and appeared to many" (Matthew 27:52,53). This tremendous miracle of resurrecting the bodies and souls of many of the Old Testament saints declared that Christ defeated the power of sin and death forever.

Just as He resurrected those saints, someday soon He will resurrect the bodies of all living and departed Christian believers at the rapture of the Church. The specific word "many" reveals that some of the Old Testament believers are still waiting for the Rapture to receive their resurrection bodies. Those "many" who arose "went into the holy city and appeared to many" proving the power of the resurrection to the huge influx of visitors in Jerusalem. At Passover the city of Jerusalem was overflowing with a million visiting Jews returning to the annual festival from every city in the Roman Empire. The truth of the resurrection of Christ and these "firstfruits" spread like wildfire throughout the Roman Empire until almost half the population believed in Christ by the second century.

Paradise

A great transformation occurred in the spiritual world when Christ defeated Satan and "led captivity captive." Jesus triumphed over Satan openly and led "many" of the departed saints home to heaven. While the Bible does not specifically state that these resurrected saints ascended to heaven, the common teaching of the early Church believed this. Certainly, they would not have died again. They probably ascended into the heavens when Jesus Christ ascended forty days after His resurrection "in a cloud of witnesses." From the time of Christ's death on the Cross, the souls of believers who die go immediately to a place called Paradise. Jesus declared to the thief on the Cross, "Assuredly, I say to you, today you will be with Me in Paradise" (Luke 23:43). Instead of descending into Abraham's bosom, all believers will now ascend into heaven to enjoy the presence of Jesus Christ forever. Paradise is another word for the New Jerusalem, the city of God in heaven that Christ is preparing for the Bride. In Paradise the souls of believers enjoy the presence of Christ and other saints but they do not yet possess their resurrection bodies. They are awaiting the day of the Rapture so that they can receive their new immortal, incorruptible bodies that they might participate in all the experiences of heaven and join with Christ to rule the nations on earth. In 2 Corinthians 12:4 the Apostle Paul explains "how he was caught up into Paradise and heard inexpressible words, which it is not lawful for a man to utter." The prophet John describes his vision of the glorious New Jerusalem and records the promise of Christ, "To him who overcomes I will give to eat from the tree of life, which is in the midst of the Paradise of God" (Revelation 2:7).

The Time of the Great White Throne Judgment

John prophesied that this judgment will occur in heaven at the end of the one thousand years of millennial reign of the Messiah. This great trial will seal the final judgment of all the wicked dead who have died — from the Garden of Eden until the last rebel dies in Satan's final rebellion at the end of the Millennium. After seven thousand years the titanic spiritual struggle for the dominion of the earth and the souls of men will finally end with Satan cast into the lake of fire. After testing men in every possible spiritual test and condition, God will test the men and women born in the Millennium to prove that, apart from Christ's redemption, men will still choose to rebel rather than serve God. After the defeat of Satan's final rebellion at the end of the Millennium, the devil will be cast into the lake of fire forever demonstrating the ultimate victory of Christ over sin and evil. When the Millennium ends, the Lord will resurrect the bodies and souls of all wicked men and women. They will stand in judgment with the sinful angels who participated in Satan's rebellion against God. This great judgment will provide each sinner with a fair trial to examine his life to reveal the absolute justice of God. While the Scriptures do not reveal the length of time the trial will take, the length of the sentence for each defendant will be eternity without end.

The Justice of God

For thousands of years people have complained that the just are often punished while the wicked apparently escape true justice. Finally, after the completion of seven thousand years of sinful human history, the great week of God's dealing with mankind, those who reject God will receive the justice and punishment they truly deserve. The Bible indicates that the sinners of all ages will finally receive judgment for every deed and word of their lives. They will be judged "by the things which were written in the books" recording every deed of their life. All of the dead will be "judged according to their works" because they refused to accept the forgiveness of God purchased by Christ by His death on the Cross.

Degrees of Punishment in Hell

Many people assume that all unrepentant sinners will experience an identical degree of punishment in hell. However, the Bible reveals that a holy and just God will judge every individual sinner according to the deeds of his life and will punish him in hell according to his works. Moses recorded these words about God's justice: "Shall not the Judge of all the earth do right?" (Genesis 18:25). All of those who stand before God at the Great White Throne judgment will be sentenced to hell forever. However, individual punishments throughout eternity will vary in degree according to God's perfect justice. In Matthew 7:1,2 the Lord warned that our judgment would reflect the choices we make in our lives: "Judge not, that you be not judged. For with what judgment you judge, you will be judged; and with the same measure you use, it will be measured back to you." Jesus warned the people about some hypocritical scribes who were seeking notoriety and fame, devouring "widow's houses and for a pretence make long prayers: these shall receive greater damnation" (Mark 12:38-40). In another passage

Christ describes the different judgment given out to the servants based on their failure to do the will of their Lord but especially upon their knowledge of his instructions. "And that servant who knew his master's will, and did not prepare himself or do according to his will, shall be beaten with many stripes. But he who did not know, yet committed things worthy of stripes, shall be beaten with few. For everyone to whom much is given, from him much will be required; and to whom much has been committed, of him they will ask the more" (Luke 12:47,48). These verses reveal that degrees of punishment will exist forever in the afterlife.

Final Justice

King Solomon, the wisest man who ever lived, wrote the book of Ecclesiastes describing the lack of justice in human life. He often pondered over the fact that evil deeds appear to go unpunished in this life while righteous men often have trouble all their days. "Because the sentence against an evil work is not executed speedily, therefore the heart of the sons of men is fully set in them to do evil. Though a sinner does evil a hundred times, and his days are prolonged, yet I surely know that it will be well with those who fear God, who fear before Him" (Ecclesiastes 8:11,12). God, in His mercy, often delays the punishment for sin, allowing a man time to repent and turn from his evil path. Solomon's inspired conclusion was that God's justice, though delayed, will finally be revealed. "For God will bring every work into judgment, including every secret thing, whether it is good or whether it is evil" (Ecclesiastes 12:14). Sometimes, Satan, in his cunning attempt to destroy men's souls, delays the consequences of sin to lead a man deeper and deeper into a whirlpool of depravity. If a man's sin immediately resulted in painful and embarrassing consequences, many people would turn from their sinful path before it entrapped them. Tragically, often a man seems to "get away with it" for a time. This apparent lack of consequences leads the person step by step into a life given over to evil. Only then, when he is imprisoned in a sinful life, will he see the terrible consequences of his choices in lost health, family and peace of mind.

The Reality of Hell

God will judge the souls of unrepentant sinners and sentence them to the degree of punishment they deserve. In Genesis 18:25, Moses revealed the true justice of God who knows the inner heart of all men: "Far be it from You to do such a thing as this, to slay the righteous with the wicked, so that the righteous should be as the wicked; far be it from You! Shall not the Judge of all the earth do right?" These passages reveal that Adolph Hitler will receive greater damnation than a sinner who lives a normal life but refuses to confess his sins and ask forgiveness of Christ. One of the most horrible things about hell, aside from the torment of the lake of fire, will be the companions that will surround sinners throughout eternity. Every torturer, bully and cruel individual will be imprisoned there forever. All those in hell will possess an immortal body that can experience sensation but cannot die. For a normal citizen, a sentence of life in a prison with violent offenders would become a living hell. Those who reject Christ's salvation and heaven will have chosen to exist in hell with these evil companions forever. Christ warned that those who refuse His mercy will "go to hell, into the fire that shall never be quenched; where 'their worm does not die and the fire is not quenched'" (Mark 9:43). Another terrible aspect of hell is that sinners will still be aware of the saints and their joy in the Kingdom of God in heaven. "There will be weeping and gnashing of teeth, when you see Abraham and Isaac and Jacob and all the prophets in the Kingdom of God, and yourselves thrust out" (Luke 13:28). Another horror of hell is that these sinners will never rest. "And the smoke of their torment ascends forever and ever; and they have no rest day or night, who worship the beast and his image, and whoever receives the mark of his name" (Revelation 14:11).

Some have tried to escape the grim reality of hell as described by the Bible. They have suggested that all these descriptions are only symbolic. Obviously the biblical writer was forced to use the best language they had available to describe the terrible visions of judgment given to them by God. Regardless of how you choose to interpret these descriptions of hell, the Bible's clear warning is that hell will be the most terrible reality we could ever imagine. God's holy justice demands that sinful rebellion must be punished. The holiness of God's heaven makes it impossible for any unrepentant sinner to enter there. There is a righteous need to punish sin expressed in biblical passages such as Romans 6:23, "For the wages of sin is death, but the gift of God is eternal life in Christ Jesus our Lord." When some writers consider the boundless love of God they suggest that this love could not possibly allow unrepentant sinners to endure an eternity in hell. However, it is impossible for our finite minds, warped by years of exposure to sin, to determine what degree of punishment is consistent with God's infinite love for mankind and the demands of holy justice.

Certain writers try to soften the warnings of an eternity in torment by suggesting that hell will be limited in duration. However many biblical passages contain the clear warning of our Savior that hell is eternal. "Then He will also say to those on the left hand, 'Depart from Me, you cursed, into the everlasting fire prepared for the devil and his angels" (Matthew 25:41). Furthermore, if the passage of time would bring the suffering of hell to an end, why would Jesus Christ have left heaven to die on the Cross to save us from eternal punishment. Others have argued that hell really means the annihilation of the souls of the wicked. However, a careful examination of the many relevant passages describing hell as "everlasting fire" prevents us from accepting this interpretation. In Revelation 20:10 John prophesied that Satan will be cast into the lake of fire to join the Antichrist and False Prophet "and they will be tormented day and night forever." John's awesome vision of the Great White Throne ends with these words, "And anyone not found written in the Book of Life was cast into the lake of fire" (Revelation 20:15). Finally, the fact that Jesus went to the Cross to die horribly for our sins is the greatest proof that hell is both real and eternal. If hell was not eternal and terrible beyond words, why would Christ have paid the supreme price of the Cross and the "three days and nights" when "He also first descended into the lower parts of the earth?"

The Judge

Jesus Christ, the Son of God will be the ultimate Judge of

269

all creation including the fallen angels and the wicked dead of all generations. In John 5:22 we read: "For the Father judges no one, but has committed all judgment to the Son." Jesus Christ, who created man and the universe, chose to die for our sins. On the day of judgment He will pass sentence on those who rejected His mercy. John declared that God "has given Him authority to execute judgment also, because He is the Son of Man. Do not marvel at this; for the hour is coming in which all who are in the graves will hear His voice and come forth; those who have done good, to the resurrection of life, and those who have done evil, to the resurrection of condemnation" (John 5:27-29). The Apostle Paul revealed that Christians will participate in the judgment of these fallen angelic beings. "Do you not know that we shall judge angels?" (1 Corinthians 6:3). Though God created man to have less power than the angels, ultimately, Christ will empower resurrected believers to a position higher than angels."For You have made him a little lower than the angels, And You have crowned him with glory and honor" (Psalm 8:5).

Who Will Be Judged?

All of the wicked dead will be resurrected in an immortal body to appear before the Throne of God in heaven to receive punishment for the sins of their life. John described his awesome vision of an innumerable throng of humanity risen from the dead to stand before God. "And I saw the dead, small and great, standing before God, and books were opened. And another book was opened, which is the Book of Life. And the dead were judged according to their works, by the things which were written in the books. The sea gave up the dead who were in it, and Death and Hades delivered up the dead who were in them. And they were judged, each one according to his works" (Revelation 20:12,13). For millennia people have tried to "work their way to heaven." Many have expressed their distaste for the Bible's message of a salvation that is unearned and is received only through the grace of Jesus Christ.

Finally, those who have refused the grace of God will have the opportunity to be judged on the basis of their works.

Every single deed has been recorded in the "books" of God to be recalled at the final judgment. Tragically, they will discover that no amount of good works will ever balance out our sinful rebellion and make our souls right with God. The Scriptures reveal the basis of God's judgment: "They were judged, each one according to his works" (v. 13).

The Book of Life

Why would the Book of Life be opened during the Great White Throne judgment of wicked sinners when no one at that judgment will have their names recorded in that book? The Book of Life contains only the names of those who have accepted the salvation of Christ. This is the record of each believer's decision to follow Jesus Christ as their Lord. Whenever someone accepts Christ as their Savior, their name is enrolled in heaven's Book of Life, qualifying them for the heavenly city, the New Jerusalem. "But there shall by no means enter it [the New Jerusalem] anything that defiles, or causes an abomination or a lie, but only those who are written in the Lamb's Book of Life" (Revelation 21:27). Probably, among those judged for their works, there will be many who will claim that they are Christians. They will claim that some great mistake has been made; that they were members of a church for years; that they have done great things for God during their lives on earth. However, God declares: "Not everyone who says to Me, 'Lord, Lord,' shall enter the kingdom of heaven, but he who does the will of My Father in heaven. Many will say to Me in that day, 'Lord, Lord, have we not prophesied in Your name, cast out demons in Your name, and done many wonders in Your name?'" (Matthew 7:21,22). Only God knows the true heart of a man. Unless we truly repent of our sins, turn from our sinful rebellion and accept Christ as our Lord and Savior, we shall never experience the salvation of God. No amount of good works or theological knowledge will qualify us to enter heaven's gates. The only acceptable price for salvation and pardon from hell is the blood of Christ shed on the Cross for each one of us. However, unless we accept that pardon individually, it has no effect for us.

The only wicked people who will not be judged at the

271

Great White Throne judgment are those who have already been judged earlier at Armageddon. These individuals include the Antichrist, the False Prophet and those evil people who survive the Battle of Armageddon to be judged at the Judgment of the Nations described in Matthew 25. These evil people are the "goats," the wicked individuals of the Gentile nations who enthusiastically joined in the persecution of the Tribulation believers, the Jewish and Gentile believers in Christ. During the Judgment of the Nations "the King will answer and say to them, 'Assuredly, I say to you, inasmuch as you did it to one of the least of these My brethren, you did it to Me.' Then He will also say to those on the left hand, 'Depart from Me, you cursed, into the everlasting fire prepared for the devil and his angels'" (Matthew 25:40-41). Since these wicked individuals are judged by Christ and sent to hell at this judgment following the Battle of Armageddon, they will not appear to be judged a second time a thousand years later at the Great White Throne judgment in heaven. As described in detail in another chapter, the Antichrist and False Prophet will be defeated by Christ at the Battle of Armageddon. Revelation 19:20 declares: "These two were cast alive into the lake of fire burning with brimstone."

The Fall of Satan

Long before Adam and Eve were created in the Garden of Eden a titanic spiritual struggle took place in the heavens among the angels of God. This battle occurred when Satan rebelled against the divine government of God. Far from the medieval images of Satan as a red devil with pitchfork and horns, the Bible declares that Lucifer was "the seal of perfection, full of wisdom and perfect in beauty" and "the anointed cherub." The Word of God describes Satan as "perfect in your ways from the day you were created, till iniquity was found in you" (Ezekiel 28:15). Ezekiel reveals that pride was the cause of Satan's sinful rebellion. "Your heart was lifted up because of your beauty; you corrupted your wisdom for the sake of your splendor" (Ezekiel 28:17). Satan, an anointed cherub, with all the experience and knowledge of an angel of God, fell into sinful rebellious pride. The same spiritual pride is the cause of all our sins.

The prophet Isaiah was given a profound insight into this first rebellion of Lucifer. Satan proclaimed: "I will ascend into heaven, I will exalt my throne above the stars of God; I will also sit on the mount of the congregation on the farthest sides of the north; I will ascend above the heights of the clouds, I will be like the Most High" (Isaiah 14:12-14). Satan's true motive is revealed in his statement, "I will be like the Most High." This urge to "be like God" lies at the basis of every false cult and religion that seeks to allow man to transcend himself, "to become like God." In the Garden of Eden, Satan approached Eve and offered her the opportunity to become a "little god" in these words: "You will be like God, knowing good and evil" (Genesis 3:5). This rebellious attempt to "be like God" led to the loss of the spiritual communion between men and God. It destroyed man's life of peace and love in Paradise. Sinful rebellion produced the curse of evil, disease, physical death and, ultimately, the spiritual death which is hell.

Lucifer possessed all the knowledge anyone could ever hope to have about God and eternity. Yet he chose to rebel against the throne of heaven. This reveals that our decision to accept or reject God does not depend on intellectual knowledge; it depends on the individual choice of each soul to accept or reject Christ as the God of his life rather than choose to be the "god" of his own life. Someone must be the God of our life. In the end, either we will allow God to rule our lives or we will insist on being the God of our own lives. Each man's fundamental spiritual decision will lead to an eternity in heaven or hell.

Toward the end of Christ's ministry He asked His disciples the most important question that each of us must answer. "He said to them, 'But who do you say that I am?' And Simon Peter answered and said, 'You are the Christ, the Son of the living God'" (Matthew 16:15,16). This is ultimately the most important question because an affirmative answer will transform the rest of our lives. If we truly acknowledge that Jesus is "the Christ, the Son of the Living God" we will give Him our lives and follow Him as our Lord and Savior from that moment on.

The Judgment of the Fallen Angels

When Satan first rebelled against the government of heaven, many of the angels chose to join him in his terrible rebellion against the Lord. In Revelation 12:4 we discover that one-third of the angels joined in that original rebellion in the dateless past. The Bible declares that these sinful angels are imprisoned awaiting their final day of judgment at the Great White Throne. "God did not spare the angels who sinned, but cast them down to hell and delivered them into chains of darkness, to be reserved for judgment" (2 Peter 2:4).

Only a portion of the rebellious angels sinned in the particular way described by Genesis 6. These demonic angels violated the law of God and took on human form to become sexually involved with women. As described in my book *Heaven - The Last Frontier*, these angels were part of a diabolical plan by Satan to demonically impregnate the women on earth. Satan's goal was to prevent the possibility of a Messiah being "virgin-born" in the future to save mankind from damnation. God was forced to destroy the whole demonically infected population on earth through a worldwide flood to save Noah's family, the only people left on the planet that were "perfect in their generations." Jude declares the fate of those rebellious angels: "The angels who did not keep their proper domain, but left their own habitation, He has reserved in everlasting chains under darkness for the judgment of the great day; as Sodom and Gomorrah, and the cities around them in a similar manner to these, having given themselves over to sexual immorality and gone after strange flesh, are set forth as an example, suffering the vengeance of eternal fire." (Jude, verses 6,7). These passages confirm that the fallen angels' sin was "sexual immorality"because they had violated the forbidden line God drew between angels and humans as they had "gone after strange flesh."

The rest of the angels that did not sin in this particular manner were allowed to remain free to follow their leader Satan in his attempt to destroy mankind. These fallen angels are the demonic spirits that remain free with Satan to participate in spiritual battles until they will be sent to hell at the Great White Throne judgment. The Apostle Paul warns

Christians that we are engaged in continuous spiritual warfare involving demonic angels and heavenly angels contesting for supremacy in the hearts of men. "For we do not wrestle against flesh and blood, but against principalities, against powers, against the rulers of the darkness of this age, against spiritual hosts of wickedness in the heavenly places" (Ephesians 6:12). These fallen angels presently have access to the heavenlies as well as the earth. However, during the Tribulation period, at the mid-point, these demonic angels and Satan will be cast out of the heavenlies by Michael the Archangel and his angelic host. "So the great dragon was cast out, that serpent of old, called the Devil and Satan, who deceives the whole world; he was cast to the earth, and his angels were cast out with him" (Revelation 12:9). When these fallen angels descend to the earth the angels of heaven will rejoice. But they call out a dreadful warning to the unrepentant sinners on earth warning that Satan's wrath is about to be unleashed upon them. "Therefore rejoice, O heavens, and you who dwell in them! Woe to the inhabitants of the earth and the sea! For the devil has come down to you, having great wrath, because he knows that he has a short time" (Revelation 12:12).

Hell itself, the lake of fire, was originally prepared by God for Satan and his angels, not for mankind. God never intended man to rebel and separate himself forever from God's presence. This is revealed in Christ's words to the sinful "goat nations": "Depart from Me, you cursed, into the everlasting fire prepared for the devil and his angels" (Matthew 25:41). These angels have far more knowledge of spiritual matters than any human, yet they do not repent of their sins. In the nature of things, it may not be possible for them to repent. Possibly, because they have complete spiritual knowledge and still reject God, there is no possibility of their receiving any new spiritual revelation that would cause them to repent of their sinful rebellion. In a similar manner, those holy angels who rejected Satan's rebellion in the dateless past were never again tempted to rebel because their holy character does not change. They made their eternal choice to obey or rebel against God based on all the knowledge that exists.

The Purpose of the Great White Throne Judgment

All those who appear at the Great White Throne judgment are destined to an eternity in hell. Some may wonder why God judges them since their fate is already sealed by their sins and rejection of Christ's salvation. Each person will have his day of judgment because Jesus Christ is a holy God whose nature is pure justice. Each person will receive punishment according to his sinful works as his every single deed, thought and act is revealed by the "books" that record the deeds of men. As Matthew 12:36 indicates: "But I say to you that for every idle word men may speak, they will give account of it in the day of judgment." The Scripture declares that every secret thought and motivation will be revealed in the final day of judgment. Paul describes that "their conscience also bearing witness, and between themselves their thoughts accusing or else excusing them in the day when God will judge the secrets of men by Jesus Christ, according to my gospel" (Romans 2:15,16).

The basis of this last judgment will be the works and motives of their lives as revealed in the "books" of God that record every thought and deed. Furthermore, as Romans 2:15,16 reveals, every man's "conscience" will "bear witness" together with the "gospel" and the "law of God" which no man can ever keep perfectly. Despite a person's best efforts, it is impossible to live a sinless and perfect life before a holy God. The Bible states that"all have sinned and fall short of the glory of God" (Romans 3:23). This means that no matter how wonderfully a person might try to live, he will never reach God's standard of perfect holiness and righteousness. As Romans 3:10 declares: "There is none righteous, no, not one." No one can live a righteous life and "without holiness, no one can see God." How then, can anyone ever qualify to enter heaven to dwell with a holy God?

Escaping the Great White Throne Judgment

The Apostle Paul reveals the only hope for man to escape the Great White Throne judgment and an eternity in hell. In Romans 6:23 Paul writes that "the wages of sin is death, but the gift of God is eternal life in Christ Jesus our

Lord." The only righteousness that God will accept cannot come from our own attempts to live perfectly, because that is impossible. The "gift of God is eternal life in Christ Jesus our Lord." We must confess that we are sinners and accept the gift of eternal life that Jesus gives us through His death on the Cross. Then God will take Christ's "righteousness" and place it to our account. When we stand before God, He will not see the sins of our life, but He will see the righteousness of His Son, Jesus Christ. The promise of God belongs to anyone who will believe His words and act on His promise. It isn't intellectual ascent to a statement of theology that saves a man from hell. As the Bible shows, the devil believes in God, but it doesn't help him. Christianity isn't a religion, a man-made set of theological statements about how we can work our way back to God. Christianity is the story of how God reached down to a sinful, hurting humanity and gave them His only Son, Jesus Christ, to purchase their salvation. The price was His blood shed on Calvary to win a pardon from hell for every soul that would trust in Him. To become a Christian we must enter into a relationship with God based on our belief, our repentance and a commitment to follow Jesus Christ as our Lord and Savior. He gave everything on the Cross to win our souls, He wants nothing less than everything in return. The promise of Christ is absolute: "If we confess our sins, He is faithful and just to forgive us our sins and to cleanse us from all unrighteousness" (1 John 1:9).

CHAPTER SIXTEEN

The New Jerusalem

The Holy City of God

The New Jerusalem is the capital city of heaven, the center of God's universe. It is the home of the Church and the saints of the Old Testament who believe the promises of God. This is not the only city in heaven but it is the only one that is described. Jesus prepared the New Jerusalem to become the ultimate home of the saints. In John 14:2 Jesus promised: "In My Father's house are many mansions; if it were not so, I would have told you. I go to prepare a place for you. And if I go and prepare a place for you, I will come again and receive you to Myself; that where I am, there you may be also." Up until the moment of Christ's resurrection, the souls of the saints of the Old Testament remained in a place of waiting, called Abraham's bosom. The souls of the unrighteous went to another place of waiting, a place of torment called Hades. Jesus, Himself, described the situation of these souls as recorded in Luke 16:22: "So it was that the beggar died, and was carried by the angels to Abraham's bosom. The rich man also died and was buried. And being in torments in Hades, he lifted up his eyes and saw Abraham afar off, and Lazarus in his bosom." In this fascinating teaching the Lord revealed that the souls of those who had died were aware of their circumstances, concerned with other people and waiting for ultimate judgment. The rich man still knew his brothers and the beggar. He retained his memories and love for his brothers, requesting that someone warn them of their spiritual peril. These revelations indicate that we will retain our identity, memories and love for others in heaven. Our love and relationships transcend death. The Old Testament saints that were resurrected by Jesus Christ are now citizens of the heavenly New Jerusalem. The Scriptures affirm that Jesus defeated Satan and the powers of hell, freeing the captives of Abraham's bosom. He won the freedom for these Old Testament saints to enter the heavenly city. "When He ascended on high, He led captivity captive, and gave gifts to men" (Ephesians 4:8).

All Christians who have died during the last two thousand years are now present in their spirits in this heavenly city. However, these individual souls are present in their spirits only. They have not yet received their glorious resurrection body which they will receive at the Rapture. All living Christians and all departed saints will receive their glorious eternal resurrection bodies at the same moment, the rapture of the Church.

The New Jerusalem -- The Promise of Paradise

The New Jerusalem is described as Paradise in a number of scriptural passages. Jesus promised the thief on the cross, "Assuredly, I say to you, today you will be with Me in Paradise." This passage assures us that the moment a Christian dies, his or her soul will instantly be present in Paradise, the New Jerusalem in heaven. The Bible does not teach soul sleep. The Scriptures declare that the bodies of the dead "sleep" while they await their resurrection at the last day. Paul confirmed that the souls of Christians are "present with the Lord." "We are confident, yes, well pleased rather to be absent from the body and to be present with the Lord" (2 Corinthians 5:8). The word "Paradise" relates to the ancient word for "garden." The word reminds us inevitably of the original Paradise, the Garden of Eden, when Adam and Eve communed with the "Lord God walking in the garden in the cool of the day" (Genesis 3:8).

The name "Paradise," referring to the New Jerusalem, was used by Paul to describe his experience of being raptured "to the third heaven." In his vision the Apostle described that he was "caught up to the third heaven...how he was caught up into Paradise and heard inexpressible words, which it is not lawful for a man to utter" (2 Corinthians 12:2,4). In the letter to the churches recorded in Revelation 2:7, Jesus described the heavenly home of the Church as follows: "He who has an ear, let him hear what the

Spirit says to the churches. To him who overcomes I will give to eat from the tree of life, which is in the midst of the Paradise of God." The tree of life will be present in the midst of the New Jerusalem forever. It will remind us that our life is dependent upon the gifts of God. In Revelation 22:2 we are told that "in the middle of its street, and on either side of the river, was the tree of life, which bore twelve fruits, each tree yielding its fruit every month. And the leaves of the tree were for the healing of the nations."

The Home of the Bride

Some writers mistakenly concluded that the New Jerusalem itself is the Bride of Christ. They misunderstand the words of the prophet in Revelation 21:2: "Then I, John, saw the holy city, New Jerusalem, coming down out of heaven from God, prepared as a bride adorned for her husband." These writers fail to notice the precise words of the prophecy that reveal that the New Jerusalem is "prepared as a bride adorned for her husband." John revealed that Christ has prepared the New Jerusalem, adorned with jewels, for the coming Church in the same careful, expectant manner that a bride prepares for her prospective husband.

The Church is clearly revealed in Scripture as the Bride of Christ. The Bible uses the word "Bride" five times to describe the Church. It also describes Christ as the Bridegroom in ten passages. As an example, Christ referred to the Church as the Bride in Revelation 22:16,17: "I, Jesus, have sent My angel to testify to you these things in the churches. I am the Root and the Offspring of David, the Bright and Morning Star. And the Spirit and the bride say, 'Come!'" The Apostle Paul used the symbol of marriage to describe the intimate spiritual relationship of the saints to their Bridegroom, Christ. In Ephesians 5:25 Paul wrote: "Husbands, love your wives, just as Christ also loved the church and gave Himself for it." The book of Revelation prophesied about the wonderful Marriage Supper of the Lamb when the spiritual union between Christ and the Church will be celebrated in heaven. Finally, Jesus revealed Himself as the Bridegroom of the Church in His prophecy of His departure to heaven. "Jesus said to them, 'Can the friends of the bridegroom mourn as long as the bridegroom is with them? But the days will come when the bridegroom will be taken away from them, and then they will fast'" (Matthew 9:15).

The City of God -- The Hope of the Early Church

The early Church wrote extensively about the prophecies of the resurrection and the Heavenly City. They longed for the day when Christ would establish the Kingdom of God. Several key writers in the first few centuries of this era wrote about their understanding of the New Jerusalem. Tertullian,in his writing *Against Marcion*, wrote about the heavenly Jerusalem. "But we do confess that a kingdom is promised to us upon the earth, although before heaven, only in another state of existence; inasmuch as it will be after the resurrection for a thousand years in the divinely-built city of Jerusalem, 'let down from heaven,' which the apostle also calls 'our mother from above' and while declaring that our citizenship is in heaven, he predicates of it that it is really a city in heaven. This both Ezekiel had knowledge of and the Apostle John beheld."

The Names of the Heavenly City

"Then I, John, saw the holy city, New Jerusalem, coming down out of heaven from God, prepared as a bride adorned for her husband" (Revelation 21:2).

The Bible uses a number of names and expressions to describe the ultimate destination and home of the Church. It is called the New Jerusalem to indicate its place in the heart of God, similar to His love for the earthly Jerusalem that He chose for His holy sanctuary. The city is called "New Jerusalem" by John because it will remain forever new in the pristine holiness of heaven. As John declared, "Then He who sat on the throne said, 'Behold, I make all things new'" (Revelation 21:5).

John called it the "holy city" in Revelation 21:2 because the holy presence of God will abide there forever. Nothing of sin will ever enter this holy city of Christ. "But there shall by no means enter it [New Jerusalem] anything that defiles, or causes an abomination or a lie, but only those who are written in the Lamb's Book of Life" (Revelation 21:27). Because God will actually dwell with His saints there, John calls the New Jerusalem "the tabernacle of God." In Revelation 21:3 he records the wonderful promise of God, "Behold, the tabernacle of God is with men, and He will dwell with them, and they shall be His people, and God Himself will be with them and be their God." Jesus promised us "mansions" in heaven, "My Father's house." "In My Father's house are many mansions; if it were not so, I would have told you. I go to prepare a place for you" (John 14:2). Just as children are secure in their father's house, we will live forever in the security of our "Father's house. From the moment Adam and Eve were exiled from the earthly Paradise, we have lived in exile from our "Father's house." It is worthwhile to consider Jesus' parable of the loving forgiveness of the father for his Prodigal Son. God plans to redeem His children from spiritual exile. His plan will ultimately be realized when we will be reunited in perfect fellowship with our heavenly Father in the City of God.

Several other names were revealed in Hebrews 12:22: "Mount Zion," "the city of the living God" and "the heavenly Jerusalem." "But you have come to Mount Zion and to the city of the living God, the heavenly Jerusalem, to an innumerable company of angels" (Hebrews 12:22). God calls it "the heavenly Jerusalem" to distinguish it from the earthly Jerusalem that will continue to exist forever as a blessed throne for the Messiah Jesus Christ.

Hebrews 11 -- Faith in the New Jerusalem

Far from being a new promise, John's prophecy of the descent of the heavenly city, the New Jerusalem, was simply a confirmation of all the promises made to the Old and New Testament saints for the last six thousand years. The great faith chapter of Hebrews 11 focused on the tremendous faith of the Old and New Testament saints in the promises of God. However, many have ignored the nature of the faith that God commends in these great saints. These saints were praised by

Christ for believing the promises of God in the New Jerusalem, the heavenly city. "For he looked for a city which has foundations, whose builder and maker is God" (Hebrews 11:10 - KJV). Many of us have heard great messages preached from this chapter about the "faith of the fathers" that was commended by God. Unfortunately, many have missed the essential detail about the object of the faith of these saints. It was not simply faith in the abstract that God commended. The clear teaching of Hebrews 11 and 12 is that God approved the faith of these saints because they believed fully in His promise of the heavenly New Jerusalem. "But you have come to Mount Zion and to the city of the living God, the heavenly Jerusalem, to an innumerable company of angels" (Hebrews 12:22).

The Bible declares that the ultimate faith of Abraham, Isaac and Jacob was in God's promise of the heavenly New Jerusalem. The earthly Promised Land and Jerusalem were just a foretaste of God's final promise. "These all died in faith, not having received the promises, but having seen them afar off were assured of them, embraced them, and confessed that they were strangers and pilgrims on the earth" (Hebrews 11:13). This faith in heaven was so profound that these saints were persuaded of its truth. They embraced the hope of the New Jerusalem and confessed it with their lips to others. This faith was so real that they lived as "strangers and pilgrims on the earth." Would those who know you best, such as your spouse or children, state that you embrace the hope of heaven and live as a pilgrim? Too many Christians have lost their longing for the heavenly New Jerusalem. They live each day focused exclusively on the cares of their daily lives. Many Christians have fallen in love with this world. In past generations, some accused Christians of "being so heavenly-minded that they were no earthy good." The problem in the closing decade of this century is almost the complete opposite. Many believers today are "so earthy-minded that they are no heavenly good" to their Father.

For many Christians, their knowledge and faith in heaven is so weak that they have lost sight of their eternal destiny. It is fascinating to read the praise in Hebrews 11:16 of the faith of these Old Testament saints who believed the promises of God. "But now they desire a better, that is, a heavenly country. Therefore God is not ashamed to be called their God, for He has prepared a city for them." Hebrews declared that "God is not ashamed to be called their God" because they believed His heavenly promises and reflected that faith in their lives. God may be "ashamed to be called their God" if Christians lack faith in the heavenly promises of the New Jerusalem. In Hebrews 13:14, the writer reminds us that everything in our earthly life is temporary. The ultimate goal and home for all believers in Christ is the eternal city of God. "For here we have no continuing city, but we seek the one to come." The New Jerusalem is our spiritual home, the ultimate goal of the Christian's walk by faith. Paul wrote, "Jerusalem above is free, which is the mother of us all" (Galatians 4:26).

The Heavenly City -- The New Jerusalem

The Bible described the New Jerusalem in very real and physical terms. Some writers interpret these descriptions in Revelation as simply symbols of a deeper spiritual reality. The problem with this approach is that it contradicts the detailed descriptions of the city. Whenever the Bible uses a symbol, it always interprets the symbol to ensure that the reader understands the clear meaning of the passage. Certainly, the vivid imagery of the book of Revelation reveals the ability of John to use figurative language and symbols to express spiritual truths. However, when John described the heavenly city, he used the most precise language available to him. Therefore, we should interpret these physical details of the eternal city of God as literally as the passage demands and common sense allows.

The first question concerns the location of the city. The Scriptures described both our resurrection bodies and the heavenly city in very concrete terms. Therefore the city must exist as a real entity in another dimension, or possibly, somewhere in distant space. The Bible does not give us enough information to conclusively answer this question. Significantly, the Bible consistently refers to heaven as existing in an upward direction from earth. In Revelation 3:12, John described "the New Jerusalem, which comes down out of heaven from My God." At present, the New Jerusalem remains in the heavens. After the Millennium ends and sin is eradicated from the earth, the New Jerusalem will descend to the earth as it "comes down out of heaven."

In addition, heaven is often described as being in a northerly direction from the earth. In Psalm 48:2 King David wrote of the heavenly city, "Beautiful in elevation, the joy of the whole earth, is Mount Zion on the sides of the north, the city of the great King." The prophet Isaiah described the rebellion of Satan in heaven in the same terms. "For you have said in your heart: 'I will ascend into heaven, I will exalt my throne above the stars of God; I will also sit on the mount of the congregation on the farthest sides of the north" (Isaiah 14:13). In astronomy, locations in space can be described in relative terms to our earth and its solar system. The direction north exists relative to the north pole and in the same northerly direction from the solar system. If we extend this direction out from our solar system it is still "north" from the standpoint of the Bible's writers and its readers on earth.

The Size of the Heavenly City

In Revelation 21:16,17 John describes the dimensions of the New Jerusalem. "The city is laid out as a square, and its length is as great as its breadth. And he measured the city with the reed: twelve thousand furlongs. Its length, breadth, and height are equal.Then he measured its wall: one hundred and forty-four cubits, according to the measure of a man, that is, of an angel." The distance of each side, twelve thousand furlongs, is equal to fifteen hundred miles. There are two different geometric shapes that could be accurately expressed by this description "Its length, breadth, and height are equal." The first is a cube shape and the second is a pyramid shape. The weight of evidence has forced the majority of writers to conclude that the holy city must be in the form of an enormous city, fifteen hundred miles square, rising in tiers as a huge mountain some fifteen hundred miles in the sky. A city that size could easily hold a population of several billion citizens. Revelation 21:17 described "its wall: one hundred and forty-four cubits" (equal to 216 feet high) and verse 21 reveals that there will be twelve gates in this wall for entering and leaving the city. While it is hard to see how a cube-shaped city could have a wall 216 foot high, a pyramidal shaped city could logically rest on a base 216 feet high with twelve gates. Interestingly, the book of Revelation describes the city as "a high mountain." When the angel took John to see the New Jerusalem he wrote: "He carried me away in the Spirit to a great and high mountain, and showed me the great city, the holy Jerusalem, descending out of heaven from God."

The materials described in the New Jerusalem are precious stones and metals depicting the beauty and glory of the heavenly city. The 216 foot high wall (144 cubits) will be laid in twelve foundation layers of jasper crystal (each layer 12 cubits or 18 feet high) "garnished with all manner of precious stones." Each of the twelve foundation layers will bear the name of one of the twelve apostles in honor of their faithfulness (Revelation 21:14). The twelve layers are jasper, sapphire, chalcedony, emerald, sardonyx, sardius, chrysolyte, beryl, topaz, chrysoprasus, jacinth and amethyst (Revelation 21:19,20). The ancients sometimes used different names for precious stones than we do today. Jasper probably referred to a light blue quartz while the sapphire was a beautiful deep blue. Chalcedony can be light brown or white and the emerald is a rich green. The sardonyx is a combination of milkwhite onyx with stripes of reddish hue. Sardius stones are almost flesh-colored and chrysolyte are a beautiful golden yellow with some green. The beryl stone is probably the same as our aquamarine while the topaz of the ancients was pale green. Some authorities identify the chrysoprasus with a golden green-colored stone like an apple. The jacinth was a gorgeous violet color and the amethyst stone portrayed a deep blue and red combination with occasional purple hue. While there is some question about the exact colors of these ancient stones, it is interesting that the last seven stones from the sardius through to the amethyst parallel the order of the colors in a rainbow.

The twelve gates are named in honor of the twelve tribes of Israel, indicating God's unbreakable covenant with His Chosen People. While the foundation walls are of jasper crystal, "the city was pure gold, like clear glass." Gold can be made so malleable that a super-thin coating of gold can be used to cover the steel and glass of a modern skyscraper. Although it is transparent "like clear glass," when you see it at an angle or from outside, the buildings walls and windows appear to be pure gold. In another passage John describes that "the twelve gates were twelve pearls: each individual gate was of one pearl. And the street of the city was pure gold, like transparent glass (21:21). While some choose to disbelieve the literalness of this passage, I see no reason to reject its reality. Jesus Christ created a universe so vast we cannot measure it. The universe is so complicated that we cannot fathom all of the secrets of the D.N.A. code or the sub-atomic particles. If He can create all these wonders, and more, then Christ can certainly create gates out of a pearl substance or streets of pure gold. What reason would God have for describing such details so precisely unless they were true?

The prophet John described the "river of water of life" in the New Jerusalem. "And he showed me a pure river of water of life, clear as crystal, proceeding from the throne of God and of the Lamb. In the middle of its street, and on either side of the river, was the tree of life, which bore twelve fruits, each tree yielding its fruit every month. And the leaves of the tree were for the healing of the nations" (Revelation 22:1,2). This river of life "proceeding from the throne of God and of the Lamb" reminds us that our spiritual and physical lives are given to us and nurtured continually by God. The tree of life will also exist in the New Jerusalem. It was originally placed in the Garden of Eden to provide the means of conditional immortality to Adam and Eve. It was among the trees and fruits of the garden that were permitted to them. As long as they partook of its fruit, they would live forever. They were created to live immortally if they remained sinless, but that immortality was apparently conditional on eating from the tree of life. However, after they fell into sinful rebellion, God exiled our first parents from Paradise in the Garden of Eden. "He placed cherubim at the east of the garden of Eden, and a flaming sword which turned every way, to guard the way to the tree of life" (Genesis 3:24). The Bible reveals that the specific reason for guarding the entrance to the Garden was to prohibit Adam and Eve from returning to partake of the fruit of the tree of life. Apparently, if they had continued to eat of the leaves from the tree of life as sinners, mankind would have been locked permanently into a sinful state. In Genesis 3:22 the Lord explains the reason for man's exile from the Garden of Eden: "Lest he put out his hand and take also of the tree of life, and eat, and live forever." In one sense, it was a mercy that God removed the tree of life from man's possession. Once sinful rebellion had occurred, it was necessary that men die physically.

While earthly cities receive light from natural sunlight or artificial light, the New Jerusalem will be constantly illuminated by the supernatural light of God's Presence. The supernatural light of Christ will infuse the holy city eliminating the need for light from the sun or artificial lamps. "And there shall be no night there: They need no lamp nor light of the sun, for the Lord God gives them light" (Revelation 22:5). Unfortunately, many writers have misunderstood this passage and believed that it taught that the night and the sun will be eliminated from the universe by God. However, a close examination reveals that "there shall be no night there" applies specifically to the New Jerusalem. Other passages reveal that night and day will continue on the earth forever. Also a close reading reveals that the "need" for a lamp or the "light of the sun" will be eliminated by God's Presence in the Holy City. It does not state that the sun will cease to exist. In Revelation 7:15, John prophesied that the martyrs will be "before the throne of God, and serve Him day and night in His temple." Obviously, time, including "days and nights" will continue forever on earth and heaven.

Will There Be Time in the New Jerusalem?

The majority of Christians in the last few centuries have adopted a boring, passive view of life in heaven. The reasons for this view are two-fold: (1) an absence of teaching about heaven, and (2) a mistaken belief that there is no time in eternity. Obviously, if there is no time in eternity, we would be left with a passive, static and boring heaven. This mistake has fostered a viewpoint that our afterlife will be incredibly dull. Consequently, many Christians want to avoid heaven as long as possible. They fear they will spend eternity "floating on clouds, playing harps in an eternal church service that will never end." These passive and boring images of heavenly life have caused many believers to abandon any hope or longing for heaven. Naturally, if time does not exist in heaven, we could not accomplish anything. Activity requires time.

Where did this unbiblical concept of a timeless heaven come from? Who created this illusion of a heaven without time or activity? Unfortunately, an innocent but archaic phrase in the 1611 King James translation of the Bible has misled millions of believers about the nature of time and eternity. In Revelation 10:6 John recorded a statement about a pause during a continuing series of judgments that the angels will pour out on the earth. In the *King James Version*, it reads "There should be time no longer." In 1611 the readers understood that phrase to indicate that the "time of delay should be no longer." The original Greek phrase meant that "there should be no time of delay any longer (and then the next judgment will fall)." The correct translation, as indicated in all other modern translations (including the *New King James Version*) and the original Greek, reads as follows, "That there should be delay no longer." John wrote: "And the angel whom I saw standing on the sea and on the land lifted up his hand to heaven and swore by Him who lives forever and ever, who created heaven and the things that are in it, the earth and the things that are in it, and the sea and the things that are in it, that there should be delay no longer" (Revelation 10:5,6).

Another verse in Revelation 22:2 confirms that time exists in heaven and the New Jerusalem. In the description of the tree of life, John revealed that there will be a "tree of life, which bore twelve fruits, each tree yielding its fruit every month." This remarkable passage indicates that we will enjoy a variety of fruit in heaven with a different variety each month. Moreover, this description of the "twelve fruits, each yielding its fruit every month" confirms that time will continue forever with twelve months to the year. These passages prove that time, including days and nights, months and years will continue forever in an endlessly fascinating New Heaven and Earth. This tragic misunderstanding about time in eternity has led many Christians to abandon any study of the promises of heaven. We need to be like the Bereans of the first century who "searched the Scriptures daily to see whether or not these thing were true" (Acts 17:11).

The recovery of the truth that eternity is the fullness of time, not the absence of time, will lead to a major re-thinking by Christians in their attitudes to heaven. Once we appreciate that we will have unlimited time in heaven, we can understand that our lives in the New Jerusalem will be the greatest adventure we can possibly imagine. We will have unlimited time to visit the Old and New Testament saints, sit at Christ's feet to learn of Him, to explore heaven and the vast universe. We will "rule and reign forever" in an active, purposeful life, leading and teaching the men and women living on the earth. Imagine the knowledge you will acquire, the things you will invent or create when you have the unlimited resources of Almighty God and you know you cannot fail. You will finally be able to use 100 percent of your brain's powers, instead of the 3 percent to 10 percent most of us use today. We live in a universe of awesome complexity, incredible beauty and inconceivable vastness. When we receive our glorious resurrection bodies, we shall enjoy and explore the wonders of the universe created by our Lord Jesus Christ.

The New Jerusalem will descend from heaven to the earth at the end of the Millennium after sin has been eliminated from the universe (Revelation 21:1,2). Satan will be sent forever into the lake of fire from which he will never return to tempt man or angels. Sin will never raise its ugly head again. Once the earth is cleansed with fire and renewed as a New Earth, pristine and holy, God's Holy City will descend to the earth in fulfillment of Revelation 21:3: "Behold, the tabernacle of God is with men, and He will dwell with them, and they shall be His people, and God Himself will be with them and be their God." As a holy God, the Lord can never bring His Tabernacle and throne to earth until sin and evil are eradicated. Once the earth is made holy, God's Presence will dwell with man forever. The Gentiles (the sheep) that survive the Judgment of the Nations after the Battle of Armageddon (described in Matthew 25) will be blessed throughout the Millennium and forever in the New Earth. These nations will live under the benevolent rule of the Messiah Jesus Christ ruling from the throne of David.

The New Jerusalem will be the home of the Old and New Testament resurrected saints of all ages. "And the nations of those who are saved shall walk in its light, and the kings of the earth bring their glory and honor into it" (Revelation 21:24). This passage reveals that these Gentile nations will continue to exist as political entities and will continue to have "kings" administering their political affairs. National governments will continue because God created mankind with a wonderful diversity and variety of peoples races, tribes and tongues. Nothing in the Bible suggests that this wonderful mosaic will disappear in Christ's Messianic Kingdom. Our diversity will remain our inheritance, even in heaven, according to John's vision recorded in Revelation 7:9. In this vision He described a "great multitude" saved through martyrdom during the Great Tribulation. Note that our individual and racial characteristics, created by Christ, will continue forever. "After these things I looked, and behold, a great multitude which no one could number, of all nations, tribes, peoples, and tongues, standing before the throne and before the Lamb, clothed with white robes, with palm branches in their hands." These people in John's vision appeared to come from all of the nations and tongues.

Zechariah confirms the continued existence of Gentile nations after the Millennium. "And it shall come to pass that everyone who is left of all the nations which came against Jerusalem shall go up from year to year to worship the King, the Lord of hosts, and to keep the Feast of Tabernacles" (Zechariah 14:16). This prophecy indicates that representatives from every nation will attend the Feast of Tabernacles "from year to year" forever. Some writers have wondered why God will demand the attendance of the representatives of the Gentile nations at this annual feast. Possibly, the Feast of Tabernacles, the fifteenth of Tishri, in the fall of the year, will mark the commencement of the millennial Kingdom of the Messiah. As I indicated in my book *Armageddon - Appointment With Destiny*, many prophecies point to the three fall feasts, the Feast of Trumpets, the Day of Atonement and the Feast of Tabernacles as possibly critical days in the fulfillment of the prophecies of Armageddon and the coming Millennium. The prophecies assure us that Israel will continue to exist as the preeminent nation in the ancient Promised Land during the Millennium and the New Earth.

God's promises to Abraham, Isaac and Jacob were eternal covenants that could never be totally fulfilled in the limited duration of a one-thousand-year Millennium. Israel's mission is to bless the nations and sanctify the Holy Name of God forever

CHAPTER SEVENTEEN

A New Heaven and New Earth

"And I saw a new heaven and a new earth, for the first heaven and the first earth had passed away. Also there was no more sea" (Revelation 21:1).

The Apostle John received a vision of the massive transformation of the heavens and the earth that will occur at the end of the Millennium to create a New Heaven and a New earth cleansed of all trace of sin. The earth and its surrounding atmospheric heavens have been polluted by man's sinful rebellion for thousands of years. The prophet Isaiah also saw the restoration of all things connected with the cleansing of the earth from the curse of sin. "For behold, I create new heavens and a new earth; and the former shall not be remembered or come to mind" (Isaiah 65:17). At the end of the Millennium, God prophesied that He will purify the earth and the heavens to create a new Paradise for mankind to enjoy forever.

The Earth's First Destruction

Once before, in the days of Noah, God cleansed the earth from the pollution of sin with a worldwide flood. After the rebellion of Adam and Eve the world lived in sinful rebellion against God until the whole earth was filled with violence, pride and sin. "Then the Lord saw that the wickedness of man was great in the earth, and that every intent of the thoughts of his heart was only evil continually" (Genesis 6:5). Among the inhabitants on the earth, the only family that followed God was the family of Noah. The fallen angels had corrupted the women of earth by violating the law of God and having sexual relations with them. The result of this immoral, unnatural and unholy union was a demonic race of giants. "When the sons of God came in to the daughters of men and they bore children to them. Those were the mighty men who were of old, men of renown" (Genesis 6:4). God viewed earth as "corrupt; for all flesh had corrupted their way on the earth." The result was the flood and the destruction of all life on earth. The Lord preserved humanity through the provision of the ark to save Noah's family and representatives of every species on earth. The waters covered the planet for one whole year. The worldwide devastation of this universal flood wiped out all traces of man's civilization before Noah. The archeologists have not found any historical evidence of civilization before the deluge. When the waters finally retreated, Noah and his family came out of the ark with the animals to begin to replenish the earth.

You can imagine the despair and fear in Noah's family after floating on the water for a year while witnessing the death of all life outside the ark. They must have feared that God would again destroy mankind with a flood if they ever again fell into sinful rebellion. To encourage them to rebuild and replenish the earth God promised and covenanted with Noah that He would never again destroy life on earth with a flood. God declared: "Behold, I establish My covenant with you and with your descendants after you, and with every living creature that is with you...Never again shall all flesh be cut off by the waters of the flood; never again shall there be a flood to destroy the earth." Moses recorded that the "sign of the covenant," marked by the rainbow which God made "between Me and you, and every living creature that is with you," will continue, "for perpetual generations." Every time we see a rainbow we should be reminded of God's eternal covenant that "the waters shall never again become a flood to destroy all flesh" (Genesis 9:12-15).

The Second and Final Cleansing of the Earth

Although God promised He would never destroy the earth with water, He also promised that He would burn the earth and the heavens with fire. Then He will create a New Heaven and New Earth at the end of the Great Day of the

Lord. Why will God burn the heavens and the earth? According to the Bible, these need to be cleansed from the effects of millennia of sin. The devil has ruled the earth and its surrounding heavens as the "prince of the power of the air" (Ephesians 2:2) for thousands of years since Adam and Eve lost the dominion of the planet. God commanded them, "Be fruitful and multiply; fill the earth and subdue it; have dominion over the fish of the sea, over the birds of the air, and over every living thing that moves on the earth" (Genesis 1:28). When man rebelled against God, Satan acquired dominion over the earth. It is significant that Jesus did not dispute Satan's claim that he could offer Him the kingdoms of the world if Christ would worship him. While Christ rejected Satan's impudent offer, in the future the Antichrist will arise and accept the devil's offer of the kingdoms of this world in return for his soul. Satan's liberty will be initially curtailed when he and his angels are defeated by Michael the archangel. Revelation 12 and Daniel 12 both record the mighty battle in the heavens that will result in Satan's defeat and confinement to the earth for the last three-and-a-half years leading up to the final defeat of Antichrist. Finally, at the end of the Battle of Armageddon, Christ will defeat Satan and imprison him in the bottomless pit for a thousand years. The dominion of the earth will be returned to Christ when He defeats Satan, the Antichrist and False Prophet at the Battle of Armageddon.

Man's Final Test

At the end of the Millennium, Satan will be released for a "little season" to test mankind one final time. Incredibly, many of the people born during the Millennium will still choose to follow their sinful and rebellious impulses. Despite the fact that Christ will rule the planet from the throne of David in Jerusalem, many will secretly harbor resentment in their hearts. Apart from the grace of God, we are all rebellious sinners in our hearts. When Satan is released these rebels will join his last great rebellion against God's rule. Satan and his army of rebels will be supernaturally destroyed by fire from heaven. They will be defeated by Christ and sent to the lake of fire in hell forever. The Bible tells us that God will cleanse the earth and the heavens with nuclear fire to eliminate any trace of sin.

There are three heavens described in the Scriptures. Some scholars believe there are seven in total. The first heaven is the atmospheric heaven which has been polluted by Satan's presence as the "prince of the power of the air." The second heaven would appear to be middle heaven where Satan and his fallen angels still have access. Apparently, these two heavens will be cleansed by God's fire at the end of the Millennium. The Apostle Paul referred to his vision when he was lifted up "to the third heaven." He was "caught up into Paradise and heard inexpressible words, which it is not lawful for a man to utter" (2 Corinthians 12:2,4). This "third heaven" is Paradise, the New Jerusalem described more fully by John in Revelation 21.

These lower two heavens were polluted to some extent by the presence of Satan and his angels. In the book of Job we read of Satan's appearance with the Sons of God before the throne of heaven to accuse God's servant Job. Later, in the New Testament, Jesus promised that He will appear as our advocate to defend us daily from the accusations made against us by Satan. In Revelation 12:10 we read about the rejoicing of heaven when "the accuser of our brethren, who accused them before our God day and night, has been cast down." The earth has been afflicted with the curse and pollution of sin since the fall of Adam and Eve. Since that initial rebellion, the decree of God has been that He will someday destroy the old earth and heavens and cleanse it with fire. Then He will create a purified New Earth and New Heaven with no taint of sin.

Amazingly, despite the prophesied events of the Millennium and many predictions in the Bible about this final destruction, the sinners living in that day will still be caught by surprise when God destroys the earth. To the unbeliever, the Bible's prophecies have no value. Unbelievers never read the Bible and they will not believe these prophecies. This is the reason the sinners of the Great Tribulation and the sinners of the final rebellion at the end of the Millennium will both be caught by surprise. As Peter warns: "But the day of the Lord will come as a thief in the night, in which the heavens will pass away with a great noise, and the elements will melt with fervent heat; both the earth and the works that are in it will be burned up" (2 Peter

3:10). In past generations scoffers mocked the words of Peter that "the elements will melt with fervent heat" because scientists were convinced that elements could not be destroyed. However the work of Einstein and the invention of nuclear weapons tragically proved that the elements will truly "melt with fervent heat."

A thermonuclear explosion will totally convert matter into energy. Peter warns that men should be "looking for and hastening the coming of the day of God, because of which the heavens will be dissolved being on fire" (2 Peter 3:12). Scientists now know that a continuous chain of nuclear reactions produces hundreds of thousands of thermonuclear explosions every second in the center of our sun. This massive production of power and heat, triggered by the dissolving of the elements in nuclear fire, was anticipated by the Apostle Peter two thousand years ago.

The Renovation of the Earth and Heaven by Fire

However, the Bible does not teach that the old earth and heaven will be annihilated by this nuclear fire. It teaches that God will destroy the surface of the earth with fire in the same way that God destroyed the planet's surface with the flood thousands of years ago. The positive message is that this universal burning of the earth's surface will be replaced by God's creation of a wonderful new Paradise, a new world like the original Garden of Eden. After describing the burning of the old earth, Peter encouraged us to remember that "nevertheless we, according to His promise, look for new heavens and a new earth in which righteousness dwells" (2 Peter 3:13).

Will God Create a Totally New Earth?

Many believe that the Bible teaches the complete planet will be annihilated and replaced by a newly created earth. However, a close examination of the Scriptures reveals that this is not true. A number of significant verses teach that the earth, the sun and the moon will continue eternally. If this is correct, then the burning of the earth must be confined to the surface as I have suggested. An examination of these passages reveals the Bible's teaching on this matter.

The Earth and Sun Will Continue Forever

A number of scriptural passages confirm that the earth and the sun will continue forever, renewed by the Lord by fire, creating a New Earth and Heaven. A careful examination of the relevant verses shows that the Bible does not claim that God will create the New Earth and Heaven out of nothing as He originally created the universe. "I saw a new heaven and a new earth, for the first heaven and the first earth had passed away" (Revelation 21:1). The Greek word used in this passage, *Parerchomai,* indicates something that passes from one condition into another, not the annihilation and replacement of something. The words of this verse do not describe the annihilation of the existing heaven and earth but that they "passed away." Just as "the world that then existed perished, being flooded with water" (2 Peter 3:6) in the days of Noah, the present earth will be burnt with fire after the Millennium. Nothing of man's proud creations and buildings will remain. The world will start over. It will be young again as it was in the Garden of Eden.

In proof that the earth and sun will continue forever, consider these passages. King David prophesied that the earth would continue forever. In Psalm 72:5 God promised that the Messiah will rule in righteousness forever. David also wrote that "they shall fear You as long as the sun and moon endure, throughout all generations" (Psalm 72:5). This passage affirms that men, the sun and the moon will all endure throughout eternity. In Psalm 78:69 David prophesied: "He built His sanctuary like the heights, like the earth which He has established forever." In Ecclesiastes 1:4, his son, King Solomon, also declared: "One generation passes away, and another generation comes; but the earth abides forever." After the horrors of the flood, God pledged to Noah that the seasons and day and night would continue as long as the earth continued (forever). "While the earth remains, seedtime and harvest, and cold and heat, and winter and summer, and day and night shall not cease" (Genesis 8:22).

When Will the Earth Be Destroyed by Fire?

The Apostle Peter tells us that "the heavens and the earth which now exist are kept in store by the same word, reserved for fire until the day of judgment and perdition of ungodly men" (2 Peter 3:7). This fiery destruction will be the final judgment of sinful men upon the earth. It will occur at the end of seven thousand years from the creation of Adam and Eve. Just as God created everything in the universe in a microcosm of one week of seven days, the Bible indicates that God has set aside seven thousand years as a great week of His dealing with mankind. Once the last thousand year period, the seventh Millennium, is completed, God will create a New Heaven and Earth filled with righteousness and justice forever. The Bible reminds us of God's timetable, the great week of human history, with these words. "But, beloved, do not forget this one thing, that with the Lord one day is as a thousand years, and a thousand years as one day" (2 Peter 3:8).

The Bible clearly teaches that God has set an appointment for the final destruction of the proud works of mankind at the end of the Millennium. Peter explains that "the heavens and the earth which now exist are kept in store by the same word, reserved for fire until the day of judgment and perdition of ungodly men" (2 Peter 3:7). This "day of judgment" referred to by Peter is also described by the prophet John in the book of Revelation as the Great White Throne judgment. This final judgment will occur in heaven after God defeats Satan's final rebellion at the end of the Millennium. It will include all of the unrepentant sinners from Cain until the last rebel who dies in Satan's final rebellion at the completion of the Millennium. The Apostle Paul refers to this "day of judgment" in Romans 2:16 where he speaks of "the day when God will judge the secrets of men by Jesus Christ, according to my gospel." More details about this final judgment day are examined in the chapter on the Great White Throne judgment.

The Return to Eden - The Removal of the Curse

In a sense, the creation of the New Heavens and the New Earth will be a return to the paradise in the Garden of Eden that was lost by man's rebellion so long ago. In that glorious time, when the world was young, man and woman walked with God "in the cool of the day," living in perfect harmony with a peaceful creation. Finally, when the Messiah reigns, the redeemed of the Lord will live once more in perfect harmony in a peaceful universe under the rule of a loving God. The Lord promised that He will "send Jesus Christ, who was preached to you before, whom heaven must receive until the times of restoration of all things, which God has spoken by the mouth of all His holy prophets since the world began" (Acts 3:20,21).

From the moment of Adam and Eve's first rebellion, man has lived under the curse of sin. Three curses resulted from the sinful rebellion of Adam and Eve. First Adam, and all his seed fell under the curse of sin, depriving them of immortality and intimate communion with God until they repented. Secondly, the earth itself was cursed because Adam's sin had transferred the dominion of the planet to the wicked serpent, Satan. In Genesis 3:17 Moses recorded these terrible words of judgment: "Cursed is the ground for your sake; in toil you shall eat of it all the days of your life." The third curse was pronounced on Cain, Adam's murderous son, for his violent killing of his righteous brother. In Genesis 4:11 God announced the curse that would follow Cain and all who chose violence: "So now you are cursed from the earth, which has opened its mouth to receive your brother's blood from your hand." Adam's sinful rebellion tragically led to the murder of his righteous son, Abel, by his evil son, Cain. Even in this first murder, God's mercy was revealed in the fact that Abel's soul went to Abraham's bosom. Abel, the world's first martyr, became the first man to enter heaven's glorious holy city. Hebrews 11:4 assures us that, "by faith Abel offered to God a more excellent sacrifice than Cain, through which he obtained witness that he was righteous, God testifying of his gifts; and through it, he being dead, still speaks."

When God created the universe His intention was that man would live in a sinless and harmonious world, in perfect communion with his Maker, without sin, violence or death. Even the animal kingdom was intended to live without killing other animals for food. The universe was created without entropy, without the tendency to run down and decay. This means that the original sinless universe was so perfectly designed and renewable that it would never have run down or died. The Second Law of Thermodynamics records the decaying state of the universe after the Fall when everything in the universe is running down, from the sun to the human body. Entropy and decay resulted from the curse of sin. This was not the way God originally created the universe. Remember, before the Fall and the curse of sin, when God created everything in the universe, "God saw that it was good" (Genesis 1:18).

The Apostle Paul prophesied the redemption of all creation when Christ will create the New Heaven and New Earth. "The creation itself also will be delivered from the bondage of corruption into the glorious liberty of the children of God" (Romans 8:21). When the curse of sin is lifted by Christ from the earth, the law of entropy will be replaced by a harmonious, sustainable universe. Today moths and rust are obvious examples of entropy where everything disintegrates over time. However, God reveals that entropy has no part in the New Earth and Heaven to come when He commands us as follows: "Lay up for yourselves treasures in heaven, where neither moth nor rust destroys" (Matthew 6:20). The curse of disease and death will be replaced with eternal life. Instead of killing other animals for food, "The lion will lay down with the lamb." God will transform the biology of the animals He created to convert them back to a vegetarian state. The prophet Isaiah (11:7) prophesied, "The cow and the bear shall graze; their young ones shall lie down together; and the lion shall eat straw like the ox." Describing this marvelous restoration of Paradise, God declares: "The wolf and the lamb shall feed together, the lion shall eat straw like the ox, and dust shall be the serpent's food. They shall not hurt nor destroy in all My holy mountain" (Isaiah 65:25)

Isaiah tells of the new creation in this wonderful prophecy. "They shall build houses and inhabit them; they shall plant vineyards and eat their fruit. They shall not build and another inhabit; they shall not plant and another eat"

(Isaiah 65:21,22). Today, under the curse of sin, everything we do is governed by our knowledge that nothing lasts forever. In this age, a man builds a house but another inhabits that house because the builder dies or becomes sick. Today, a farmer plants but another eats because the farmer dies prematurely or loses the farm to his creditors. The prophet promises that the curse of sin and death will be lifted by Christ. Man will live forever in the glorious New Earth. "My elect shall long enjoy the work of their hands" (Isaiah 65:22).

How Can We Ever Enjoy Heaven If Loved Ones Are Lost?

Some ask how we will ever be able to enjoy the glories of heaven if we are haunted by memories of loved ones who rejected Christ's salvation. The Bible suggests the answer in the prophecies of Isaiah. "For behold, I create new heavens and a new earth; and the former shall not be remembered or come to mind" (Isaiah 65:17). God will not allow the rebellious decision of sinners to veto the joy of those who chose the salvation of Christ in heaven. If we are not able to find happiness in heaven unless every soul we know also accepts salvation, then hell will truly win the victory over heaven's joy. God will not allow it. The Lord promised, "The former shall not be remembered or come to mind." While people will certainly remember their loved ones who rejected salvation, the pain of their loss will not be allowed to destroy our joy throughout eternity. In Revelation 21:4 we learn that "God will wipe away every tear from their eyes; there shall be no more death, nor sorrow, nor crying; and there shall be no more pain, for the former things have passed away."

Life in the New Heaven and Earth

"But be glad and rejoice forever in what I create; for behold, I create Jerusalem as a rejoicing, and her people a joy" (Isaiah 65:18).

For thousands of years the vast majority of people have had their lives shortened due to poverty, pain and unhappiness. Less than 1 percent of all humanity throughout history lives as well as we do in North America today. Yet sin, greed and evil have resulted in lives of unhappiness and pain for the majority of mankind. Even those fortunate enough to live in wealthy countries often live "lives of quiet desperation." This was not how God created man to live. Finally, when Satan's evil rule will be defeated by Christ, mankind will enter into the long-awaited Promised Land of an eternal Paradise under the Messiah Jesus Christ.

The Duration of the Kingdom of God on Earth

In considering the future messianic Kingdom of God, many have focused exclusively on John's prophecies in Revelation 20 about the one-thousand-year millennial Kingdom on earth. They assume that the entire duration of Christ's Kingdom on earth will be limited to one thousand years. However, a close examination of the Bible's prophecies will reveal that God consistently promised an eternal Kingdom on earth. The book of Revelation reveals that there will be a crisis one thousand years after the Battle of Armageddon and the establishment of Christ's Kingdom. In this crisis, Satan will be released "for a little season" to test mankind one final time. When the devil is finally defeated, Christ will renovate the earth and the heavens by fire. They will continue in their renewed state forever. This biblical revelation of an eternal Kingdom of Christ on the New Earth is vital if we are to fully appreciate the tremendous future promises of God to His Bride, the Church of Jesus Christ. We shall rule with Him forever, not simply for a thousand years.

Some have focused exclusively on the promise in Revelation 20:6 that "Blessed and holy is he who has part in the first resurrection. Over such the second death has no power, but they shall be priests of God and of Christ, and shall reign with Him a thousand years." If that verse was God's only promise to us we would be justified in limiting the kingdom promises to a one-thousand-year duration. However, when we examine the whole counsel of God we find an abundance of passages that affirm Christ's Kingdom will continue forever. The Christian saints will rule with Christ forever on the New Earth as shown in the following passages. The Lord promised an eternal reward to those who are faithful because He has "made us kings and priests to our God; and we shall reign on the earth" (Revelation 5:10). The whole focus of the Bible's prophecies is directed at the glorious victory of Christ over sin and death. When the battle is won, Christ will establish His eternal kingdom on the earth, where He was rejected two thousand years ago. There is not a single verse in the Bible that limits the extent and duration of Christ's kingdom to one thousand years. In Revelation 11:15 the Seventh angel declares: "The kingdoms of this world have become the kingdoms of our Lord and of His Christ, and He shall reign forever and ever!"

The Children of the New Earth

The Kingdom of God on the New Earth will include billions of humans living in Gentile nations and Israel. These men and women will be the children of those who survived the Great Tribulation and the Battle of Armageddon. Not everyone on earth will die during that terrible period. According to the book of Revelation, it is possible that one third of the six billion humans on the planet will survive. Therefore, up to two billion people will be living in the world the day after Armageddon when Christ begins His millennial Kingdom. Some of these people will be living in areas like Brazil, New Zealand and other places remote from the major battlegrounds in the Revived Roman Empire in Europe and the Middle East.

The Bible teaches that mankind will continue having children on the New Earth forever. The Bible says nothing about Christians having children in heaven, nor does it say anything about married physical love existing for the Church members after the resurrection. Possibly, because the Church is the Bride of Christ, a "royal priesthood" of believers, there will be no additions biologically to the Church. There will be no need for reproduction to replace lost individuals in the Church because there will be no death. Most Bible scholars conclude that the words of Jesus eliminate the possibility of marriage in heaven. "But those who are counted worthy to attain that age, and the resurrection from the dead, neither marry nor are given in marriage" (Luke 20:35). In my book *Heaven - The Last Frontier* I provide a detailed examination of this fascinating issue. Certainly, the Bible indicates we will know our loved ones and family as our spiritual friends. In 2 Samuel 12:23 the Scriptures indicate that King David will go to meet his beloved son in heaven. Our relationships and love will not end at death. Even the rich man who went to Hades was aware of his brothers and cared enough to ask that someone warn them to avoid hell. Jesus promised that we will retain our identities and interests in heaven. As He indicated, we will enjoy new and old friendships and "sit down with Abraham, Isaac, and Jacob in the kingdom of heaven" (Matthew 8:11).

However, the teaching of the Scriptures is clear that the Jews and Gentiles who live in the Millennium and beyond in the New Earth will continue having children forever. Who would the saints rule over if no one survived Armageddon? God promised Abraham and Israel repeatedly that He would give him "children as the sand of the sea and the stars in the sky." These extensive promises could not be fulfilled in a short period of only one thousand year in the millennial Kingdom. After the Millennium, when sin and evil are destroyed, there will never be any disease or death in the universe again. Even the possibility of sin and evil will be eliminated from God's holy universe. The children born in the New Earth will grow up as God originally planned for Adam and Eve in the Garden of Eden. They will live in perfect harmony with their brothers and their Messiah. Christ will no longer rule "with a rod of iron" after the Millennium because all humanity will then live sinlessly in peace and justice. Instead of an outwardly applied law, which man could never keep, God will transform the hearts of men, placing His law within their inward hearts forever. As the prophet Jeremiah prophesied (31:33): "But this is the covenant that I will make with the house of Israel: After those days, says the Lord, I will put My law in their minds, and write it on their hearts; and I will be their God, and they shall be My people." This inward spiritual transformation will occur first with the nation Israel after the Battle of Armageddon. Interestingly, not one reference in the Bible indicates that any of the Jews will rebel during the Millennium. After Satan is cast into hell at the end of the Millennium, the Lord will also transform the hearts of all the Gentile nations that are saved. There will never be another rebellion against God's Kingdom.

The Scriptures describe the perpetual generations of humanity that will continue inhabiting the New Earth forever. Isaiah 65:23 prophesied about future generations of children in the Kingdom of God: "They shall not labor in vain, nor bring forth children for trouble; for they shall be the descendants of the blessed of the Lord, and their offspring with them" (Isaiah 65:23). This passage tells us that, in the future Kingdom of God, there will be no stillborn babies and no rebellious children. Moses confirms in Deuteronomy 29:29 that children will be born forever in the New Earth: "The secret things belong to the Lord our God, but those things which are revealed belong to us and to our children forever, that we may do all the words of this law." In describing the New Covenant with Israel, the Lord promised that it would continue with their seed and descendants forever: "This is My covenant with them: My Spirit who is upon you, and My words which I have put in your mouth, shall not depart from your mouth, nor from the mouth of your descendants, nor from the mouth of your descendants' descendants...from this time and forevermore" (Isaiah 59:21).

Israel Will Continue Forever

The Bible clearly teaches that Israel will continue as a nation under the Messiah forever. The triumphant words of Isaiah declare that Christ will rule forever in Jerusalem from the throne of David. "For unto us a Child is born, unto us a Son is given; and the government will be upon His shoulder. And His name will be called Wonderful, Counselor, Mighty God, Everlasting Father, Prince of Peace. Of the increase of His government and peace there will be no end, upon the throne of David and over His kingdom, to order it and establish it with judgment and justice from that time forward, even forever" (Isaiah 9:6,7).

After almost two thousand years of exile among the nations, the Jews finally returned to the Promised Land in fulfillment of the prophecies of Ezekiel 37, the vision of the valley of dry bones. No other ancient nation, which had ceased to exist, has ever returned to national life. Yet Israel was reborn in "one day" as Isaiah 66:8 declared. "Who has heard such a thing? Who has seen such things? Shall the earth be made to give birth in one day? Or shall a nation be born at once? For as soon as Zion travailed, she gave birth to her children. " In my book *Armageddon - Appointment With Destiny*, I show that Israel was reborn on May 15, 1948 at the precise time foretold by the prophecy of Ezekiel 4:4-6. Furthermore, Israel recovered its ancient Hebrew language, exactly as foretold by the prophet Zephaniah. "For then I will restore to the peoples a pure language, that they all may call on the name of the Lord, to serve Him with one accord" (Zephaniah 3:9). None of the other ancient nations speak their age-old languages. Today, King David could walk the streets of Jerusalem and be understood in his biblical language, Hebrew. This is both a great miracle and a tremendous fulfillment of prophecy.

In the prophecies of Jeremiah, God declared that His covenant with Israel was unbreakable and will continue forever, comparing it with the eternal nature of the sun, moon and stars. "Thus says the Lord, Who gives the sun for a light by day, and the ordinances of the moon and the stars for a light by night, Who disturbs the sea, and its waves roar, the Lord of hosts is His name: 'If those ordinances depart from before Me,' says the Lord, 'Then the seed of Israel shall also cease from being a nation before Me forever'" (Jeremiah 31:35,36). After describing the miraculous return to the Holy Land, Ezekiel confirmed that Israel will remain in the Promised Land forever. "Then they shall dwell in the land that I have given to Jacob My servant, where your fathers dwelt; and they shall dwell there, they, their children, and their children's children, forever; and My servant David shall be their prince forever." This passage proves that God's promise to Israel will continue forever. It also shows that the men and women of the Millennium and New Earth will continue having children forever.

The Gentile Nations Will Also Continue Forever

Furthermore, the prophecies teach that the Gentile nations will continue to exist in the Millennium and in the New Earth. In Revelation 21:24 we read: "And the nations of those who are saved shall walk in its light, and the kings of the earth bring their glory and honor into it." The unrighteous Gentiles (the goats) will be judged by Christ after the Battle of Armageddon in the Valley of Jehoshaphat. Those who persecuted the Chosen People and the tribulation saints will be destroyed by Christ at the Judgment of the Nations before the millennial Kingdom begins. The Gentile nations of the saved will be blessed throughout eternity and will live under the administration of the saints of the Church. After the Battle of Armageddon, the representatives of the Gentile nations will come up to Jerusalem to "worship the King, the Lord of Hosts, and to keep the Feast of Tabernacles" forever. "And it shall come to pass that everyone who is left of all the nations which came against Jerusalem shall go up from year to year to worship the King, the Lord of hosts, and to keep the Feast of Tabernacles" (Zechariah 14:16). The expression "year to year" implies that this commemorative Feast of Tabernacles will continue forever.

The Eternal Festival and Feasts of Israel

The prophet Isaiah also saw a vision of the festivals continuing forever with all of the nations, "all flesh," participating in the worship of the Lord in Jerusalem. Isaiah addressed these words to Israel: "'For as the new heavens and the new earth which I will make shall remain before Me,' says the Lord, 'So shall your descendants and your name remain. And it shall come to pass that from one New Moon to another, and from one Sabbath to another, all flesh shall come to worship before Me,' says the Lord" (Isaiah 66:22,23). This remarkable prophecy reveals a number of key elements regarding the future of the earth. These inspired words confirm that these things will continue forever: the New Heavens and New Earth, Israel's descendants and name, Israel's Sabbath and the festivals of the New Moon, Rosh Hodash.

The New Heavens

When we look out at the magnificent heavens on a clear night we are filled with awe at God's power and creation. Now, with our satellite probes moving out beyond the solar system toward interstellar space, we are beginning to grasp that the universe is far larger than we can ever possibly measure. God does nothing without a purpose. Why did Christ create such a vast universe if the tiny earth is the only place that will ever be inhabited? The Bible clearly teaches that, after the Millennium, the Jews and Gentiles will continue to have children forever "as the sand of the sea" and that no one will ever die because there is no more sin. God's promise to Abraham was as follows: "In blessing I will bless you, and in multiplying I will multiply your descendants as the stars of the heaven and as the sand which is on the seashore" (Genesis 22:17). Since the known stars are numbered in the millions of trillions, the future population of mankind is beyond numbering. If only one star in a million has planets, then there are millions of planets to be explored someday.

Our own small galaxy, one of millions observed to date, is so large that a space ship traveling at the speed of light (187 thousand miles per second) would take over 100 thousand years to cross it. Recently, astronomers discovered several nearby stars that possess planets. Interstellar space travel in our human bodies, with a seventy-year lifespan, is practically impossible. However, our resurrection bodies, which we will receive at the Rapture, can travel at the speed of thought, just as Christ and the angels appeared at will wherever they wanted. Once we receive our new resurrection bodies, we may be given the opportunity to explore the vast reaches of God's creation in His immeasurable universe.

The Incredible Promise

The promise to Israel alone is staggering: "As the host of heaven cannot be numbered, nor the sand of the sea measured, so will I multiply the descendants of David My servant and the Levites who minister to Me" (Jeremiah 33:22). The logical conclusion is that the future population explosion of mankind, after the Millennium, will finally exceed the capacity of the earth. Perhaps, the Lord's ultimate plan for a sinless humanity is to explore and inhabit His vast universe. King David wrote an inspired psalm that suggests that mankind will finally have dominion, under the Messiah Jesus, of far more than the planet earth. Consider carefully the words of King David recorded in Psalm 8: "When I consider Your heavens, the work of Your fingers, the moon and the stars, which You have ordained, what is man that You are mindful of him, and the son of man that You visit him? For You have made him a little lower than the angels, and You have crowned him with glory and honor. You have made him to have dominion over the works of Your hands; You have put all things under his feet." (Psalm 8:3-6).

Note that the focus of the prophecy is not the earth, but "the moon and the stars." When David considered the immensity of God's creation in the heavens he asked: "What is man that You are mindful of him?" The amazing God-inspired answer was this: "You [God] have crowned him with glory and honor. You have made him to have dominion over the works of Your hands; You have put all things under his feet." Note that "the works of Your hands" and "all things" included the "the heavens, the work of Your fingers, the moon and the stars, which You have ordained." These verses suggest that God's plans for the Church include reigning and ruling forever, not only over the earth, but over "the heavens" and "the stars" in a universe beyond measuring.

What an amazing prospect! Is this possible? In considering the answer to this question we need to think about what would have occurred if Adam and Eve had resisted Satan's temptation and man had never fallen into sinful rebellion. Man was created to live forever without disease or death. God told Adam and Eve to "be fruitful and multiply; fill the earth and subdue it" (Genesis 1:28). Without sin, disease or death, the sinless generations would have produced an ever-increasing population until the earth was covered with human settlements. Once the earth was full of humans, possibly a sinless humanity would have been allowed to colonize inhabitable planets throughout the universe. God did not limit man to a single area on the globe. There is no logical reason why a righteous humanity will be limited to this earth alone once our ever-increasing population makes emigration desirable. Once Satan is sent to the lake of fire forever and sin exists no more, a sinless humanity will return to a condition similar to the one which would have existed if Adam and Eve had never sinned.

Is is possible that God will allow a sinless humanity, after the Millennium, to explore and inhabit a vast, endless universe? Perhaps, someday, the whole of the immense universe will be home to an ever-expanding humanity that will sanctify the name of Jesus forever. Isaiah the prophet (66:22) spoke of these things: "For as the new heavens and the new earth which I will make shall remain before Me," says the Lord, "so shall your descendants and your name remain."

The role of the Church, the Bride of Christ, will be to rule and reign with the Messiah forever. We may enjoy an adventure beyond our finest dreams as we experience all of the wonders of a vast and beautiful universe created by Jesus Christ.

Alpha and Omega -- From Eternity to Eternity

John recorded these words of Jesus Christ: "And He said to me, 'It is done! I am the Alpha and the Omega, the Beginning and the End. I will give of the fountain of the water of life freely to him who thirsts'" (Revelation 21:6). Using the first and last letters of the Greek alphabet, Alpha and Omega, Christ declared that He both created and will destroy the old earth to cleanse it forever. Someone wrote that "History is His Story" -- that the whole of history reveals the story of Christ's plan to redeem the earth and the souls of men from the curse of sin. Any attempt to understand God's plan for mankind must begin at the Alpha -- the book of Genesis -- the book of beginnings. The Bible commences with these critical words: "In the beginning, God created the heavens and the earth" (Genesis 1:1). Significantly the Bible concludes with the final chapters of Revelation revealing the final cleansing of the old earth with fire and the beginning of an eternal Paradise on a New Earth.

Truly the words of Christ take on a new meaning in light of these possibilities. "Eye has not seen, nor ear heard, nor have entered into the heart of man the things which God has prepared for those who love Him. But God has revealed them to us through His Spirit. For the Spirit searches all things, yes, the deep things of God" (1 Corinthians 2:9,10). The

Apocalypse reveals the awesome and climactic events that will usher in the long-awaited Kingdom of God on earth. John ends his prophecy with these words: "He who testifies to these things says, 'Surely I am coming quickly.' Amen. Even so, come, Lord Jesus!" (Revelation 22:20).

APPENDIX

Prophetic Views Held by the Early Church

In the midst of an ongoing correspondence, a critic of prophecy made the statement that the views on prophetic interpretation held by people like Hal Lindsey, myself and others were totally different than the historic beliefs of the early Church. My research over the last thirty years had provided ample evidence that our views of the future fulfillment of prophecy were very similar to those held by the Christians of the first two centuries. In the various chapters of this book I shared with my readers a number of specific areas what these Christian writers wrote about the Antichrist and the deliverance of the Church. However, this critic's comments encouraged me to embark on a more systematic study of church writings prior to 325 A.D and the Council of Nicea. These writings were translated into English and assembled in the 1890s into a ten-volume set called the Ante-Nicene Library. Although not exhaustive, the following material will provide the serious prophecy researcher with an overall survey of the major prophetic views of these Christian writers. A list of these writers and their works appears at the end of this appendix.

This survey proved conclusively that, while some writers held unusual views, the majority of these Christians believed in the premillennial coming of Christ to establish a literal kingdom on earth for a thousand years. They expected an "any moment," imminent, coming of the Lord to resurrect the saints. They looked for a personal Antichrist and False Prophet to deceive the world after defiling a rebuilt Temple in Jerusalem. Christians in the first two centuries believed that the Roman Empire would revive in the form of ten nations. The Antichrist would conquer three of them and the other seven would submit to his literal Mark of the Beast system. Interestingly, they understood that the last week of seven years in Daniel's prophecy of the seventy weeks would be separated from the first sixty-nine weeks by a gap during the Church Age. A literal millennial Kingdom where the saints will rule with Christ will be followed by a New Heaven and New Earth. These beliefs are so close to our own as to be almost identical. While these shared beliefs and methods of interpretation do not prove that we are correct, they certainly provide the strongest possible evidence in favor of the fact that our interpretation is similar to that taught by the Apostles in the early Church.

Major Prophetic Views	Church Writers Holding the View
1. Premillennial Return of Christ	*Epistle of Barnabas*, 15 Papias, *Fragments*, 6 Justin M., *First Apology*, 52 Eusebius , *Proof of Gospel*, 15 Nicene Creed, Last Clause Gelasius, *Commentarius Actorum Concilii Nicaeni*, 2. 30 Athanasius, *On the Incarnation of the Word*, 56 Lactantius, *Divine Institutes*, 14; 24 Tertullian, *Against Marcion*, 25 Methodius, *Banquet Ten Virgins*, 9.1; 5 Justin M., *Dialogue With Trypho*, 53; 80 Irenaeus , *Against Heresies*, 28 Victorinus, *Comm. on Apocalypse*, 20
2. Literal, not Allegorical Interpretation	Tertullian, *On the Resurrection of the Flesh*, 22 Hippolytus, *Treatise on Christ & Antichrist*, 5 Irenaeus, *Against Heresies*, 35
3. Antichrist will rule for seven years; Daniel's seventieth week	Lactantius, *Comm. on Apocalypse*, 11 Hippolytus, *Treatise on Christ & Antichrist*, 43 Victorinus, *Comm. on Apocalypse*, 11 Hippolytus, *Appendix* , 21 *Pseudo-Titus Epistle* *Instructions of Commodianus*, 41
4. A literal personal Antichrist	Irenaeus, *Against Heresies*, 25 *Instructions of Commodianus*, 41 *Pseudo-Clementines*
5. A literal Mark of the Beast	Lactantius, *Comm. on Apocalypse*, 13 *The Didache*, 1

6.	A literal False Prophet	Lactantius, *Divine Institutes*, 17 *Instructions of Commodianus*, 41
7.	Israel to be reborn as a nation	Hippolytus, *Treatise on Christ &* *Antichrist*, 6; 54 *Apocalypse of Peter*, 2 *Assumption of Moses* Irenaeus, *Against Heresies*, 34
8.	Israel as the Fig Tree of Matt. 24	*Apocalypse of Peter*, 2
9.	Revelation refers to a future Tribulation not to the Destruction of Jerusalem in A.D. 70	Lactantius, *Comm. on Apocalypse*, 13 Irenaeus, *Against Heresies*, 26. 1
10.	Revelation written approx. A.D. 96 during reign of Emperor Domitian (by John)	Lactantius, *Comm. on Apocalypse*, 17 Fragments, *Irenaeus*, 2 Irenaeus, *Against Heresies*, 30 Papias, *Fragments* Victorinus, *Comm. on Apocalypse*, 17
11.	A literal one-thousand-year millennial reign	Lactantius, *Divine Institutes*, 14 Tertullian, *Against Marcion*, 25 Methodius, *Banquet of Ten Virgins*, 9. 1, 5 *Epistle of Barnabas*, 15 Papias, *Fragment*, 6 Justin M., *Dialogue With Trypho*, 53; 80 Irenaeus, *Against Heresies*, 28 Victorinus, *Comm. on Apocalyps*, 20 *Instructions of Commodianus*, 41 *Banquet of the Ten Virgins*, 9. 1
12.	Antichrist and seven kings out of Roman Empire	Lactantius, *Comm. on Apocalypse*, 12; 17 Irenaeus, *Against Heresies*, 26 Victorinus, *Comm. on Apocalypse*, 12; 17 Hippolytus, *Appendix*, 19
13.	The Antichrist will be Jewish	Hippolytus, *Treatise on Christ &* *Antichrist*, 6. 54 Hippolytus, *Appendix*, 20 Irenaeus, *Against Heresies*, 30
14.	Rebuilding of Roman Empire	Irenaeus, *Against Heresies*, 26 Hippolytus, *Treatise on Christ &* *Antichrist*, 6. 54

15. The Temple will be rebuilt	Lactantius, *Divine Institutes*, 17
	Comm. on Apocalypse, 13
	Hippolytus, *Fragments - Comm*
	    Daniel, 2. 22, 39
	Hippolytus, *Treatise on Christ &*
	    Antichrist, 6
	Appendix, 20. 25
	Epistle of Barnabas, 16
	Irenaeus, *Against Heresies*, 25; 28
	Victorinus, *Comm. on Apocalypse*,
	    13

16. Future Antichrist will defile the Temple with the abomination of desolation	Lactantius, *Divine Institutes*, 17
	Comm. on Apocalypse, 13
	Hippolytus, *Fragments - Comm.*
	    Daniel, 2. 22, 39
	Irenaeus, *Against Heresies*, 25; 28
	Victorinus, *Comm. on Apocalypse*,
	    13

17. Daniel's seventy weeks stands for 490 years	Julius Africanus Chronography,
	    16. 1
	Live, *Testament Twelve Patriarchs*,
	    16
	Eusebius, *Proof of Gospel*, 8. 2

18. Half of Daniel's seventiethth Week equal to three and a half years	Irenaeus, *Against Heresies*, 25
	Hippolytus, *Fragments - Comm.*
	    Daniel, 2. 22
	——— *Treatise- Christ &*
	    Antichrist, 43; 47; 61; 64
	——— *Appendix*, 21; 25; 36
	Irenaeus, *Against Heresies*, 30
	JUstin M., *Dialogue With Trypho*,
	    32

19. The "gap" between Daniel's sixty-nine weeks and the last seventieth week of years
 	
(Gap before last week)
	Hippolytus, *Fragments - Comm.*
	    Daniel, 2. 22
	——— *Treatise on Christ &*
	    Antichrist, 43; 47; 61; 64
	——— *Appendix*, 21; 25; 36
	Irenaeus, *Against Heresies*, 25
	Eusebius, *Church History*, 2

20. Daniel's last "week" of seven years just before the return of Christ	Hippolytus, *Fragments - Comm.*
	    Daniel, 2. 22, 39
	——— *Treatise on Christ &*
	    Antichrist, 43
	——— *Appendix*, 21; 36
	Justin M., *Dialogue With Trypho*, 32
	Irenaeus, *Against Heresies*, 25

317

tongue" will be saved during Tribulation	Victorinus, *Comm.on Apocalypse*, 7,8,9
29. Antichrist will persecute the saints 1260 days	Lactantius, *Divine Institutes*, 17 Hippolytus, *Fragments - Comm. Daniel*, 2:7, 39 Irenaeus, *Against Heresies*, 25
30. Those who refuse his mark will be slain	Lactantius, *Divine Institutes*, 17 Hippolytus, *Treatise - Christ & Antichrist*, 49
31. Antichrist's time of power over the saints will be limited to 42 months	Lactantius, *Divine Institutes*, 17 Hyippolytus, *Frag. Comm. on Daniel*, 3:7 ——— *Appendix*, 25
32. Antichrist will imitate Christ	Lactantius, *Divine Institutes*, 18 Hippolytus, *Appendix*, 20 *Ascension of Isaiah*, 4 *Instructions of Commodianus*, 41
33. Saints will rule in the Millennium	Lactantius, *Divine Institutes*, 24 Justin M., *Dialogue with Trypho*, 80
34. Satan will be bound for one thousand years	Lactantius, *Divine Institutes*, 24 Lactantius, *Epitome of Div. Instit.*, 72
35. The New Jerusalem will descend on the Earth	Lactantius, *Divine Institutes*, 24 *Revelation of John the Theologian* Tertullian, *Against Marcion*, 25
36. God will literally transform biology eliminating violence in animals	Lactantius, *Divine Institutes*, 24
37. Satan will gather all nations to attack the city of God after the 1000 years	Lactantius, *Divine Institutes*, 26 Victorinus, *Comm. on Apocalypse*, 20
38. The Judgment of the Wicked at the end of the 1000 years	Lactantius, *Divine Institutes*, 26 Justin M.., *Dialogue with Trypho*, 80 Victorinus, *Comm. on Apocalypse*, 20
39. False Prophet will set up an image of Antichrist	Lactantius, *Epitome of Divine Institutes*, 71 Victorinus, *Comm. on Apocalypse*, 13 *Instructions of Commodianus*, 41

40. Christ will judge the nations after Armageddon	Lactantius, *Epitome of Divine Institutes*, 71 Hippolytus, *Appendix*, 41
41. Believers will be transformed into an immortal body	Lactantius, *Epitome of Divine Institutes*, 71 Tertullian, *On Marcion*, 25 Tertullian, *On Resurrection of the Flesh*, 42
42. Literal Famine – 3rd Horseman	Lactantius, *Comm. on Apocalypse*, 7 Victorinus, *Comm.on Apocalypse*, 6
43. Supernatural Deliverance of Church	Lactantius, *Comm. Apocalypse*, 6; 15 Victorinus, *Comm.Apocalypse*, 6; 15 *Shepherd of Hermes*, 4. 1,2 Cyprian, *Epistle*, 55. 7
44. God will send Elijah to warn men, stopping rains, destroying with fire	Lactantius, *Divine Institutes*, 17 Hippolytus, *Treatise on Christ & Antichrist*, 46
45. Two Witnesses witness for 1260 literal days equalling "three years and six months"	Lactantius, *Comm. Apocalypse*, 11 Hippolytus, *Appendix*, 21 ———— *Treatise on Christ & Antichrist*, 43; 47 Victorinus, *Comm.Apocalypse*, 11
46. Elijah as one of the Two Witnesses	Lactantius, *Comm. Apocalypse*, 7 Hippolytus, *Fragments - Comm. Daniel* 2:22 – *Treatise on Christ & Antichrist*, 46 *Revelation of John the Theologian* Victorinus, Comm.Apocalypse, 11 Instructions of Commodianus, 41
47. Two Witnesses Slain by Antichrist	Lactantius, *Comm. Apocalypse*, 11 Hippolytus, *Fragments - Comm. Daniel*, 2:39 Victorinus, *Comm.Apocalypse*, 11
48. Two Witnesses Raised after 3 1/2 days	Lactantius, *Comm. Apocalypse*, 11
49. Two Witnesses killed in Jerusalem	Lactantius, *Comm. Apocalypse*, 11
50. The Sun Clothed Woman - Israel	Lactantius, *Comm. Apocalypse*, 12

The Ancient O. T. Church	Victorinus, *Comm.Apocalypse*, 12
51. The Man Child is Christ	Lactantius, *Comm. Apocalypse*, 12 Victorinus, *Comm.Apocalypse*, 12
52. Woman Fleeing 1260 days - Israel "flee to hills of Judah"	Lactantius, *Comm. Apocalypse*, 12 Victorinus, *Comm.Apocalypse*, 12
53. 144,000 Jews respond to Witnesses	Lactantius, *Comm. Apocalypse*, 12 Victorinus, *Comm.Apocalypse*, 12
54. Antichrist's Defeat at Christ's return	Irenaeus, *Against Heresies*, 30 *Seventh Book of Apostolic Constitutions* *Ascension of Isaiah*, 4
55. Satan Drew 1/3 of angels away	Lactantius, *Comm. Apocalypse*, 12 Victorinus, *Comm.Apocalypse*, 12
56. Satan's Expulsion from Heaven - mid-week. Gives Antichrist satanic power for 3 1/2 yrs	Lactantius, *Comm. Apocalypse*, 12
57. 666 relates to the numeric value of Antichrist's name in original language	Lactantius, *Comm. Apocalypse*, 13 Hippolytus, *Treatise - Christ & Antichrist*, 50 Irenaeus, *Against Heresies*, 30 Victorinus, *Comm.Apocalypse*, 13
58. The Second Beast from the sea is False Prophet	Lactantius, *Comm. Apocalypse*, 13
59. False Prophet actually brings fire down from Heaven to deceive men	Lactantius, *Comm. Apocalypse*, 13 Lactantius, *Div. Inst*, 71 Victorinus, *Comm.Apocalypse*, 13
60. False Prophet makes satanic image of Antichrist to be worshipped	Lactantius, *Comm. Apocalypse*, 13 *Instructions of Commodianus*, 41 *Ascension of Isaiah*, 4
61. A literal Mark of the Beast on on the right hand or forehead	Lactantius, *Comm. Apocalypse*, 13 Hippolytus, *Appendix*, 28 Cyprian, *Epistle*, 55: 7
62. Christ's reference to Daniel's "abomination of desolation" as an event under the future Antichrist in the future Tribulation	Lactantius, *Comm. Apocalypse*, 13
63. Antichrist stops the daily sacrifice	Hippolytus, *Fragments - Comm. Daniel*, 2: 43
64. Daniel's "little horn" of Dan. 2 is Antichrist	Hippolytus, *Fragments - Comm. Daniel*, 2:2

65. Antichrist will take over Israel "he shall set up the kingdom of Judah" and "build the city of Jerusalem"	Hippolytus, *Fragments - Comm. Daniel*, 2:2, 39 —— *Treatise on Christ & Antichrist*, 25
66. The "clay toes" represent democracies	Hippolytus, *Fragments - Comm. Daniel*, 2:3 —— *Treatise on Christ & Antichrist*, 27
67. The "stone" that destroys the "ten toes"is Jesus Christ coming to establish His Kingdom	Hippolytus, *Fragments - Comm. Daniel*, 2:2 —— *Treatise on Christ & Antichrist*-36
68. Identification of Great Whore of Babylon with Rome – 7 heads – 7 mountains –	Lactantius, *Comm. Apocalypse*, 17 *Instructions of Commodianus*, 41 Hippolytus, *Treatise on Christ & Antichrist*, 28
69. Antichrist will have great military power	Hippolytus, *Treatise on Christ & Antichrist*, 15
70. Antichrist will appear in "the last days"	Hippolytus, *Treatise on Christ & Antichrist*, 19
71. The Fourth Beast of Dan. 2 is Rome	Hippolytus, *Treatise on Christ & Antichrist*, 25 —— Appendix, 1
72. Two Advents – Two Resurrections	Hippolytus, *Treatise - Christ & Antichrist*, 44 – *Appendix,* 21 *Recognitions of Clement,* 49 Justin.M., *Dialogue With Trypho,* 32, 110 Victorinus, *Comm.Apocalypse,* 20 *Pseudo-Titus Epistle* Justin M., *First Apology,* 52 Tertullian, *Apology,* 21 Lactantius, *Divine Institutes,* 20 Lactantius, *Epitome -Div. Inst.,* 72
73. Resurrection of Saints	Polycrates, Bishop of Ephesus *Revelation of John the Theologian Recognitions of Clement,* 52 Irenaeus, *Against Heresies,* 29; 34 Victorinus, *Comm.Apocalypse,* 6; 13 *Pseudo-Titus Epistle* Tertullian, *On the Resurrection of the Flesh,* 24; 42

SELECTED BIBLIOGRAPHY

Anderson, Robert. *The Coming Prince.* London: Hodder & Stroughton, 1894

Blackstone, Wm. E. *Jesus is Coming.* London: Fleming H. Revell Co., 1908

Bloomfield, Arthur, E. *A Survey Of Bible Prophecy.* Minneapolis: Bethany Fellowship, Inc., 1971.

Boston, Thomas. *Human Nature In Its Fourfold State.* Philadelphia: Ambrose Walker, 1814.

Bullinger, E.W. *The Apocalypse or The Day Of The Lord.* London: Eyre & Spottiswoode, 1909.

Charles, R.H. *A Critical and Exegetical Commentary on the Revelation of St. John.* 2 Vols. Edinburgh: T. & T. Clark, 1959.

Coates, C.A. *An Outline of the Revelation.* London: Stow HIll Bible Depot., 1985.

Cohen, Gary, G. *Understanding Revelation.* Chicago: Moody Press, 1978.

Criswell, W. A. *Expository Sermons on Revelation.* Grand Rapids: Zondervan Publishing House, 1962.

Davidson, John. *Discourses on Prophecy.* London: John Murray & Co. 1825

Dean, I. R. *The Coming Kingdom - The Goal Of Prophecy.* Philadelphia: Philadelphia School Of The Bible, 1928.

Dewart, Edward, Hartley. *Jesus The Messiah.* Toronto: William Briggs, 1891.

Feinberg, Charles. *PreMillennialism Or Amillennialism?* Grand Rapids: Zondervan Publishing House, 1936.

Fruchtenbaum, Arnold, G. *The Footsteps of the Messiah.* Tustin: Ariel Press, 1982.

Gaebelein, A. C. *Revelation.* Glasgow: Pickering & Inglis, 1915.

Haldeman, I.M. *The Coming of Christ.* New York: Charles C. Cook, 1906.

Hallifax, Dr. Samuel. *Twelve Sermons On The Prophecies Concerning The Christian Church*, London: T. Cadell, 1776

Hawley, Charles A. *The Teaching of Apocrypha and Apocalypse.* New York: Association Press, 1925

Hindson, Ed. *The New World Order.* Wheaton: Victor Books, 1991.

Hovery, Alvah. *Biblical Eschatology.* Philadelphia: American Baptist
Publication Society, 1888.

Huffman, Jasper. *The Messianic Hope in Both Testaments.* Winona Lake:
The Standard Press, 1945.

Ironside, H.A. *Lectures on the Book of Revelation.* New York: Loizeaux
Brothers, 1930.

Jarvis, Rev. Samuel Farmar. *The Church of the Redeemed.* London: Wm.
Jones Cleaver, 1850.

Keith, Rev. Alexander. *The Signs Of The Times.* Edinburgh: William
White & Co., 1832.

LaHaye, Tim. *No Fear Of The Storm.* Sisters: Multnomah Press Books,
1992.

Larkin, Rev. Clarence. *Rightly Dividing The Word.* Philadelphia: Erwin W.
Moyer Co., 1943.

Leonard, Bernard. *The Book of Destiny.* Belleville: Buechler Publishing Co.,
1955.

Litch, Josiah. *Messiah's Throne And Millennial Glory.* Philadelphia:
Joshua V. Himes, 1855.

Lockyer, Herbert. *All The Messianic Prophecies Of The Bible.* Grand
Rapids: Zondervan Publishing House, 1960.

Ludwigson, R. *A Survey Of Bible Prophecy.* Grand Rapids: Zondervan.
1951

Maimonides, Moses. *Treatise On Resurrection.* New York: KTAV
Publishing House, Inc. 1982.

Newton, Bishop Thomas. *Dissertations On The Prophecies.* London: R & R
Gilbert, 1817.

Pember, G. H. *The Antichrist, Babylon and the Coming of the Kingdom.*
Miami Springs: Schoettle Publishing Co., Inc., 1988.

Pentecost, Dwight, J. *Things To Come.* Grand Rapids: Zondervan
Publishing House, 1958.

Peters, George. *The Theocratic Kingdom.* Grand Rapids: Kregel
Publications, 1957.

Pember, G.H. *The Church, The Churches and the Mysteries.* Miami
Springs: Conley & Schoettle Publishing Co., Inc., 1984.

Rossetti, Christina. *The Face Of The Deep.* London: Society For Promoting
Christian Knowledge, 1895.

Scott, Walter. *Exposition of the Revelation of Jesus Christ.* London: Pickering & Inglis, Ltd., 1970.

Seiss, J. A. *The Apocalypse,* Grand Rapids· Zondervan Publishing House, 1960.

Smith, Chuck. *The Tribulation & The Church.* Costa Mesa: The Word For Today, 1980.

Stanton, Gerald, B. *Kept From The Hour.* Miami Springs: Schoettle Publishing Co., Inc., 1991.

Tatford, Dr. Frederick. *The Revelation.* Minneapolis: Klock & Klock Christian Publ., 1983.

Taylor, Rev. G. F. *The Second Coming Of Jesus.* Franklin Springs: The Publishing House, 1950.

Thompson, Rev. J. L. *That Glorious Future.* London: Morgan and Scott, 1887.

Tristam, Rev. H.B. *The Seven Golden Candlesticks.* London: The Religious Tract Society, 1871.

Withers, James. *The Messiah King.* London: S. W. Partridge & Co., 1888.

Wordsworth, Chr. *Lectures on the Apocalypse.* Philadelphia: Herman Hooker, 1852.

Speaking Engagements
or
Teaching Seminars

Mr. Grant Jeffrey is available for seminars or other speaking engagements throughout the year for churches, conferences and colleges.

Subjects included are Prophecy, Apologetics, Evangelism Training and General Bible Teaching.

Please Contact:

Grant Jeffrey Ministries
P.O. Box 129, Station "U"
Toronto, Ontario, M8Z 5M4
Canada